Jerusalem, the Temple,
and the New Age in Luke-Acts

Jerusalem, the Temple, and the New Age in Luke-Acts

J. Bradley Chance

MERCER

PEETERS

ISBN 0-86554-301-1

Jerusalem, the Temple,
and the New Age in Luke-Acts
Copyright © 1988
Mercer University Press
Macon, Georgia 31207
All rights reserved
Printed in the United States of America

Library of Congress Cataloging-in-Publication Data
Chance, J. Bradley.
    Jerusalem, the temple, and the new age in Luke-Acts /
    J. Bradley Chance.
    xii + 168pp. 6x9in. (15x23cm.)
    Revision of thesis (Ph.D.)—Duke University, 1984.
    Includes bibliographies and index.
    ISBN 0-86554-201-1 (alk. paper)
    1. Bible. N.T. Luke—Criticism, interpretation, etc.
2. Bible. N.T. Acts—Criticism, interpretation, etc.
3. Jerusalem in the Bible.
4. Temple of Jerusalem (Jerusalem) in the Bible.
5. Eschatology—Biblical teaching. I. Title.
BS2589.C48   1988
226'.4064—dc19

88-6850
CIP

Contents

Abbreviations

APOT *The Apocrypha and Pseudepigrapha of the Old Testament.* Two volumes. Ed. R. H. Charles. Oxford: Clarendon Press, 1913.

ATR *Anglican Theological Review*

BA *The Biblical Archaeologist*

BARev *Biblical Archaeology Review*

BASOR *Bulletin of the American Schools of Oriental Research*

Bib *Biblica*

CBQ *Catholic Biblical Quarterly*

CBQMS CBQ Monograph Series

ExpTim *Expository Times*

FRLANT *Forschungen zur Religion und Literatur des Alten und Neuen Testaments*

HTR *Harvard Theological Review*

IB *The Interpreter's Bible.* Twelve volumes. Ed. George Arthur Buttrick. New York and Nashville: Abingdon Press, 1952–1957.

IDB *The Interpreter's Dictionary of the Bible.* Four volumes plus supplementary volume. Ed. George Arthur Buttrick and Keith Crim (supplementary volume). New York and Nashville: Abingdon Press, 1962 and 1976.

IEJ *Israel Exploration Journal*

Imm *Immanuel*

Int *Interpretation*

JAAR *Journal of the American Academy of Religion*

JBL *Journal of Biblical Literature*

JBLMS JBL Monograph Series

JETS *Journal of the Evangelical Theological Society*

JQR   *The Jewish Quarterly Review*

JSJ   *Journal for the Study of Judaism in the Persian, Hellenistic, and Roman Period*

JSNT   *Journal for the Study of the New Testament*

JSS   *Journal of Semitic Studies*

JTS   *Journal of Theological Studies*

NICNT   *The New International Commentary on the New Testament*

NovT   *Novum Testamentum*

NovTSup   NovT Supplements

NTS   *New Testament Studies*

OJRelSt   *Ohio Journal of Religious Studies*

PRS   *Perspectives in Religious Studies*

RB   *Revue Biblique*

RefTheoRev   *The Reformed Theological Review*

RevQ   *Revue de Qumran*

RHPR   *Revue d'Historie et de Philosophie religieuses*

SBLDS   Society of Biblical Literature Dissertation Series

SBLMS   Society of Biblical Literature Monograph Series

SJT   *Scottish Journal of Theology*

SNTSMS   Society for New Testament Studies Monograph Series

TDNT   *The Theological Dictionary of the New Testament.* Nine volumes. Ed. Gerhard Kittel and Gerhard Friedrich. Trans. Geoffrey W. Bromiley. Grand Rapids MI: Eerdmans, 1964–1974.

TRu   *Theologische Rundschau*

TZ   *Theologische Zeitschrift*

VT   *Vetus Testamentum*

WTJ   *Westminster Theological Journal*

ZNW   *Zeitschrift für die neutestamentliche Wissenschaft und die Kunde der altern Kirche*

Translations Used

Unless otherwise indicated, all translations come from the sources as listed below.

The Bible and the Deuterocanonicals/Apocrypha
The Holy Bible: Revised Standard Version containing the Old and New Testaments with the Apocrypha/Deuterocanonical Books. Nashville: Thomas Nelson & Sons, 1973.

Classical Works
The Loeb Classical Library. Cambridge MA: Harvard University Press.

Midrash Rabbah
Midrash Rabbah. Ed. H. Freedman and Maurice Simon. London: Soncino, 1951.

The Mishnah
The Mishnah. Trans. Herbert Danby. London: Oxford University Press, 1933.

The Pseudepigrapha
The Apocrypha and Pseudepigrapha of the Old Testament. Volume 2. Ed. R. H. Charles. London: Oxford University Press, 1913.

Qumran Scrolls
The Dead Sea Scrolls in English. Second edition. Trans. Geza Vermes. New York: Penguin Books, 1975.

The Talmud
The Babylonian Talmud. Trans. I. Epstein. London: Soncino, 1935–1948.

Acknowledgments

This monograph is a revision of my doctoral dissertation, submitted to Duke University in 1984. Much of that work, like so many others, was burdened with prolegomena which in this book have been radically reduced. I am grateful to the editors and referees of Mercer University Press who reviewed the manuscript and made helpful suggestions which helped alleviate the text of much of its dissertation baggage. Material in the chapters dealing specifically with the Lukan concept of Jerusalem and the temple remains essentially unchanged; the bibliography has been updated and some arguments have been restated and clarified.

It is not possible to accomplish a task as monumental as one's first book without finding oneself in debt to many persons. Several members of my dissertation committee, Franklin W. Young, D. Moody Smith, and Eric Meyers, all encouraged me to pursue publication of the text. John Schütz, who served as a model professor for me while I was an undergraduate at the University of North Carolina and who also served on my dissertation committee, was especially helpful in giving me guidance on publishing the manuscript. My colleagues at William Jewell College were always supportive and gracious enough to show continued interest in the progress of the manuscript. Good students are always an inspiration to a professor, and I offer a word of appreciation to them, especially the group that participated in my seminar on Luke-Acts in the spring of 1987. My student assistant, Lisa Bill, whose sister Terri's help was so indispensable in my completion of the dissertation, carried on the tradition by offering invaluable help regarding the many technical matters of the manuscript, including the grinding task of preparing the indexes. My wife Mary was always kind enough to show interest in what I was doing and to offer moral support when the frustrations of "teaching in the real world" seemed to conflict with my passions for the ivory-colored, ivy-covered tower.

The publication of academic monographs requires financial assistance. I am greatly indebted to William Jewell College and the Department of Religion that awarded me special grants to subsidize this project.

A very special word of appreciation is extended to Ms. Ann Bailey. Following the death of her sister and my grandmother, Myrtle Huke, she wished to make an enduring contribution dedicated to her sister's memory. I am happy that she has deemed this book worthy of such an offering. I know my grandmother would have been pleased.

Finally, I dedicate this work to my Southern Baptist colleagues who, in many places and under many different conditions, live out their calling in the context of teaching religion. I dedicate it to them because I, along with them, live in the earnest hope that Baptist people will never abandon the important truth that one of the greatest assets to the open Bible is an open mind.

September 1987   —*J. Bradley Chance*

Introduction

Even a casual reading of Luke-Acts reveals the prominent place that Luke[1] assigns to the city of Jerusalem and the temple. The first two chapters of Luke focus on this city and its holy place. Luke's record of Jesus' passion and resurrection takes place in Jerusalem or its environs. Following the ascension of Jesus, Luke concludes his gospel by stating that the disciples returned to Jerusalem and were continually in the temple praising God (Lk. 24:52-53). The action of the first seven chapters of Acts is virtually confined to Jerusalem, and much of what takes place there is focused on the temple (2:26-27; 3:1-4:4; 5:12-32, 42; 6:13-14; 7:44-50). Intermittently throughout Acts Jerusalem comes to the fore (9:26-30; 11:27-12:25; 15:1-29), though the temple plays no role in these places. Finally, both the city and the temple play a prominent role toward the end of Acts (21:15-23:35).

Statistically, Luke refers to Jerusalem and the temple quite often when compared to the rest of the New Testament. He mentions the city in the Gospel alone some thirty-one times, as compared to Matthew and Mark who together mention the city only twenty-three times.[2] While Luke and Acts together constitute only one-third of the New Testament, they contain almost two-thirds of the references to Jerusalem.[3] The same sort of dis-

---

[1]The name "Luke" is used to denote the author of the two-volume work known as Luke-Acts, with no intention of prejudging the question of authorship. Details regarding this issue and the justification for interpreting Luke and Acts as works of the same writer may be found in Werner Georg Kümmel, *Introduction to the New Testament*, rev. ed., trans. Howard Clark Kee (Nashville: Abingdon Press, 1975) 147-50, 156-59.

[2]Numerical statistics are based on data located in *Computer-Konkordanz zum Novum Testamentum Graece: von Nestle-Aland, 26, Auflage und zum Greek New Testament, 3rd Edition* (Berlin and New York: Walter de Gruyter, 1980) s.v. Ἱεροσόλυμα and s.v. Ἰερουσαλήμ, 879-82.

[3]Michael Bachmann, *Jerusalem und der Tempel: Die geographisch-theologischen Elemente in der lukanischen Sicht des judischen Kultzentrums*, Beiträge zur Wissenschaft vom Alten und Neuen Testament, Sechste Folge, Heft 9 (Stuttgart: Kohlhammer, 1980) 1-2.

proportional statistics may be seen with respect to references to the temple, which for Luke is usually designated by the term ἱερόν. While Luke-Acts is approximately twenty-eight percent longer than Matthew and Mark combined, it contains almost twice as many references to the ἱερόν.[4] The above data alone justify an inquiry into Luke's interest in Jerusalem and the temple.

The following chapters will discuss Luke's interpretation of the significance of Jerusalem and the temple in the context of Luke's eschatology. Narrowing the context of this interpretation to Lukan eschatology is justified by the fact that two investigations have recently appeared that deal directly and in depth with the motif of the temple and Jerusalem in the Lukan writings. The first study is an unpublished dissertation by Francis David Weinert; the second is the published dissertation by Michael Bachmann.[5]

Weinert, following the lead of Conzelmann,[6] tended to dissociate Jerusalem from the temple,[7] a position that Bachmann thoroughly and rightly rejects.[8] Yet both Weinert and Bachmann are in agreement that Luke did not invest the temple or Jerusalem with a peculiarly Christian symbolic significance, as Conzelmann was inclined to do. Rather, as Weinert states concerning the temple, it is understood by Luke ''as that ancient, well recognized and accepted national religious institution in Israel.''[9] Bachmann especially argues that any explication of the theological importance the city and the temple held in the mind of Luke must begin with the recognition that Luke viewed these entities first and foremost within the context of traditional Jewish perceptions.[10]

----

[4]In the Nestle edition of the New Testament the total number of words in Matt. and Mk. is 29,547, whereas the total number of words in Lk.-Acts is 37,810, an increase of slightly less than 28% (27.7%). Source: Robert Morgenthaler, *Statistik des Neustestamentlichen Wortschatzes* (Zurich: Gotthelf-Verlag, 1958) 164, §3. The total occurrences of the word ἱερόν in Matt. and Mk. is twenty, while the total in Lk.-Acts is thirty-nine, one less than exactly twice the frequency. Source: ibid., 106, s.v. ἱερόν.

[5]Francis David Weinert, ''The Meaning of the Temple in the Gospel of Luke,'' (Ph.D. diss., Fordham University, 1979); Michael Bachmann, *Jerusalem und der Tempel.*

[6]Hans Conzelmann, *The Theology of Saint Luke,* trans. Geoffrey Buswell (London: Faber and Faber; New York: Harper & Brothers, 1960) 73-79.

[7]Weinert, ''Meaning of the Temple,'' 15-22.

[8]Bachmann, *Jerusalem und der Tempel,* 13-66, 132-70.

[9]Weinert, ''Meaning of the Temple,'' 316.

[10]Bachmann, *Jerusalem und der Tempel,* 380.

These careful studies have served to acquaint the scholarly community with the significant data revolving around Luke's presentation of the temple and Jerusalem. Further investigation along similar lines would only be redundant. Rather, the path has been cleared for investigations with a more focused interest, such as the present task of interpreting Luke's perception of Jerusalem and the temple in the context of his eschatology.

Because of the enduring impact of Conzelmann's *Theology of Saint Luke,* some might question from the outset the legitimacy of interpreting Luke's perception of Jerusalem and the temple in an eschatological context. Conzelmann has argued that Luke has systematically de-eschatologized the gospel tradition. It is Conzelmann's contention that the delay of the parousia created a problem for the early church. Luke addressed this problem by emphasizing the remoteness of the parousia and replacing imminent eschatological hope with a noneschatological concept of *Heilsgeschichte.*[11] Succinctly stated, Conzelmann proposed that Luke viewed the history of God's redemptive work as divided into three periods, that of Israel, Jesus, and the church. Hence the church, along with her mission, became in Luke's scheme of things the final segment of God's ongoing and potentially long-term history of redemption. There is nothing intrinsically eschatological about the work of Christ or the church.

However, Conzelmann has hardly created a consensus with respect to Lukan eschatological expectations. The various nuances of his noneschatological interpretation of Luke-Acts have been challenged by numerous interpreters.[12] Conzelmann's thesis has received enough negative criticism to justify the pursuit of the following investigation. The study will proceed on the presumption that Luke, like many of his Christian contemporaries, shared the conviction that with the arrival of Jesus the eschatological age of salvation had dawned. The term eschatological is used in its fully apocalyptic sense: Luke believed that the end-time, new age of salvation had

---

[11]Conzelmann, *Theology,* 95-136.

[12]W. C. Robinson, *The Way of the Lord: A Study of History and Eschatology in the Gospel of Luke* (Ph.D. diss., University of Basel; privately published, 1962) 1-42; Fred O. Francis, "Eschatology and History in Luke-Acts," JAAR 37 (1969): 51-52; Charles H. Talbert, "The Redaction Critical Quest for Luke the Theologian" in "Jesus and Man's Hope," special edition of *Perspective* 11 (1970): 173-84; E. Earle Ellis, *Eschatology in Luke* (Philadelphia: Fortress Press, 1972) 17-18; A. J. Mattill, Jr., *Luke and the Last Things: A Perspective for Understanding Lukan Thought* (Dillsboro NC: Western North Carolina Press; Macon GA: Mercer University Press, 1979) 41-112; Eric Franklin, *Christ the Lord: A Study in the Purpose and Theology of Luke-Acts* (Philadelphia: Westminster Press, 1975) 9-47; Robert Maddox, *The Purpose of Luke-Acts,* ed. John Riches (Edinburgh: T. & T. Clark, 1982) 105-15.

broken into this world. It was in the context of this eschatological faith that Luke attempted to understand the significance of Jerusalem and the temple. It is the purpose of the remainder of this book to argue for the truth of this thesis statement.

It should be noted that I have assumed for this study the standard two-source hypothesis regarding the order of the Synoptic Gospels and a post-70 CE dating of Luke-Acts. With respect to the two-source hypothesis, I do not believe that this presupposition will skew the presentation of the data. In many instances I interpret the text as it stands without explicit reference to Luke's use of Mark. In many of those instances where I do make specific appeal to Luke's use of Mark (and where such appeal does help to justify my argument) I would note for the sake of "neo-Griesbachians" that much of what I assume Luke would have seen in Mark he would just as readily have seen in Matthew (see, for example, Mk. 11:19, 27 ‖ Matt. 21:17, 23; Mk. 13:3 ‖ Matt. 24:3; Mk. 15:33 ‖ Matt. 27:45-54).

The proceeding investigation will unfold in accordance with the following outline. Chapter one will examine the eschatological expectations revolving around Jerusalem and the temple in Judaism and the non-Lukan New Testament documents. Chapter two will address the question of whether Luke tended to "spiritualize" the temple and transfer its functions either to Jesus or the church. Chapter three will investigate Luke's understanding of the role of the temple and Jerusalem in God's salvation of Israel. Chapter four will examine the same saving activity in relation to the Gentiles. Chapter five will focus on the third Evangelist's interpretation of the destruction of Jerusalem and the temple. In the conclusion some suggestions regarding the implications of this investigation for Luke's theology and life-setting will be offered.

The Eschatological Jerusalem and Temple
in Judaism and Early Non-Lukan Christianity

Chapter I

Introduction

The ultimate purpose of this monograph is to examine Luke's perception of the eschatological functions of Jerusalem and the temple. It is appropriate, therefore, to survey Jewish and non-Lukan Christian conceptions of Jerusalem and the temple in order to establish a context for this study of Luke's own perceptions. The following survey will by no means be exhaustive, but shall attempt only to portray the broad contours of these eschatological conceptions.

The Eschatological Jerusalem and Temple in Judaism

While Israel's expectations about the eschatological Jerusalem and temple find their roots in the deep attachments and loyalties of preexilic Israel to its cultic centers and the land, it was after the Exile that such conceptions came to fruition.[1] These eschatological expectations may be summarized as consisting of four interrelated motifs. First, there would occur the glorious restoration of Jerusalem and the temple which, second, would serve as the focal centers of God's restored people of Israel and, third, as important places in Yahweh's dealings with the nations. Fourth, in some

---

[1]W. D. Davies, *The Gospel and the Land: Early Christianity and Jewish Territorial Doctrine* (Berkeley: University of California Press, 1974) 15-48.

expectations the Messiah would play an important role in relation to the temple and the city.

The Restoration and Glorification of Jerusalem and the Temple. Despite Ezekiel's vivid and harsh descriptions of Jerusalem's destruction, he offered consolation to the people during the Exile by speaking of their miraculous restoration to the land (see 20:42; 34:13; 36:34-35; 37:12, 14, 21). The eschatological program of Ezek. 40-48 described a restored community centered around a new temple.[2] To this new temple the glory of Yahweh would return (43:4, cf. 44:4), and due to this presence Yahweh would dwell in the midst of his people (43:7). Indeed, Yahweh dwells in this city (48:35) only because he has established his presence in the temple. Zadokites would serve as the priests (44:15-16) and judges (44:24) of this cultic community where they would teach the people the laws of purity (44:23). Despite this focus on the temple mount, the "city" was not a mere appendage in the restored Israel. Ezekiel ends his description of the restored community with the declaration that the city itself would be called "The LORD is there" (48:35).

Postexilic portions of Isaiah express particular interest in the hope of a restored Jerusalem and temple. The operating premise of the prophet was that Yahweh had not forgotten Zion (49:14-18). She was to be comforted (40:1-2; 51:3) by a declaration of good news (52:7; cf. 41:27). The salvation of Yahweh was going to visit the forgiven city (46:13; 62:11; cf. 52:9). Zion would be filled with justice and righteousness (33:5-6). She would be rebuilt in splendor (54:11), and her glory would be beheld by all (60:1-22).

The postexilic prophets Haggai and Zechariah also envisaged the grand restoration of Jerusalem and the temple. "My cities shall again overflow with prosperity, and the LORD will again comfort Zion and again choose Jerusalem" (Zech. 1:17). It would be the place of God's dwelling; the entire city would be the mountain of the Lord (Zech. 8:3). The miraculous character of the restored city is reflected in the fact that it would need no walls to protect it, for Yahweh himself would be its protection (Zech. 2:5; cf. Ezek. 38:11).

Haggai and Zechariah also gave the new temple a prominent place in the time of eschatological blessing.[3] For these two men, particularly Hag-

---

[2]See Jon Douglas Levenson, *Theology of the Program of the Restoration of Ezekiel 40-48,* Harvard Semitic Monograph Series 10 (Cambridge MA: Scholars Press for the Harvard Semitic Museum, 1976).

[3]See W. J. Dumbrell, "Kingship and Temple in the Post Exilic Period," *Reformed*

gai, the building of the temple was the precondition for the coming of Yahweh (Hag. 1:8). Failure to rebuild the house had produced blight, famine, and scarcity (Hag. 1:10-11; 2:15-17). Proper attention to the temple produced abundance (Hag.2:18-19). Its rebuilding was the necessary prerequisite for the eschatological upheaval of the nations (Hag. 2:6-7).

In the postbiblical period speculation concerning the temple and Jerusalem of the New Age multiplied. At times, the restored, glorified city and temple were seen as standing on a continuum with the old city and temple. In other sources, the glorified centers of salvation were perceived as entirely new entities, sometimes envisioned as a heavenly temple or city which would descend to earth.[4] In either case, these important geographical centers would be renewed, restored, and refurbished in order to fulfill their important salvific functions.

Numerous texts in the Apocrypha and Pseudepigrapha look forward to the glorification of the city of Jerusalem and the temple. Jud. 10:8 and 13:4 make reference to the exaltation of Jerusalem. Sib. Or. 5:414-33 envisages the glorious restoration of Jerusalem and the temple: "And the city which God loved he made more radiant than the stars and the sun and the moon; and he set it as the jewel of the world" (420-22). Second Bar. 4:2-7, while clearly denigrating the earthly city, looks forward to the earthly manifestation of the eternal city which is now stationed in the heavenly sphere.

Second Esdras makes a number of references to the manifestations of the new Jerusalem. Key texts are 7:26-28, 9:38-10:59 and 13:36. In 7:26 reference is made to the appearance of "the city which now is not seen," and the disclosure of "the land which is now hidden," while 13:37 (cf. 13:6) speaks of a Zion "carved without hands." In light of these references, the woman of chapters 9-10 is generally interpreted as representing the heavenly Jerusalem. This woman is mourning the loss of her son (9:41-10:4), the earthly Jerusalem (10:46-47). It is clearly implied in 7:26 and 10:51 that this heavenly city will one day be established on earth, on an entirely new foundation.

Theological Review 37 (1978): 33-42; Paul D. Hanson, *The Dawn of Apocalyptic: The Historical and Sociological Roots of Jewish Apocalyptic Eschatology,* rev. ed. (Philadelphia: Fortress Press, 1979) 240-62; D. L. Petersen, "Zerubbabel and Jerusalem Temple Reconstruction," *CBQ* 36 (1974): 366-72.

[4]A number of interpreters have noted these two versions of expectation. See, e.g., Paul Volz, *Die Eschatologie der judischen Gemeinde im neutestamentlichen Zeitalter, nach der Quellen der rabbinischen, apokalyptischen und apokryphen Literatur* (Tübingen: J. C. B. Mohr, 1934) 372-73; Bertil Gärtner, *The Temple and the Community in Qumran and the New Testament,* SNTSMS 1 (Cambridge: Cambridge University Press, 1965) 16-17.

First Enoch 25:3 also implies the descent of a heavenly temple and city: "This high mountain which thou hast seen, whose summit is like the throne of God, is His throne, where the Holy Great One, the Lord of Glory, The Eternal King, will sit, when He shall come down to visit the earth with goodness." If this descending mountain is interpreted as Zion, the hope of the earthly manifestation of the heavenly city and temple comes to expression here. T. Levi 5:1 refers to the heavenly temple, though nothing is explicitly said of the establishment of this temple on earth: "And thereupon the angel opened to me the gates of heaven, and I saw the holy temple, and upon a throne of glory the Most High."

First Enoch 90:28-29 speaks of the "folding up" of the old house, along with its pillars, beams and ornaments, after which "a new house greater and loftier than that first . . . [is] set up in the place of the first which had been folded up" (90:29). There is, however, no explicit indication that such a temple descends from heaven.

A number of texts which were written during the existence of the second temple still looked forward to the future glorification of the cultic center. In Tob. 14:5 reference is made to the return of God's people to Jerusalem. "They will rebuild the house of God, though it will not be like the former one until the times of the age are completed." Similar sentiments are expressed in As. Mos. 4:7-9 and 2 Bar. 68:5-6. Second Macc. 2:4-8 draws attention to the fact that certain implements from the first temple, (the tent, the ark, and the altar of incense) were hidden away, not to be disclosed "until God gathers his people together again and shows his mercy. And then the Lord will disclose these things" (vv. 7b-8a). The clear indication is that the author of 2 Maccabees did not view the present temple as completely "restored."

The covenanters of Qumran believed that the temple of Jerusalem was thoroughly corrupt (CD 11:18-21; 1QpHab 8:8-13;12:1-10) and hence saw themselves as the true temple of the present age.[5] The community used the term "house" (בית) to depict itself (e.g. 1QS 5:6; 8:5, 9; 9:6; CD 3:19). Twice this "house" is linked with the noun "holiness" (1QS 8:5; 9:6). Like the Jerusalem temple, the primary function of this temple community was to provide atonement, but in the case of the Essenes such atonement was limited to the sectarians themselves and the land they would one day occupy (1QS 5:5-7; 8:4-10; 9:3-5; 1QSa 1:3). The means of atonement were the prayers and good works of the community (1QS 9:4-5).

---

[5]See, e.g., Gärtner, *Temple and Community*, 1-46, and Georg Klinzing, *Die Umdeutung des Kultus in der Qumrangemeinde und im Neuen Testament* (Göttingen: Vandenhoeck und Ruprecht, 1971) esp. 50-93.

Despite its contempt for the current temple of Jerusalem, the Qumranic community looked forward to the restoration of Jerusalem in the eschatological era. The Qumranic fascination with the city is readily apparent in such documents as 5Q15, 11QTemple, and 1QM. Scroll 1QM assumes the capture of the city by the sectarians during the first stages of the eschatological war (1QM 1; 3:11; 7:4). Concern for the purity of the city in 11QTemple allows the conclusion that the recaptured Jerusalem would adhere to strict laws of purity.[6] Scroll 11QTemple itself does not *describe* the eschatological temple or the eschatological city, but 29:7-10 clearly states that a new temple, and implicitly, therefore, a new city, is coming:

> I will accept them, and they will become my people, and I myself will be with them for ever. I will dwell with them all the days and I will sanctify by my glory my sanctuary, upon which I will cause to rest my glory until that blessed day when I will build my sanctuary, establishing it for all time, conforming to the convenant which I have made with Jacob at Bethel.[7]

The rabbinic materials offer abundant expression of the hope of Jerusalem's and the temple's restoration/glorification. The fourteenth and fifteenth petitions of the Babylonian recension of the *Shemoneh 'Esreh* express the hope that God will again restore the holy city forever.[8] In *Pesikta de Rab Kahana* numerous rabbis, many of whom lived in a relatively early period of the Common Era, speak of the glorious future of Jerusalem. R. Eleasar the Modite (120-140 C.E.), commenting on Jer. 3:17, envisaged the expansion of Jerusalem so that it might hold all the eschatological pilgrims (Pes. de Rab Kah. 20:17). R. Johanan (d. 279 C.E.) speculated that Jerusalem would extend as far as Damascus (20:17). R. Nehemiah (140-165 C.E.) also envisaged the expansion of the holy city (20:7). R. Eliezer ben Jacob (80-120 or 140-165 C.E.) foresaw the heavenward extension of the city (20:7).

The rabbinic materials echo the hope for a new, restored temple. The seventeenth benediction contains a prayer for the restoration of the temple service. Liturgical utterances express the hope that the temple be quickly

---

[6]See 11QTemple 45:7-18; 47:2-18. Also Jacob Milgrom, " 'Sabbath' and 'Temple City' in the Temple Scroll," BASOR 232 (1978): 25-28.

[7]My translation, following the text as found in Yigael Yadin, *The Temple Scroll*, vol. 3 (Jerusalem: The Israel Exploration Society, 1977).

[8]For a critical introduction to and translation of both the Babylonian and Palestinian recensions of the *Shemoneh 'Esreh* see Emil Schürer, *The History of the Jewish People in the Age of Jesus Christ (175 B. C.–A. D. 135)*, 2 vols., rev. English ed. by Geza Vermes, Fergus Millar, and Matthew Black (Edinburgh: T. & T. Clark, 1973, 1979) 2:454-63.

rebuilt (b. B. Mes. 28b; m. Ta'an 4:8; m. Tamid 7:3). Priests are encouraged to remain continually in a state of readiness for temple service lest "the Temple may speedily be rebuilt and the need will arise for priests to do service therein and there will be none available" (b. Ta'an. 17b; see also b. Sanh. 22b).

The rabbis shared in speculation concerning the heavenly temple. Testimony said to stem from R. Johanan (d. 279 C.E.) states that there was a correspondence between the earthly and the heavenly temple (b. Ta'an 5a). R. Simeon ben Yohai (140-165 C.E.) is reported to have said that the heavenly sanctuary stood 18 miles above the earthly one (Gen. Rab. 69:7).

The most thorough description of the heavenly temple which is to be established on earth is found in the eleventh century midrash *Bereshit Rabbati*. Despite the late date of the manuscript itself, the traditions contained within it may be quite old.[9] The text is a midrash of Jacob's vision in Gen. 28, focusing on the statement of 28:17: "This is none other than the house of God." The midrash on Gen. 28:17 purports to contain a vision of Moses which he received on the day of his death. In this vision, Moses is privileged to speak both with God (lines 36-37) and the Messiah (line 18). The vision makes reference to a heavenly temple made by the hand of God (lines 7, 19-20, 22, 33). The Messiah tells Moses that it is this temple, revealed to Jacob (lines 20-21), "which will stand for Israel for ever and ever until the end of all generations" (lines 23-24, cf. lines 31-33). While the descent of the temple to earth is never *described,* it is specifically stated that this heavenly building will be fashioned by God on earth (line 33).

Within both biblical and postbiblical Judaism there existed expectant anticipation for the renewal of the temple cult and the city. The new temple and city of God would play centrally significant roles in the eschatological deliverance which was to be revealed.

Jerusalem: The City of God's Restored People. Closely associated with the restoration of the city and the temple was the restoration of the people of God. Jeremiah promises the restoration of the people employing the imagery of the Exodus (Jer. 23:3). Isa. 27:12-13 also sounds the hope of a worldwide gathering of the people of God. The most colorful description

---

[9]So Harold A. Attridge, "The Ascension of Moses and the Heavenly Jerusalem," in *Studies in the Testament of Moses,* ed. George W. E. Nickelsburg, Jr., Septuagint and Cognate Studies 4 (Cambridge MA: Society of Biblical Literature, 1973) 122. The antiquity of the tradition may very well be attested by 11QTemple 29:10. Here reference is made to the "covenant which God made with Jacob at Bethel." This "covenant" refers to the building of the new temple indicating that a tradition similar to that behind *Bereshit Rabbati* was known at Qumran.

of such hope is found in Ezek. 37:1-14 where the restoration of the people is viewed as a literal resurrection of a dead nation. These texts attest to the fact that the Old Testament has virtually no conception of a restored people apart from a definite place of restoration. This place was Jerusalem and the land.

The people who returned were to be the holy and redeemed people of God (Isa. 62:12). The restored Jerusalem would not be the abode of the unclean (Isa. 52:1; Ezek. 36:39; cf. Joel 3:17, [Hebrew 4:17]). It was to be the abode of the righteous and faithful of Israel (Isa. 26:1-2; 60:21; Zech. 8:8). The filth of sin would be removed from the people (Isa. 4:4; Zech. 13:1). They were to be redeemed remnant (Zech. 8:6-8); a people born of God (Isa. 66:8-9); a new people with a new heart and a new spirit (Ezek. 36:26-28), with a new covenant written upon their hearts (Jer. 31:31-34). The restored city would be the abode of the righteous, redeemed remnant of the eschatological people of God.

The Apocrypha and Pseudepigrapha make numerous references to Jerusalem and/or the temple as the central place of God's restored people. First Enoch 90:28-36 describes the building of the new Jerusalem and temple by God, which is followed by the gathering of the sheep "in that house" (90:33). Jub. 1:28-29 closely relates the "elect of Israel" to the holy places. Second Esdr. 13:12-13, 39-50 also makes clear that the central location of the restored, ingathered people will be Jerusalem/Zion. In numerous passages the return of the people of God is described in thoroughly miraculous terms, thereby indicating the significance of the return to Jerusalem (Bar. 5:5-9; Ps. Sol. 11:5-7; 2 Esdr. 13:46-47). In some passages it is even said that the returned and restored people of God would rebuild Jerusalem and the temple (Tob. 14:5; Adam and Eve 29:6).

It is particularly emphasized that the eschatological people of God who inhabit the new Jerusalem will be a holy people. The setting of Ps. Sol. 17:28-31 is Jerusalem (see v. 25). The text states that the Messiah will "gather together a holy people" (v. 28) who have been "sanctified by the Lord" (v. 28). No unrighteousness will be found in their midst (v. 29), "nor shall there dwell with them any man that knoweth wickedness" (v. 29b). The people are called "sons of their God" (v. 30). Furthermore, "neither sojourner nor alien shall sojourn with them any more" (v. 31).

The Qumranic materials also saw Jerusalem as the focal place of God's people in the eschatological era. Scroll 4QpPs 37, III:10-11 speaks of the "Congregation of the Poor" who will possess the high mountain of Israel and enjoy the delights of God's sanctuary. It is expressly stated in this passage that "the wicked of Israel . . . shall be cut off and blotted out for ever." Concerning the eschatological temple 4QFlor 1:2-5 states: "This is the House into which [the unclean shall] never enter, [nor the uncircumcised] nor the Ammonites, nor the Moabites, nor the half-breed, nor the foreigner, nor the stranger, ever; for there shall My Holy Ones be.''

The close association of the people and the city is also reflected in the rabbinic materials. B. B. Bat. 75b records the saying of R. Johanan (d. 279 C.E.): ''The Jerusalem of the world to come is unlike the Jerusalem of this world. The Jerusalem of this world all can enter who will; the Jerusalem of the world to come they only can enter who are appointed for it.'' R. Eleazar (3rd century C.E.) expresses a similar view in the same Talmudic passage. In numerous places the rabbis speculated that Jerusalem would need to be considerably enlarged so as to house all the people who would dwell there in the age to come.[10]

In many circles of postexilic and postbiblical Judaism it was assumed that a close relationship would exist between the restored people of God and the city of the temple. Jerusalem in the eschatological age would be the focal point of the eschatological people.

The Restored Jerusalem and the Nations. Restored Jerusalem affects not only the people of God. A definitive eschatological feature of the city consists of its universal and cosmic import: the new Jerusalem would affect the nations as a whole. A number of texts describe the relationship between Yahweh and the nations in polemical terms, viewing Jerusalem as the place of the nations' subjugation (e.g. Ezek. 38-39; Zech. 14; Ps. Sol. 17:23-27; and 2 Esdr. 13:24-38). Many other texts, however, envision the eschatological Jerusalem as being closely associated with the salvation of the nations. It is these texts that are most relevant to this investigation.

According to von Rad, the earliest expression of this tradition is found in Isa. 2:2-4 (‖ Mic. 4:1-3).[11] Numerous other postexilic passages speak of a universal pilgrimage to pay homage to Yahweh. Zeph. 3:8-10 describes the conversion of the nations following God's judgment of them. As a result of Yahweh's cosmic demonstrations of his power Haggai proclaims that the nations will come to his temple bearing material tribute (Hag. 2:7). A passage from Jeremiah which is often dated after the destruction[12] says of Jerusalem: ''And all nations shall gather to it, to the presence of

---

[10]Pes. de Rab Kah. 20:7; b. B. Bat. 75b. See also Louis Ginzberg, *The Legends of the Jews,* 7 vols., trans. Henrietta Szold, Paul Radin (vol. 3), and Boaz Cohen (vol. 7) (Philadelphia: The Jewish Publication Society of America, 1909–1938) 6:73n373.

[11]Gerhard von Rad, *Old Testament Theology,* 2 vols., trans. D. M. G. Stalker (Edinburgh: Oliver and Boyd, 1962, 1965) 2:294.

[12]Ibid., 272.

the LORD in Jerusalem, and they shall no more stubbornly follow their own evil heart'' (Jer. 3:17).

Isa. 60:3 foresees the pilgrimage of the nations to the light shining forth from Jerusalem. Verse 14 of the same chapter states: ''The sons of those who oppressed you shall come bending low to you; and all who despised you shall call you the City of the LORD, the Zion of the Holy One of Israel''. The pilgrimage is not solely for the glorification of Jerusalem. The final purpose of such a pilgrimage is summed up in two texts:

> And the foreigners who join themselves to the LORD, to minister to him, to love the name of the LORD, and to be his servants, every one who keeps the sabbath, and does not profane it, and holds fast my covenant—these I will bring to my holy mountain and make them joyful in my house of prayer; their burnt offerings and their sacrifices will be accepted on my altar; for my house shall be called a house of prayer for all peoples. (Isa. 56:6-7)

> From new moon to new moon, and from sabbath to sabbath, all flesh shall come to worship before me, says the LORD. (Isa. 66:23)

Within the Apocrypha and Pseudepigrapha there is also testimony that Jerusalem would play a central role in the conversion of the nations. Tob. 13:11-12 refers to the pilgrimage of the nations to Jerusalem. The conversion of the nations is made explicit in Tob. 14:6-7, the context implying that Jerusalem is to be the place of this conversion. The pilgrimage of the nations is echoed in Sib. Or. 3:702-31. In the first passage this pilgrimage is said to follow the punishment of the Gentiles. In this context it is said that the pilgrim nations will ''ponder the law of the Most High God'' (3:719) and repent of their idolatry (721-23). Ps. Sol. 17:34-35 also employs the image of a pilgrimage to Jerusalem by the nations. The gifts they bear, however, are the dispersed people of Israel (17:34; cf. Isa. 49:22-23). The conversion of the nations is implied in 17:35-36 where it is said that the nations shall be ruled over by the Messiah-king: ''And there shall be no unrighteousness in his days in their midst, For all shall be holy and their king the anointed of the Lord'' (17:36).

Not surprisingly, the Qumranic materials do not envisage the conversion of the nations. Gentiles are not members of the covenant, nor do they have a chance of becoming so. They are ''beyond redemption.''[13]

The rabbis shared in the expectation that the nations would come to know God at Jerusalem. In Tanhuma one finds the statement of R. Johanan

---

[13]See also in this connection the discussion by E. P. Sanders, *Paul and Palestinian Judaism: A Comparison of Patterns of Religion* (Philadelphia: Fortress, 1977) 243-54.

(d. 279 C.E.): "In the time to come God will make Jerusalem a mother-city for the whole world, as it is said, 'And I will give them to thee as daughters, though they be not of thy covenant'."[14] A similar view is attributed to R. Simeon ben Gamaliel (d. ca. 140 C.E.) in *Aboth de R. Nathan* 35. Finally, R. Hoshaia (third century C.E.) said in the name of R. Aphes: "Jerusalem is destined to become a beacon for the nations of the earth, and they will walk in its light" (Pes. de Rab Kah. 21:4).

The restored Jerusalem was to play a central role in God's dealing with the nations. At Jerusalem the nations would come to recognize the sovereignty of Yahweh and worship him.

Restored Jerusalem, the New Temple, and the Messiah. In much of the expectation concerning Jerusalem and the temple a messianic figure is given an important place. Haggai and Zechariah especially saw a close relationship between the Messiah, the city, and the cult. Many interpreters are convinced that these two prophets saw one of their contemporaries, Zerubbabel the son of Shealtiel, as this Messiah.[15] Haggai explicitly associates the apocalyptic-like shaking of the cosmos and the overthrow of the nations with Yahweh's choosing of Zerubbabel (Hag. 2:20-21). Though it is Yahweh who accomplishes this act, Zerubbabel is clearly viewed by Haggai as God's chosen representative. Zechariah shared similar hopes with respect to Zerubbabel. By means of the Spirit of Yahweh Zerubbabel would possess the earth-shaking power reminiscent of that spoken of by Haggai (Zech. 4:6-7). While Haggai speaks of the messianic figure Zerubbabel in contexts dealing with the temple (Hag. 1:14-15; 2:2-9), Zechariah establishes an explicitly close relationship between Zerubbabel and the cult. He specifically states that Zerubbabel would lay the foundation of the second temple and oversee its completion (Zech. 4:9; cf. 6:11-14).

Assuming the messianic identity of the *nasi* of Ezek. 40-48, it is clear that Ezekiel looked forward to a close relationship between the future Davidic ruler and the restored cult. It would be his responsibility to provide the offerings for the feasts, new moons, and sabbaths as well as necessary offerings to make atonement for Israel (45:17; cf. 46:6-15). He would provide special offerings on behalf of himself and the people during the feast

---

[14]From C. G. Montefiore and H. Loewe, *A Rabbinic Anthology* (N.p.: Meridian Books, n.d.) 564-65.

[15]E.g., Joseph Klausner, *The Messianic Idea in Israel: From its Beginning to the Completion of the Mishnah,* trans. W. F. Stinespring (New York: The Macmillan Company, 1955) 185-205; Sigmund Mowinckel, *He that Cometh,* trans. G. W. Anderson (New York/ Nashville: Abingdon, 1954; Oxford: Basil Blackwell, 1956) 119-22.

of passover (45:21-25). He would be accorded a special place in the cultic life of the community (44:3; 46:2).

What comes forth most prominently in the Apocrypha and Pseudepigrapha is the motif that Jerusalem/Zion is the focal point of messianic activity. In some texts the appearance of the Messiah occurs simultaneously with the manifestation of the new Jerusalem (2 Esdr. 7:26-28; 13:35-36). In 1 Enoch, the Messiah does not appear until *after* the building of the "new house" (90:28-29) and the gathering of Israel and the nations (90:30-36). What is significant is that despite alternative chronological speculations, the Messiah and the new Jerusalem stand in a close relationship. In one text it is even said that the Messiah will build the new Jerusalem (Sib. Or. 5:420-27).

A clear indication of the close association of the Messiah and the temple is found in Sib. Or. 5:422-27. Here it is said that in the newly built Jerusalem the Messiah "made a temple exceeding fair in its sanctuary, and fashioned it in size of many furlongs, with a giant tower touching the very clouds and seen of all, so that all the faithful and all the righteous may see the glory of the invisible God, the vision of delight."

The Qumranic materials betray an underlying assumption that the Messiah would be closely associated with Jerusalem. The motif, however, is not prominent. A primary text is 4QFlor 1:11-13 which consists of a midrash on 2 Sam. 7:11c, 12b, c, 13, 14a: "He is the Branch of David who shall arise with the Interpreter of the Law [to rule] in Zion [at the end] of time. As it is written, I will raise up that tent of David that is fallen (Amos ix, 11). That is to say, the fallen *tent of David* is who shall arise to save Israel." If the "Branch of David" of 4QFlor 1:11 is the Messiah of Israel, then it is clear from line twelve that Zion will be the center of his rule. However, the Messiah was not to play a role in the building of the eschatological sanctuary, for it is explicitly stated in 11QTemple 29:10 that God would build the new temple.

It was firmly embedded in rabbinic tradition that the coming of the Messiah would go hand-in-hand with the reestablishment of the temple (Gen. Rab. 2:5, 56:2; Ex. Rab. 31:10). There are even statements which declare that it would be the Messiah who would rebuild the temple. The most pertinent passages from the targumim are Tg. Zech. 6:12 and Tg. Isa. 53:5:

> And you shall say to him,
> Thus says the LORD of hosts,
> This man, Messiah is his name.
> He will be exalted,
> And he will build the temple of the LORD. (Tg. Zech. 6:12)

He will build the temple
Which was profaned for our transgressions
And delivered up because of our sins. (Tg. Isa. 53:5)[16]

In Tg. Zech. it is specifically said that the Messiah "will build the temple of the LORD." What is most significant about the Isaiah Targum is that the phrase "he will build the temple" is *added* to the Hebrew text.

The date of this conception must be addressed. Some are convinced that these traditions do not antedate the destruction of 70 C.E. Donald Juel is confident that this Targum is to be dated after the destruction: "One need only glance through the targum to Isaiah to observe how profoundly the destruction of the temple has influenced the interpretation of the passages."[17] However, one's interpretation of Tg. Isa. 53:5 is most significant: "He will build the temple that was profaned because of our transgressions." In this context the observation of Koch should be noted.

It is significant that there stands here in the Aramaic "handed over" (*msr*), whereas there stands here in the original Hebrew the much stronger "dashed into pieces" (*dk'*). This probably means that the temple is indeed profaned (because of wicked priests?), however, it is still certainly in existence.[18]

One must be cautious, but there is reason to give serious consideration to the possibility that this portion of of Targum Isaiah antedates 70 C.E.

The above survey indicates that there was an expectation within the Old Testament and postbiblical Judaism that there would exist a close association between the Messiah and the new Jerusalem and temple. Speculation was not uniform, but there was widespread conviction that when the Messiah came Jerusalem and the temple would be significant centers of activity.

Josephus and the Jewish Revolutionaries. Despite the evidence presented above that Jerusalem and the temple would be important places in the eschatological age, some might object that such "importance" existed only in the ideal world of religious literature. However, there is good evidence that in the first decades of the Common Era such expectations were powerfully influential not only in shaping the dreams and visions of those

---

[16]Text and translation found in Donald Juel, *Messiah and Temple: The Trial of Jesus in the Gospel of Mark,* SBLDS 30 (Missoula MT: Scholars Press, 1977) 181.

[17]Ibid., 188.

[18]"Messias und Sundenvergebung in Jesaja 53-Targum. Ein Beitrag zu der Praxis der aramäischen Bibelübersetzung," JSJ 3 (1972): 120.

who produced the literature, but also in motivating people to concrete, and even dangerous activity.

Using primarily Josephus as a source of information, Martin Hengel has argued that the zealot movement was essentially a religious movement deeply immersed in intense, eschatological expectation.[19] Their conviction that the kingdom of God was imminent motivated the Zealots to action, even in the face of impossibly difficult odds. In War 6:310-15 Josephus states that the war was motivated by a misunderstanding of Old Testament prophecy "to the effect that at that time one from their country would become ruler of the world." The revolutionaries misunderstood this to refer to a messianic deliverer. Furthermore, Josephus often points out how Jerusalem was the focal point of revolutionary activity. He related, for example, how the Egyptian false prophet gathered together a group of enthusiastic followers and, having promised that miraculous signs would be given at Jerusalem (Ant. 20:170), engaged in rebellious activity against the Romans in the area of Mount Olivet and Jerusalem (War 2:261-263; cf. also in a similar vein War 2:254, 275-276; 4:135-137; Ant. 20:214, 252-255). Finally, Josephus says that even in the face of certain destruction, false prophets predicted the inviolability of the temple (War 6:285-287).

The same spirit and motivation stood behind the Bar Kokhba revolt of 132-135 C.E. The revolt possessed an eschatological character. This is most immediately evidenced by the fact that Simon bar Cosiba was viewed by many as the Messiah. Such a view was shared by Jewish leaders no less prominent than R. Akiba.[20] Simon's new name, Bar Kokhba (son of a star), and his official title of *nasi,* both point to his messianic character and identity. His name was derived from Num. 24:17b: "A star shall come forth out of Jacob, and a scepter shall rise out of Israel." This text was interpreted messianically at Qumran in the previous century. Bar Kokhba's official title of *nasi* also points to his messianic identity in that again the Qumran scrolls indicate that *nasi* was considered by some Jews to be a messianic title (CD 7:18-20).

Numismatic evidence points to the importance of Jerusalem and the temple for the participants of this revolt.[21] The Jewish coins indicate that Eleazar *the priest* was one of the leaders of the revolt. This, plus the pres-

---

[19]Martin Hengel, *Die Zeloten: Untersuchungen zur Jüdischen Freiheitsbewegung in der Zeit von Herodes I. bis 70 N. Chr.* (Leiden: E. J. Brill, 1961) esp. 235-318.

[20]See Lam. Rab. II. 2, sec. 4.

[21]The definitive numismatic study is that of Y. Meshorer, *Jewish Coins of the Second Temple Period* (Tel-Aviv, 1967) esp. 92-101.

ence of numerous temple symbols found on the Bar Kokhba coins,[22] strongly imply that a main aspiration of the rebels was the reconstitution of the cult. The religious concerns of the first-century Zealots appear to have continued to influence the followers of Bar Kokhba. One particular feature of this symbolism is quite interesting. On many of the coins there sits a star immediately above the symbolic representation of the temple. The star is clearly a reference to Bar Kokhba, the "son of a star." This might indicate that the close association between Messiah and temple to which both the Old Testament and postbiblical literature testified was shared by the followers of Bar Kokhba. This conclusion would be strengthened if the view of some interpreters is correct that reconstruction of the temple was actually begun during the early years of the second revolt.[23] This brief examination of the two Jewish revolts would seem to indicate that the eschatological expectations that circulated around Jerusalem and the temple were quite operative in revolutionary Palestine.

Conclusion. In summation, the conviction was widespread among Jews of the second temple period that Jerusalem and the temple would play significant roles in the eschatological age. The actions of anti-Roman revolutionaries indicate that the eschatological expectations expressed in the literature were not limited to the wild imaginations of recluse sectarians or speculative scholars. Such expectations were so firmly entrenched in the cultural stream of the Jewish people that they could motivate these people to action.

The Eschatological Jerusalem and Temple
in Early Non-Lukan Christianity

The following investigation will be confined to the New Testament, recognizing that this collection of ancient Christian documents is not the only available source of information concerning early Christianity. Nonetheless, there is even within this corpus a significantly abundant amount of material dating from across the latter half of the first century of the Common Era so as to ensure that the conceptual patterns discerned herein are representative of the broad stream of early Christianity.

---

[22]Such symbols are found as a facade of the temple itself. Also symbols of musical instruments which were important in the temple service are found on the coins: lyres, harps, and trumpets. Various sacred vessels (such as an amphora) associated with the temple betray the cultic interest of the revolt.

[23]Mary Smallwood, *The Jews Under Roman Rule: From Pompey to Diocletian,* Studies in Judaism in Late Antiquity 20 (Leiden: E. J. Brill, 1976) 445, and Schürer, *History of the Jewish People,* 1:546. Both view this as a good possibility.

The Conceptual Pattern in Mark and Matthew. A survey of the Markan gospel indicates that the second Evangelist has replaced Jerusalem and the temple with a new entity: the Christian community. It must first be noted that Mark is careful to juxtapose the Jewish leaders, the temple, and Jerusalem (3:22, 7:1, 10:32-33, and 11:1, 15, 27). The distinct impression offered by Mark is that the Jewish leaders, the temple, and Jerusalem form one unit; a unit in opposition against Jesus.[24]

Mark establishes a direct link between the rejection and death of Jesus and the destruction of the temple/Jerusalem. In 15:37-38 the death of Jesus and the rending of the veil of the sanctuary (ναός) are juxtaposed.[25] The linking of the Jewish leaders to this death is made explicit in 11:18, 12:12, and 14:1. Mark has prepared the reader for this proleptic destruction of the temple in 15:38 by enclosing the pericope of the cleansing (11:15-19) within the cursing and destruction of the fig tree (11:13-14, 20-21). Such compositional activity by Mark indicates that the cleansing represents an enacted prophecy of the temple's destruction. The parable of the vineyard (12:1-12) indicates that the destruction of the tenants of the vineyard (the Jewish leaders, who are linked with Jerusalem and the temple) is directly tied to their rejection of Jesus (vv. 8-9). It is in this sense that the enigmatic saying of 14:58 is to be understood. Jesus did not actually predict that *he* would destroy the temple, hence the testimony of the witnesses is said to be false. Yet, on the deeper, more ironic level, he is the agent of destruction in that his rejection by the Jewish leaders brings about the destruction of the place.[26]

Indissolubly linked with the rejection/destruction of Jerusalem, the temple, and its leaders is the promise that the Christian community will *replace* them. The major passages that testified to the destruction of the temple and its leaders also pointed to their replacement. Immediately following Peter's observation that the cursed fig tree had withered (11:21), Jesus' word to his disciples indicates that they will be the new circle of faith, forgiveness, and prayer. Such replacement may also be seen in the parable of the vineyard (see 12:8-9). The motif of replacement is then made explicit in 14:58b which promises that the destroyed temple of the old or-

---

[24]John R. Donahue, S. J., "Temple, Trial and Royal Christology," in Werner H. Kelber, ed., *The Passion in Mark: Studies on Mark 14-16,* (Philadelphia: Fortress Press, 1976) 61-79.

[25]Juel, *Messiah and Temple,* 137-38.

[26]Ibid., 124, 137-38.

der would be replaced by a new temple "not made with hands." This is most likely a reference to the postresurrection community.[27]

Mark 13:14, found in the context of the so-called "little apocalypse," also points to the radical de-emphasis of the temple and Jerusalem. Here two things are made clear. First, the place which had been the holy precinct is now desecrated—it is the seat of Satan.[28] Second, verse 14b depicts the movement of the people of God *away* from the city. The effect of the chapter is to rob both city and sanctuary of any positive role in the fulfillment of the eschatological promises.

The result of Mark's treatment of Jerusalem and the temple is a radical reinterpretation of Jewish eschatological expectation. The idea that Jerusalem and the temple would play significant roles in the realization of God's eschatological promises has been thoroughly rejected. To be sure, Mk. 14:58b indicates that Mark has retained the concept that a "new temple," built by the Messiah, would play a decisive role in the dawning of the eschatological age. Yet the fact that Mark has defined this "new temple" in *ecclesiological* terms makes clear that a thorough redefinition of the concept has transpired. For Mark, Jerusalem and its temple have been replaced permanently by the Christian community.

Matthew offers a similar understanding of Jerusalem and the temple, viewing it as a guilty city destined for destruction and desolation (22:7; 23:37-39; chapter 24). This relegation of the temple and Jerusalem to virtual insignificance is evidenced in numerous non-Markan passages. The pericope of the temple tax (17:24-27) betrays the assumption that the temple, or what its memory might represent, is of penultimate significance to Matthew and his community. The focus of the community is no longer the temple but Jesus, who is greater than the temple (12:5-6). Matthew 12:5-6 does not explicitly assert that Jesus is a new temple, but his person certainly takes precedence over the Jerusalem temple.

The pericope concerning Judas's return of the money tinged with "innocent blood" (27:3-10) portrays the temple as a vile, polluted place, thereby deprived of playing any positive role in the realization of God's promises. W. C. van Unnik has studied this text against the background of the motif of innocent blood in the Old Testament.[29] In the Old Testa-

---

[27]Ibid., 143-57.

[28]Cf. W. H. Kelber, *The Kingdom in Mark: A New Place and a New Time* (Philadelphia: Fortress Press, 1974) 122.

[29]"The Death of Judas in Saint Matthew's Gospel," ATR Suppl. Series 3 (1974): 44-57.

ment the shedding of innocent blood was a defiling and polluting offense (Ps. 106:38-39), the punishment for which was destruction (Jer. 26:15). Matthew makes it a point to state that the blood money was cast into the ναός (27:5). Matthew could have understood the result of this to be a defiling of the temple making it fit now only for destruction, a destruction which was proleptically enacted with the tearing of the veil of the ναός (27:51). By means of the motif of blood Matthew has directly associated the destruction of the temple (and the people, 27:25) with the Jewish rejection of Jesus. As a polluted place, attended by a polluted people, the temple and the Jews remain true to their perverse character, for theirs is a history of the shedding of "righteous blood" in the very precincts of the sanctuary (23:35). Jerusalem, the temple, and its people are destroyed for their guilt has polluted them, making them unfit for the presence of God and certainly unqualified to be the center of eschatological fulfillment.

Matthew 16:17-19 may indicate that the first Evangelist, like Mark, viewed the Christian church as the new temple. In the first place, the "rock" imagery within this saying gives the statement immediate affinity with Jewish temple motifs.[30] Second, the idea that Peter is the foundation rock gives the verse an association with Eph. 2:20 which declares the apostles and prophets to be the foundation of the *temple*-community (cf. also Rev. 21:14). Third, the declaration that Jesus (whom Peter just confessed to be the Christ, v. 16) would build the church/temple gives the text an affinity with Mk. 14:58b, a text which declares the church to be the new temple built by Christ. Also, it may betray Matthew's conscious reflection upon and reinterpretation of the popular Jewish idea that the Messiah would rebuild the eschatological temple.[31] Hence, like Mark, Matthew sees Jerusalem and its temple as no longer playing any positive role in the realization of God's eschatological promises; the prerogatives of the old temple now belong to the new temple, the church.

The Conceptual Pattern in Paul and the Deutero-Pauline Texts.[32] Paul and the later texts which bear his name show awareness and appropriation

---

[30]See Joachim Jeremias, *Golgotha*, ΑΓΓΕΛΟΣ, Archiv für neutestamentliche Zeitgeschichte und Kulturkunde (Leipzig: Verlag von Eduard Pfeiffer, 1926) 43-45, 51-58, 70-73.

[31]Adolf Schlatter, *Der Evangelist Mattäus: Seine Sprache, sein Selbtständigkeit* (Stuttgart: Calwer Verlag, 1948) 506-507, argues that the idea of Jesus "building" the church is a conscious reflection upon Zech. 6:12 where it says of the "Branch," that "he shall build the temple of the LORD."

[32]I shall assume the authenticity of Rom., 1 and 2 Cor., Gal., 1 Thess., Phil., and Phile. All other texts in the New Testament ascribed to Paul are referred to as "deutero-Pauline."

of traditional expectations concerning Jerusalem and the temple. Yet to Paul's way of thinking the church was the sphere of the concrete realization of these expectations.

First, he assumes a close association to exist between the Christ and the church/temple. In 1 Cor. 3:10-11 Jesus is described as the θεμέλιον upon whom the "building" (3:9) or "temple" (3:16) is built. In the deutero-Pauline materials a similar image is found. In Eph. 2:20 Christ is called the ἀκρογωνιαῖος, the cornerstone of the foundation. Ephesians, similarly to 1 Corinthians, assumes a close relationship between the Christ and the new temple. Christ is the one in whom the structure grows and is built (Eph. 2:21-22; cf. 4:16-17). Clearly the idea represented here is that the community-temple is wholly dependent upon the Messiah for its growth. In effect, Jesus builds the temple, reflecting the expectation that the Messiah would build the eschatological temple of God. While this idea has influenced Paul and his followers, the fulfillment of the expectation was found in the church.

Second, the temple motif expresses for Paul the idea that the church is the dwelling place of God (1 Cor. 3:16, 2 Cor. 6:16b).[33] One aspect of the hope of Judaism was that in the eschatological age God's presence among his people would again be realized.[34] Paul believed that this hope was finding full realization in the community-temple. In 2 Cor. 6:16b-18, Paul offers a collage of Old Testament texts which, according to Paul's own testimony (see v. 16a), have to do with the church as the temple of God. In the church, the hope of a new temple in which the presence of God is manifested finds realization.

Third, a deutero-Pauline text proclaims the temple/church to be the center of the Gentiles' salvation. In Eph. 2:19 it is said that the Gentiles are "no longer strangers and sojourners but . . . are fellow citizens with the saints and members of the household of God." The Pauline disciple does not abandon the *form* of Jewish expectation, he simply affirms that by virtue of the peace preached to the Gentiles "who were far off" (v. 17) they have now become fully a part of the people of God (ἡ πολιτεία τοῦ Ἰσραήλ, v. 12) and, hence, may gain access into the ναὸν ἅγιον (v. 21), the church. By insisting on this ναός as the sphere of the Gentiles'

---

[33]It is legitimate to consider 2 Cor. 6:14-7:1 as Pauline. See Werner Georg Kümmel, *Introduction to the New Testament,* rev. ed. trans. Howard Clark Kee (Nashville: Abingdon Press, 1975) 287-88.

[34]See Joel 3:17 (Hebrew, 4:17) and Zech. 2:10. The coming and continued abiding presence of God as the essence of Old Testament eschatological hope is discussed and documented in Edmund P. Clowney, "The Final Temple," WJT 35 (1973): 164-65.

reconciliation to God, the author is at the same time reflecting the Jewish expectation that Jerusalem and the temple would be the place of the Gentiles' redemption. The deutero-Pauline text has retained the form of Jewish expectation, but has reinterpreted it in terms of its ecclesiology.

The transferral to the church of expectations concerning Jerusalem and the temple deprived these literal entities of any importance in the realization of God's eschatological promises. In the deutero-Pauline text of 2 Thess. 2:3-4, for example, the author reflects traditional apocalyptic expectations concerning the end-time abomination of the ναός (See Dan. 9:27; 11:31; 12:11). The defeat of this agent of Satan (2:9) by the power of Christ (2:8) may indicate that the author believed the temple to be the place of the final revelation of the victory of God. It should be noted, however, that while the text shares in the tradition that the temple will be desecrated, there is no mention of its subsequent consecration as a result of the defeat of the man of lawlessness. Second Thess. 2:3-4 may, therefore, be attesting to the expectation, similar to that found in Mark and Matthew, that the Jerusalem temple would be only a place of desolation and desecration—not a place of salvation.

Second, the role of Jerusalem itself in Paul's thought is related to this issue. Rom. 11:26-27 may indicate Paul's belief that Jerusalem was to be associated with eschatological salvation. But here "Zion" may refer to the church, which would indicate that Paul has retained the *form* of Jewish expectation, while altering the material meaning.[35]

Another important text is Gal. 4:26, where reference is made to a "Jerusalem above." Even if Paul did view the heavenly city as some type of literal "place," it is clear that it has nothing to do with the earthly Jerusalem. Furthermore, Paul says nothing of the descent of this heavenly Jerusalem to earth.

It is enlightening to interpret Gal. 4:26 in light of Phil. 3:20 where Paul makes reference to a heavenly πολίτευμα. H. C. G. Moule argues that Paul may have conceived of the πολίτευμα of Philippians as a type of locality, though he does not note an association with Gal. 4:26.[36] If in some way the heavenly πολίτευμα of Phil. 3:20 is closely associated, even if not explicitly identified, with the heavenly Jerusalem of Galatians, it is

---

[35]So E. Earle Ellis, *Paul's Use of the Old Testament* (Grand Rapids MI: Baker Book House, 1981, rpt. of 1957 original) 123n5. He argues that Zion is the "true Israel," the church, whereas Jacob is the nation Israel.

[36]*The Epistle to the Philippians,* Thornapple Commentaries (Cambridge: 1897; rpt.: Grand Rapids MI: Baker, 1981) 73.

made clear in Philippians that the saints' heavenly place of citizenship does not descend to earth. Rather, it explicitly states that *Jesus* descends from (οὗ) this πολίτευμα[37]in order to resurrect the saints (3:21) who meet the Lord *in the air* and forever remain with the Lord (1 Thess. 4:16-17). Following this resurrection, according to 1 Cor. 15:23-28, the eternal reign of God begins. There is simply no room in Paul's eschatological schema for the establishment on earth of a literal city which would house the saints of God.

Nonetheless, Johannes Munck has argued that Paul believed that Jerusalem was to be the scene of the End, with the nations' pilgrimage to the holy place bringing 'tribute' being the event which triggered the Eschaton.[38] Paul understood the Gentile churches' gift to the Jerusalem saints, brought to the holy city by him and representatives of the "nations," to be this eschatological pilgrimage. Davies raises two formidable objections.[39] One, if Paul believed the End would manifest itself at Jerusalem with the arrival of the "nations," why did he appeal to Caesar? Second, Paul's plans to go to Spain following the delivery of the collection are simply inexplicable if the apostle genuinely believed that the End would manifest itself in Jerusalem of Judea.

Neither Jerusalem of Judea nor the temple located there retained in the thought of Paul or his followers any significance in the realization of God's eschatological promises. Furthermore, he did not envision the literal establishment upon the earth of a new Jerusalem descended from heaven. His consistent appropriation and transferral of temple and city motifs to the church would indicate that the church, built on Christ, was the temple of the eschatological age.

The Conceptual Pattern in John. Even a cursory reading of the Fourth Gospel indicates that John, like other New Testament writers, believed that the temple had been displaced and replaced by something else. He believed that it was Jesus himself, and not the believing community, to whom the function and prerogatives of the Jewish temple had passed. There are a number of texts that allude to Jesus as the temple.

---

[37]Interpreters debate whether the antecedent of οὗ is οὐρανοῖς (so F. W. Beare, *The Epistle to the Philippians,* 3rd ed., Black's New Testament Commentaries [London: Adam and Charles Black, 1973] 136-37) or πολίτευμα (so Moule, *Philippians*). It must be noted that the pronoun is singular, and that could tend to favor the singular πολίτευμα as the antecedent.

[38]*Paul and the Salvation of Mankind,* trans. Frank Clarke (London: SCM Press, 1959), 282-308.

[39]Davies, *Gospel and the Land,* 202-203.

John 1:14. The two key words that point to the theme of Jesus as the temple are σκηνοῦν and δόξα. Σκηνοῦν literally means "to pitch a tent," and, therefore, conveys the image of the tabernacle (σκηνή) of the Old Testament.[40] The σκηνή represented the place where God met his people (see especially Ex. 40). Closely associated with the tabernacle was the glory of God (Ex. 40:34), an association seen also in Jn. 1:14. In the word-become-flesh the community beholds the glory of the eternal one who is God (Jn. 1:1). In associating Jesus with the tabernacle and the glory which was present there the author of John has laid the foundation for transferring to Jesus the function and prerogatives of the temple.

John 1:51. This statement appears to find its background in Gen. 28:12 since each text makes reference to angels "ascending and descending" onto some object. What is significant is that the passage in Genesis has to do with the house of God (Gen. 28:17). As might be imagined, this was a ripe text for speculation concerning the temple. In point of fact, the stone upon which Jacob laid his head (Gen. 28:11) was often interpreted as the foundation stone of the temple.[41] The place where the angels ascended and descended was the place of the Lord; the "house of God" and "the gate of heaven." Knowledge of this background easily leads to the conclusion that John wished this to be said about Jesus; he is the "place" and "gate" where heaven and earth meet.

John 2:19-22. This text declares unambiguously that Jesus has replaced the temple. The Jews totally misunderstand the meaning of Jesus' statement in verse 19 ("destroy this temple"). But there is no doubt for the reader that Jesus is referring to himself when he says "and in three days I will raise it up," for the Evangelist explicitly states this in verse 21: "But he spoke of the temple of his body." The fact that the Evangelist has placed this story at the beginning of the Gospel may indicate that from his point of view Jesus' displacement of the temple is not the culmination of Jesus' work, but its foundation.[42]

This brief look at some selected texts indicates that Jesus in the Fourth Gospel has displaced the temple of Jerusalem. What is more, the Johannine Jesus assumed within himself many of the functions of the eschato-

---

[40]Raymond E. Brown, *The Gospel according to John*, 2 vols., The Anchor Bible 29 and 29a (Garden City NY: Doubleday & Co., 1966) 1:32-35.

[41]See Gen. Rab. 68:12; 69:7.

[42]Rudolf Schnackenburg, *The Gospel according to St. John*, 2 vols., trans. Kevin Smyth, Herder's Theological Commentary on the New Testament (New York: Herder and Herder; London: Burn and Oater, 1968, 1980) 1:356.

logical temple and city. First, it was believed that living water would flow from the eschatological city and temple (Ezek. 47:1; Zech. 14:8), a feature of eschatological expectation which was associated with the Tabernacles' festival in Jesus' time. Interpreted in this context, the saying of Jesus, uttered during the Feast of Tabernacles, that living water would flow from *him*, points to Jesus as the new temple (Jn. 7:37-39). Second, just as the nations would come to the "lifted up" Jerusalem (Isa. 2:2), all men will come to Jesus when he is "lifted up" (12:32). Third, it was believed that the eschatological city would function as the light of the world (Pes. de Rab Kah. 21:4,5). Such is the explicit function of Jesus in John (8:12).

It would appear, therefore, that John, like his Christian contemporaries, believed that the temple of Jerusalem had been displaced by a new temple. Unlike his contemporaries, the new temple finds realization in Jesus himself and not in the church. John's displacement of the temple with Jesus also led to the transferral of certain specific functions of the temple to Jesus: he is the source of living water, the center of the eschatological redemption of the nations, and the light of the world.

The Conceptual Pattern in Hebrews. As was true of his Christian contemporaries, the denigration of the old cult is one motive of the author of Hebrews. In Hebrews, the displacement of the old temple has been realized by the work of Jesus and the life of the existing Christian community. Unlike the preceding materials, however, the author of Hebrews does not "ecclesiologize" or "christologize" the temple, for in Hebrews neither the church nor Jesus actually becomes the new eschatological temple.

The cultic focus of attention in Hebrews is actually the Old Testament "tabernacle" (8:2, 5; 9:2, 6, 8, 11, 21), and "holy place" or "sanctuary" (see, e.g., 9:2-3), with neither the ναός nor the ἱερόν, the standard words for "temple," being explicitly mentioned. Heb. 8-10 is the heart of the epistle, for there is described herein the work of Christ in the heavenly sanctuary; work which makes God immediately accessible to his people (10:19-22). The superiority of the work of Christ as it effects access to God is expressed in dualistic language pertaining to the tabernacle and sanctuary. The sanctuary wherein Christ has performed his once-for-all sacrifice (7:27; 9:25-28; 10:12) is described as being "heavenly" (8:5; cf. 9:23-24) as opposed to "worldly" (9:2). It is "true" or "genuine" (8:2; cf. 9:24) as opposed to being merely a "copy," "shadow" (8:5), or "type" (9:24). This heavenly, true sanctuary is described as being "not made with hands" (9:11), as opposed to "made with hands" (9:24). The sanctuary of Christ's work is not of this age (9:11), while the "first tabernacle" was actually "symbolic for the present age" (9:9).

It is extremely difficult to get a grasp on a precise definition of the heavenly sanctuary. Dissimilarities with Philo caution against defining it in pure, Platonic categories.[43] Jewish apocalyptic often speculated concerning the heavenly temple, but the differences in form, style, and content that exist between Hebrews and Jewish apocalyptic caution against defining the heavenly temple as a concrete entity that one day would descend to earth to replace the earthly temple.[44] It would appear that for the author of Hebrews the heavenly, true sanctuary represents primarily the presence of God.[45] Clearly, the purpose of Christ's work in this "place" is to make available to the people of God access to the divine presence (9:24; 10:19).

O. Hofius has argued that standing behind the image of the veil (6:19-20; 10:19-20) is Jewish tradition that employed similar imagery to express the transcendent grandeur of God, a holiness that set him radically apart and at a distance from his creation. What has resulted from the death of Jesus is nearness to God.[46] On humanity's behalf he has entered in to the immediate presence of God (6:19-20). For the author of Hebrews, therefore, the heavenly sanctuary is not simply a pure form, nor a place envisioned by an apocalyptic seer. It is an all-inclusive symbol which functions to capture the result of the work of Christ: nearness to God which hitherto had been unavailable (see 9:8-14).

The author of Hebrews also employs the image of the pilgrimage to Zion to portray access to God and the heavenly world (12:22-24). George Wesley Buchanan has argued that a type of Christian Zionism which would find a literal fulfillment in the land of Canaan stands behind this image.[47]

---

[43]On the issue of the relationship between Philo and Hebrews, see Sidney G. Sowers, *The Hermeneutics of Philo and Hebrews: A Comparison of the Interpretation of the Old Testament in Philo Judaeus and the Epistle to the Hebrews,* Basel Studies of Theology 1 (Zurich: EVZ-Verlag, 1965), and R. Williamson, *Philo and the Epistle to the Hebrews,* Arbeiter zur Literature und Geschichte des hellenistischen Judentums 4 (Leiden: E. J. Brill, 1970).

[44]So Franz Joseph Schierse, *Verheissung und Heilsvollendung: Zur theologischen Grundfrage des Hebräerbriefs,* Münchener Theologische Studien 9 (Munich: Karl Zink Verlag, 1955) 26.

[45]Yves M.-J. Congar, *The Mystery of the Temple: The Manner of God's Presence to His Creatures from Genesis to the Apocalypse,* trans. Reginald F. Trevett (London: Burns and Oater, 1962) 173-75.

[46]Otfried Hofius, *Der Vorhang vor dem Thron Gottes: Eine exegetischreligionsgeschichtliche Untersuchungen zu Hebräer 6,19f. und 10,19f.,* Wissenschaftliche Untersuchungen zum Neuen Testament 14 (Tübingen: J. C. B. Mohr, 1972) 95-96.

[47]*To the Hebrews: Translation, Comment and Conclusions.* The Anchor Bible 36 (Garden City NY: Doubleday, 1972) 256-57.

But his literalistic interpretation seems out of touch with the hermeneutical style of Hebrews for which Old Testament entities function primarily as "types" of that which is now finding fulfillment on a more nonliteral level.[48] He is, however, correct to argue that what may very well stand behind the Zion imagery is the motif of the eschatological pilgrimage to Zion, for the motif of the pilgrimage functions symbolically to give expression to the close relationship between the community and God.

The author of Hebrews believes that in some proleptic sense the faithful have arrived at the destination of their eschatological pilgrimage. This is indicated by the use of the perfect tense (προσεληλύθατε) in 12:22, denoting the continuance of *completed* action. Since the author of Hebrews perceived the community as having already arrived at Zion, it is clear that he interpreted this pilgrimage symbolically. In all likelihood, worship was the context in which the sharing of eschatological redemption found realization. In the first place, the Old Testament could use προσέρχεσθαι in a cultic sense (Num. 18:4; Jer. 7:16), and in Hebrews it is often used with a cultic nuance (4:16; 7:25; 10:1, 22; 11:6). Second, worship is described in cultic language in 13:15. This description of worship, which employs the language of sacrifice, directly follows a statement concerning the city which is to come (13:14b).

Hebrews views neither Jesus nor the church as the eschatological temple or city. Nonetheless, he does believe that "in these last days" (1:2) the old temple has been displaced by a hitherto unavailable access to God. Such access is made possible by the once-for-all atoning work of Jesus in the past, and is realized in the present in the context of Christian worship. Hence, while Hebrews does not share the precise interpretation of the other Christian writings examined thus far, he does share broadly in the same pattern: Jesus and his community render the old temple obsolete in the new age of salvation.

The Conceptual Pattern in First Peter. First Peter 2:4-10 contains an interesting complex of images, all of which may serve to point to the church, related inextricably to Christ, as the new eschatological temple of God. There are two primary reasons why one can conclude that this text portrays the church as the new temple. First, the cultic language of priesthood (ἱεράτευμα, 2:5, 9) and sacrifice (θυσία, 2:5) has led some interpreters to view the "spiritual house" of 2:5 as a temple.[49] Second, inter-

---

[48]See Sowers, *Hermeneutics,* 89-97.

[49]E.g., Richard J. McKelvey, *The New Temple: The Church in the New Testament,* Oxford Theological Monographs (New York: Oxford University Press, 1969) 128; Klinzing, *Umdeutung des Kultus,* 192n5.

preters tend to believe that this text portrays the community as the temple because the image of the community as a house stands in close relation to a complex of images focusing on a "stone" (λίθος) motif.

What is particularly striking is the close association between this Petrine passage and some Qumranic texts, two of which are particularly striking: 1QH 6:25ff. and 1 QS 8:1-10. First Peter's association with 1QH 6:25ff. consists of the common use of Isa. 28:16 to describe the community. In both 1 Peter and 1QH the members of the community are viewed as the "stones" which form the edifice. Furthermore, in both texts there exists a differentiation between the stone-of-foundation (see 1QH 6:26a; 1 Pet. 2:4) and the stones which comprise the community (see 1QH 6:26b; 1 Pet. 2:5), whereas Isa. 28:16 makes no such differentiation. Isaiah speaks only of a single foundation stone. This leads Gärtner to conclude that there must exist some link between 1 Peter and 1QH.[50] If temple imagery lay ultimately behind the passage of 1QH 6, as Gärtner contends, then 1 Peter's link with this Qumranic text would provide a link with community-as-temple symbolism.

The second important Qumranic text is 1QS 8:1-10 where numerous specific associations can be noted.[51] "Spiritual house" (1 Pet. 2:5) corresponds to the "House of Holiness" (1QS 8:5) and "House of Perfection and Truth" (1QS 8:9); "holy priesthood" (1 Pet. 2:5) corresponds to the "Assembly of Supreme Holiness for Aaron" (1QS 8:5-6) and the "Most Holy Dwelling for Aaron" (1QS 8:8-9); the offering of "spiritual sacrifices" (1 Pet. 2:5) corresponds to the offering up of fragrance (1QS 8:9); "acceptable to God" (1 Pet. 2:5) corresponds to "what is acceptable" in 1QS 8:10 (cf. 8:6). What is significant is that standing behind 1QS 8:5-10 is the concept of the community as the temple. If 1 Peter shows so many affinities with such a temple-as-community tradition, it seems that he would share in the same conception of his community. The "spiritual house," therefore, is probably a temple.[52]

---

[50]See Gärtner's discussion, *Temple and Community*, 76-79.

[51]David Flusser, "The Dead Sea Sect and Pre-Pauline Christianity," in *Scripta Hierosolymitana* IV: "Aspects of the Dead Sea Scrolls," ed. Chaim Rabin and Yigael Yadin (Jerusalem: Magnes Press, 1965) 233-34.

[52]So Gärtner, *Temple and Community*, 75-78; McKelvey, *New Temple*, 127-128; Lloyd Gaston, *No Stone on Another: Studies in the Significance of the Fall of Jerusalem in the Synoptic Gospels*, NovTSup 23 (Leiden: E. J. Brill, 1970) 188-89; Klinzing, *Umdeutung des Kultus*, 191-96. A strong objection to this broad consensus may be found in John Hall Elliott, *The Elect and the Holy: An Exegetical Examination of 1 Peter 2:4-10 and the Phrase* βασίλειον Ἱεράτευμα, NovTSup 12 (Leiden: E. J. Brill, 1966).

First Peter stands in the broad context of other New Testament authors in that he sees the community as a new temple. Its status as such is inextricably related to its association with Jesus, the living stone. Because the Christians believe in Jesus, he is a cornerstone and foundation of the edifice. The author clearly assumes that the new eschatological temple is the locus of God's eschatological work. The living stones which comprise this temple are the eschatological people of God (1 Pet. 2:9-10). Just as the people who would gather at the eschatological temple and city in Jewish speculation would be a holy people, so too are the Christians to be a holy people (1:15-16, 22; 2:1, 5, 9-10, 11; 3:8-16; 4:15). Like the eschatological temple of Jewish expectation, the new temple is the locus for the witness to the Gentiles (2:12) and is even the "place" of the Gentiles' salvation (2:10). While 1 Peter betrays no direct association with the traditions that the Messiah would build the eschatological temple, he clearly does believe that it is the relationship of the believers to Jesus the Messiah that transforms them into the living stones which are "built into a spiritual house" (2:5).

The Conceptual Pattern in the Apocalypse. Revelation has numerous explicit points of contact with Jewish eschatological traditions pertaining to Jerusalem. First, the idea of the heavenly temple, found in many Jewish sources, is present, though the emphases concerning the temple are redirected. Second, like the eschatological Jerusalem of Jewish expectation, the new Jerusalem of Revelation would be inhabited only by those who were holy (21:8, 27; 22:3, 14-15). Third, Jerusalem is envisaged as the place of the Gentiles' salvation (21:24-26; 22:2). Finally, while the Messiah is not portrayed as building the new city or a new temple, there is an intimate connection between Messiah and temple (19:7; 21:2, 9, 22). While such specific points of contact with Jewish tradition are easily detected, the Seer has been greatly influenced by the Christian appropriation of the Jerusalem/temple traditions. The fusion of Jewish and Christian motifs come to clear expression in the Apocalypse.

Within Revelation there are a number of explicit references to a heavenly temple (11:19; 14:15, 17; 15:5, 6, 8; 16:1, 17). While such a concept was widespread in Judaism, it takes on a different quality and character in Revelation. In the first place, there is nowhere present the idea that this heavenly temple is the perfect heavenly pattern of the earthly sanctuary in Jerusalem. To the Seer of the Apocalypse the literal temple of Jerusalem plays no important role at all. The empirical city of Jerusalem in point of fact is an evil city, known primarily as the place where Jesus was crucified (11:8). Second, there is no conception that this temple which now stands in heaven would one day descend to earth. In the perfect, consummated age no temple structure would exist at all (21:22).

Revelation betrays contact with Christian tradition in its appropriation of the image of the *earthly* church as a temple. A significant text in this regard is 11:1-3. Here the "measured" temple, that is, the divinely protected temple, can easily be understood as the earthly church, the people of God. The "protection" of the ναός does not indicate preservation from the physical tribulation and suffering, but from being conquered spiritually by the Satanic forces. It denotes the people who are saved—the church. The outer court of 11:2 is generally interpreted to mean those who will not survive spiritually the onslaught of Satan and his forces; that is to say, it denotes those who are not "saved."[53]

Rev. 20:9 may share in related imagery. Here the church is not portrayed as the temple, but as the holy city Jerusalem. To understand the city as a symbol for the saints one must translate the phrase τὴν παρεμβολὴν τῶν ἁγίων καὶ τὴν πόλιν τὴν ἠγαπημένην by understanding τῶν ἁγίων appositionally and καί epexegetically. This would render the following translation: "the camp which is the saints, which is the beloved city." Such an interpretation may be justified since it is virtually impossible that the Seer would have understood the earthly Jerusalem to be "the beloved city" for he emphatically disparages the empirical Jerusalem. In 11:8 he views it only as the city which is known as the place which crucified Jesus and persecuted his witnesses, the church.

Temple/city imagery is used also to describe the *consummated* people of God. It is explicitly stated in 3:12 that the people of God will form the constitutive elements of the temple in the new Jerusalem. This creates a possible tension with 21:22 which states that there is no temple at all in the new city, for God and the Lamb are the temple. However, what comes to expression in this "tension" is the promise of perfect communion between God and his people in the new Jerusalem (21:3). The focus of this communion is not a special holy *place,* but a special holy *people.* Hence, the conquering saints of 3:12 may quite understandably be called the temple of God. Yet since the people of God share in the experience of the unmediated presence of God and the Lamb, it might also be said that the temple consists of God and the Lamb themselves. Both ideas, that of the consummated community-as-temple and God and the Lamb as temple, serve to give symbolic expression to the idea that perfect communion is shared between God and his people in the new age.

---

[53]So, e.g., R. H. Charles, *A Critical and Exegetical Commentary on the Revelation of St. John,* 2 vols., The International Critical Commentary (New York: Charles Scribner's Sons, 1920) 1:276, and G. R. Beasley-Murray, *The Book of Revelation,* New Century Bible (London: Oliphants, 1974) 176.

Imagery of the new, restored Jerusalem, complete with paradisical motifs, is used to describe this perfect communion. Like the restored Jerusalem of many circles of Jewish expectation, the Gentiles also share in this experience of the divine presence in Jerusalem. It is by the light of this city that the nations walk (21:24-26; cf. Pes. de Rab Kah. 21). The nations shall share in the healing which goes forth from this city as well (22:2). The influence of Christian tradition on the Seer is seen in the "ecclesiologizing" of the motif of the new Jerusalem. The city is described as the bride of the Lamb (21:9; cf. 21:2), which is most generally recognized as a reference to the church, the people of God.[54] Yet at the same time temple imagery comes into play with emphasis on the *cubical* dimension of the *golden* city (21:16, 18). This perfect golden cube is clearly an allusion to the cubed Holy of Holies (1 Kgs. 6:20), the place of the presence of God among his people. In the eternal age, God's presence would not be experienced in a special place among the people; the locus of God's presence would be the people themselves. They are the Holy of Holies.

It would appear, therefore, that while the Seer has shown himself to be thoroughly familiar with common Jewish eschatological traditions revolving around Jerusalem and the temple, he has fallen into the broad stream of Christian tradition by finding the realization of such hopes in the *people* of God. The people of God, in perfect rest, will be the locus of God's presence and salvation. They will fulfill in every respect the hopes associated with Jerusalem and the temple by Jewish visionaries. Jerusalem and the temple as empirical entities have been totally displaced.

Conclusion. Early Christianity, as it is reflected in the non-Lukan materials of the New Testament, was aware of Jewish expectations concerning Jerusalem and the temple in the eschatological age. First, many early Christians, like many Jews, held to the hope of a restored "temple" and "city" (Mk. 14:58b; Matt. 16:17-19; 1 Cor. 3:12; cf. Gal. 4:26; Rev. 3:12; 14:1; 20:9; 21:2-22:5). Second, this restored "city" and "temple" would be the locus of God's holy and redeemed eschatological people (1 Cor. 3:17b; 2 Cor. 6:17; Eph. 2:21; cf. 1 Cor. 6:19; Heb. 12:22-24; 1 Pet. 2:9-10; Rev. 21:8, 27; 22:3, 14-15). Third, the restored "temple" and "city" would be the center from which God would deal with the Gentiles, ultimately for their salvation (Eph. 2:12, 17, 19; Jn. 2:21; 7:37-39; 8:12; 12:32, 35-36; 1 Pet. 2:10, 12; Rev. 20:7-10; 21:24-26; 22:2). Finally, they saw a close relationship between the restored "temple-city" and the Messiah (1

---

[54]So Congar, *Mystery,* 215, and McKelvey, *New Temple,* 176.

Cor. 3:10-11; Eph. 2:20; Mk. 14:58b; Matt. 16:17-19; 1 Pet. 2:4-10; Rev. 19:7; 21:2, 9, 22). One would be hard pressed to argue that early Christianity formulated its temple-Jerusalem ideology in a cultural vacuum, separated from Jewish thought.

Early Christianity also thoroughly reformulated traditional Jewish expectations. There took place a thorough disparaging, or at least disregarding, of the *literal* temple and city (2 Thess. 2:3-9; Gal. 4:26; Mk. 13:14; Matt. 24:15; 27:3-10; Hebrews; Rev. 11:8). Jewish texts often indicated that the second temple, either before or after its destruction, was perceived as being imperfect (Tob. 14:5a; 2 Macc. 2:4-8; 2 Bar. 2:4-7; 1 En. 90:28-29; Sib. Or. 3:286-294; 4QpIsa[b]:6-9). But this was coupled with the expectation that the less-than-perfect city and temple would be replaced by a perfect *literal* and *physical* temple and city in the age to come (Tob. 14:5b, 2 Macc. 2:7-8; 2 Bar. 6:9; 1 En. 90:29; Sib. Or. 3:286-294; 4QFlor 1:1-3; 11QTemple). The dominant pattern among the earliest Christians was to reserve *no* place for a new physical temple or city. These had been totally and forever displaced either by the community itself as the new temple/city (Paul, Mark, Matthew, 1 Peter, Revelation), by Jesus himself as the new temple (John, Revelation) or by the redemptive work and liturgical activity of Jesus and the community respectively (Hebrews). There is no hint of the restoration of the literal holy precincts in the Christian materials. Revelation is most explicit: even in the fully consummated new creation there is no literal city and no literal temple, for the people of God, along with God himself and the Lamb, joined together in perfect communion, form the new temple. Jerusalem of Judea and the temple located there are of no positive significance in the eschatological work of God.

This discussion had no intention of explaining the origin of the conceptual patterns concerning the eschatological Jerusalem and temple in Judaism and early Christianity. Its only purpose was to provide a backdrop against which Luke-Acts could be interpreted. It is now to this task that attention is directed.

The Identification of Jesus and the Church with Jerusalem and the Temple in Luke-Acts

Chapter II

Introduction

The prevailing pattern in early non-Lukan Christianity was to transfer to Jesus or to the church the prerogatives and functions of the eschatological Jerusalem and temple. In investigating the role of Jerusalem and the temple in Luke-Acts, it is necessary to ask whether the third Evangelist shared in the broad conceptual pattern of his Christian contemporaries. Is there evidence that Luke transferred to Jesus and/or the church the eschatological functions of the temple?

The Transferral of Temple Motifs to the Church

A number of factors indicate that Luke did not explicitly transfer to the church the functions of the temple.

1. A survey of the concordance reveals the primary fact that Luke simply did not explicitly equate ἱερόν, ναός, τόπος (when used of the temple), or the city with the church.

2. Luke omits from his account of the trial of Jesus the statement of Mk. 14:58 (cf. Mk. 15:29, which is also struck from Luke) in which Jesus indirectly promises the establishment of a new spiritual temple, the church. It would not be illegitimate to conclude that Luke omitted the saying of Mk. 14:58 precisely because he saw that it could (and according to modern interpreters, it *should*) be understood to be a promise for the restoration of

the temple on a "spiritual" level, a restoration which would find its fulfillment in the church.

3. Luke did not see the postresurrection community as a substitute for the temple. Luke concludes his gospel with the statement that the disciples "returned to Jerusalem with great joy, and were continually in the temple blessing God" (Lk. 24:52). Furthermore, the temple played a central role in the life of the community in the early chapters of Acts (2:46; 3:1-3, 5; 5:20-21, 42). It would be incorrect to insist that the community's attachment to the temple was thoroughly a noncultic one, and that the community used the temple exclusively as a place to teach Israel,[1] for Luke explicitly states in Acts 21:23-26 that Paul made the necessary offering at the temple in relation to the Nazarite vow.

4. A survey of the Lukan materials indicates that Luke did not transfer cultic language from the temple to the church, as though he wished to imply that the church was now the proper locus of the cult. Christians are never referred to generally as priests, or as a priesthood. Neither is the priesthood of the temple dismissed as a defiled office (Lk. 5:14; 17:14). It is true that Luke quite often pictures members of the priesthood, and especially its leaders, in a negative light.[2] Yet, priests can be said to accept the eschatological revelation of God (Lk. 1:5; Acts 6:7). The priesthood as such, therefore, is neither supplanted by the church, nor polemically rejected.

Neither does Luke spiritualize the idea of offering (προσφορά, δῶρον) or sacrifice (θυσία), nor does he use such language to describe the Christian life.[3] The language of sacrifice is employed literally, and is often employed in the context of the temple cult. When it is found in this context, it is presented in a positive light (Lk. 2:24; 5:14; 21:1-4; Acts 21:26; 24:17). Explicitly negative attitudes revolve around the cultic terms only in the context of the Stephen speech (Acts 7:41-42), where Stephen is describing the idolatrous incident of the golden calf (7:41) and the lack of a sacrificial cult during Israel's period of desert wanderings (7:42). The latter reference can hardly be understood as Luke's rejection of all sacrifice and offering, given Acts 21:26 and 24:17 where Paul's participation in the Jewish cult is viewed as an act of true piety.

---

[1]So Ernst Lohmeyer, *Lord of the Temple: A Study of the Relation Between Cult and Gospel,* trans. Stewart Todd (Edinburgh and London: Oliver and Boyd; Richmond: John Knox Press, 1961) 112-13.

[2]See, e.g., Lk. 19:47; 20:1, 19; 22:2, 4, 52, 54, 66; 23:4, 10, 13, 24:20; Acts 4:1-22; 5:17-40; 9:1-2.

[3]Contrasting such New Testament texts as Rom. 12:1; 15:16; Eph. 5:2; Phil. 2:7; 4:18; Heb. 13:15-16.

5. Luke offers no explicit indications that the church has supplanted the temple as the place of worship. Lk. 2:37 clearly denotes the Jerusalem temple as a place of worship (λατρεύειν). The gospel concludes with the note that the disciples returned joyfully to Jerusalem where they praised God in the temple (Lk. 24:53). In one instance (Acts 24:14), "the Way" is said to provide a proper way of worshipping God, yet there is no hint here that Christian worship displaces that of the Jews. In fact, the validity of non-Christian Jewish worship is affirmed in Acts 26:6-7 where Paul refers to the Jews' hope in "the promise made by God to our fathers, to which our twelve tribes hope to attain, as they earnestly worship night and day." This attitude toward Jewish worship contrasts greatly with that of other New Testament authors who portray the Jewish places of worship as Satanic (Rev. 2:9; 3:9), desolate (Mk. 13:14), or strongholds of persecution (Jn. 16:2).

With regard to the issue at hand, one text deserves special attention. In the context of Acts 15 James is said to offer the following quotation from Amos:

> After this I will return, and I will rebuild the dwelling [lit. "tabernacle" (σκηνήν)] of David, which has fallen; I will rebuild its ruins, and I will set it up, that the rest of men may seek the Lord, and all the Gentiles who are called by my name, says the Lord, who has made these things known from of old. (Acts 15:16-17; cf. Amos 9:11)

It is not necessary to attempt to solve the numerous critical problems surrounding the fifteenth chapter of Acts in order to come to some helpful conclusions concerning the meaning of the "*skene* of David" (v. 16). The issue for this study is simply this: Did Luke understand this "tabernacle of David" to be a reconstituted temple? This question must be addressed in two parts.

First, it is necessary to determine the group or person that the tabernacle is representing. A few argue that the reconstructed tabernacle refers to Jesus or the messianic kingdom which he inaugurates. Ernst Haenchen argues that the tabernacle represents the whole of the Jesus story, culminating in the resurrection of Jesus and the mission to the Gentiles.[4] Haenchen fails to show how the imagery of verse 16 with its references to the "rebuilding" and "restoration" of "ruins" is to be understood as a clear reference to the Jesus story. J. C. O'Neill implies that the restructured tabernacle is a reference to the messianic rule of David, though it is

---

[4]*The Acts of the Apostles: A Commentary,* trans. Bernard Noble and Gerald Shinn with Hugh Anderson, rev. trans. R. McLeod Wilson (Philadelphia: Westminster, 1971) 448.

unclear precisely what he means by this.[5] Jacques Dupont would appear to share a similar view in that he sees the tabernacle as referring to the throne of David,[6] but he also provides no meaningful elaboration.

A number of other interpreters view the rebuilt and restored tabernacle as the church, the people of God.[7] This seems reasonable, for it is clear from verse 17 that the purpose of the restored tabernacle is to bring the Gentiles to God. As important as the "Jesus event" is to this purpose, it is primarily the function of the community to engage in this activity (Acts 1:8). It should be noted, however, that understanding the tabernacle to represent the whole church (inclusive of the Gentiles) makes verse 17 something less than sensible. The purpose of rebuilding the tabernacle is so the Gentiles may also seek the Lord and call upon his name. Apparently, therefore, the tabernacle is not inclusive of the Gentiles, but is the instrument by means of which the nations will come to know the Lord. Clearly the thrust of Acts 15:16-17 differentiates between the tabernacle of David and "the rest of men," with the latter being understood as "all the Gentiles." It would be better to understand the tabernacle, therefore, as a portion of the church, specifically the Jerusalem church, or perhaps the Jewish Christians, wherever their location.

Such an interpretation is not original. J. Jervell has also argued that the restored tabernacle denotes the restored Israel.[8] He believes that the restoration of empirical Israel was, in Luke's view, the prerequisite for the Gentile mission. It is only on the foundation of the *restored* empirical Israel, which is restored on the basis of its acceptance of Jesus as the Messiah, that the Gentiles can be incorporated into the people of God. This principle is laid down in Acts 3:25, where it is stated that through the seed

---

[5]*The Theology of Acts in Its Historical Setting*, rev. ed. (London: S.P.C.K., 1970) 14.

[6]"Apologetic Use of the Old Testament in the Speeches of Acts" in *The Salvation of the Gentiles: Essays in the Acts of the Apostles*, trans. John R. Keating (New York: Paulist, 1979) 139.

[7]So, e.g., I. H. Marshall, *The Acts of the Apostles: An Introduction and Commentary*, Tyndale New Testament Commentaries (Grand Rapids MI: Wm. B. Eerdmans, 1980) 252; and Otto Bauernfeind, *Kommentar und Studien zur Apostelgeschichte*, Wissenschaftliche Untersuchungen zum Neuen Testament 22 (Tübingen: J. C. B. Mohr, 1980) 192.

[8]Jacob Jervell, "The Divided People of God: The Restoration of Israel and Salvation for the Gentiles," in *Luke and the People of God: A New Look at Luke-Acts* (Minneapolis: Augsburg, 1972) 51-69. Cf. similarly Earl Richard, "The Divine Purpose: The Jews and the Gentile Mission (Acts 15)," in *Society of Biblical Literature 1980 Seminar Papers*, ed. Paul. J. Achtemeier (Chico CA: Scholars Press, 1980) 272.

of Abraham (the Jews)[9] " 'shall all the families of the earth be blessed' " (quoting Gen. 22:18). Luke repeatedly stressed that thousands of the Jews of Jerusalem had accepted Jesus as Messiah, and hence the foundation in Jerusalem had been laid for the going forth of the gospel. The establishment of the foundation of the restored Israel continues throughout Acts, where in many cities numerous Jews accepted the message of the gospel.[10] The story ends in Rome, where the gospel is presented to the Roman Jews where, once again, some believed (28:24). In some sense the rebuilt tabernacle represents the foundation for the incorporation of the Gentiles into the people of God. It is the restored Israel, the Jewish Christians.

But did Luke understand this tabernacle to be a new temple? While Luke did not believe the whole church to be the new temple, might he have at least understood the Jewish Christians to be the new temple? One might initially wish to answer this question positively, since the tabernacle of Exodus 26 was viewed as the prototype of the Solomonic temple (cf. 1 Kgs. 6). But this cannot simply be assumed to be true of Acts short of a more complete investigation. This is the second factor to be considered in interpreting Acts 15:16-18.

Earl Richard has observed that a number of motifs that appear in Acts 15 are reverberations of similar motifs in Acts 7.[11] Given the echoing of motifs, Richard argues that one should not hesitate to interpret one speech in relation to the other. For example, "tabernacle," or one of its Greek cognates, appears in both speeches (7:44, 46; 15:16). What is more, the tabernacle of 7:44 is related to the nations in both texts (7:44-45; 15:16-17). If on the literary level each text informs the interpretation of the other, then one's interpretation of the tabernacle of 15:16 should be shaped by how one understands the tabernacle of 7:44, 46. If the tabernacle of 7:44, 46 is synonymous with the house built by Solomon in 7:47 (the temple), then there would be compelling reason to conclude that the restored tabernacle of 15:16, representing the Jewish-Christian community, was interpreted by Luke to be the restored temple.

Bauernfeind has argued that there does exist a continuity between the tabernacle of 7:44 and the temple of Solomon (7:47).[12] Since the taber-

---

[9]Not Christ, as in Gal. 3:15-18. Jacques Dupont, "The Salvation of the Gentiles and the Theological Significance of Acts," in *Salvation of the Gentiles*, 23.

[10]Acts 2:41; 4:4; 5:14; 13:42-43; 14:1; 17:4, 11; 18:4.

[11]Richard, "Divine Purpose," 272.

[12]Bauernfeind, *Apostelgeschichte*, 118.

nacle seems to be portrayed favorably in the speech, the words of Stephen concerning the temple are not to be considered as polemical. Bauernfeind interprets the Stephen speech to be saying that Solomon did not violate the will of God in building the temple, but only carried out David's request to build it. To be sure, he states, there is a prophetic critique of the temple. Stephen wishes to emphasize, as F. D. Weinert puts it, that the temple does not in any way limit "God's authority over or presence to the world."[13] It is to be pointed out, however, that Solomon's speech dedicating the temple (see especially 1 Kgs. 8:27) voices the same idea as does Acts 7:48. In other words, Luke is offering through Stephen no new view of the temple. All Luke is attempting to do is to emphasize that the temple does not confine God. He is not hurling polemical accusations against the sanctuary in principle.

One would not wish to argue that Luke here is advocating an absolute rejection of the temple. This would be an absurd assertion in light of the numerous texts that speak positively of the temple cult. Hence, it is correct to conclude that that the primary thrust of the critique of 7:47-50 is not to attack the temple cult itself, but to warn against trying to limit God's presence. Yet it seems to some interpreters that in the immediate context of Stephen's speech the precise means whereby Luke affirms the universal scope of God is to *contrast* the mobile tabernacle which moved with the people of God, with the stationary "house" and "place" which is a place of "rest" (χατάπαυσις, v. 49).[14] Hence, 7:47-50 is not an attack against the temple per se, but there is a polemic against the temple viewed as a "house," viewed as the "resting" place of God which confines and restricts him. A more appropriate image of God's presence would be the mobile tabernacle by means of which God can move to any place.[15]

The full implications of the speech can come forth only in the larger context of Luke's universalism, which will be discussed below in chapter 4. What is to be noted here is the fact that Luke does *not* view the tabernacle of 7:44 as synonymous with the temple of Solomon. The tabernacle

---

[13]"The Meaning of the Temple in the Gospel of Luke" (Ph.D. diss., Fordham University, 1979) 186.

[14]See, e.g., Jane Via, "An Interpretation of Acts 7:35-37: From the Perspective of Major Themes in Luke-Acts," PRS 6 (1979): 190-206.

[15]Earl Richard, *Acts 6:1-8:4: The Author's Method of Composition* SBLDS 41 (Missoula: Scholars Press, 1978) 326-30, argues along this line. He states, "the use of the term τόπος in the speech (7:7, 33, 49) suggests that he wishes to broaden the concept of 'place' so that God's promise is not limited to 'this place', i.e., the temple of 6:13, 14" (326).

symbolizes a view of God who is on the move in the world; the "house" points to a view of God who is confined and stationary. They are not the same image of God, and, hence, the tabernacle does not equate with the temple. Applied to Acts 15, it may be concluded that the tabernacle of 15:16, which denotes the restored Jewish community, is not to be perceived as a new temple by Luke. If anything, Luke sees the tabernacle as a fitting metaphor for the Jewish Christians, not because it conjures up the image of the temple, but because it calls to mind God's mobility in the world. It is through the restored tabernacle—the Jewish followers of "the Way"—that God will move into the world and call the nations to salvation. Luke does not understand the Christian community, or any portion of it, to be the new, restored temple.

The Transferral of Temple Motifs to Jesus

Did Luke "christologize" the temple? In other words, did Luke, as did the fourth Evangelist, believe that Jesus himself had replaced the functions and prerogatives of the Jewish temple? It must be stated initially that Luke never explicitly equates Jesus with the temple. In fact, like the Christian community, Jesus is portrayed by Luke as being active in the temple. This portrayal offers no hint of antagonism toward the temple out of which the impetus to replace the temple with Jesus might come (see Lk. 2:41-51; 19:28-21:30).

Interpreters who argue that Luke has consciously dubbed Jesus as the new temple to replace the old one offer such arguments on the flimsiest of grounds. F. X. Reitzel has attempted to argue that every major section of the gospel contains a reference to the temple.[16] It is his contention that each reference to the temple in these major sections marks a turning point at which something ends and something new begins. This "something old and new" is symbolic of the pattern of death and resurrection. The climax of this pattern is found in the tearing of the temple veil, which is the end of the old temple of brick and mortar which is "to be replaced forever by the eternal Temple of the Risen Christ."[17] Reitzel's exegesis is totally arbitrary. His "turning points" are not that decisive (see Lk. 18:10), and one is left wondering what to make of all the temple activity in Acts if in point of fact Jesus has replaced the temple.

---

[16]"St. Luke's Use of the Temple Image," *Review for Religious* 38 (1979): 520-39. He divides the gospel into seven sections, noting how each section contains an important temple scene or reference. The important temple scenes are located in Lk 1:8-23; 2:22-38, 41-51; 4:9-12; 18:10; 20:1-21:38; 22:45; 24:53.

[17]Ibid., 525.

Another "christologized" interpretation of the temple in Luke comes from L. T. Brodie.[18] Brodie's purpose is primarily apologetic; he wants to defend the integrity of Luke and argue against any view that minimizes the integral role of the first two chapters to the rest of the Lukan gospel. Brodie argues that Lk. 1:1-4:22a forms a continuous narrative patterned consciously after the Chronicler's history of Israel (including Ezra and Nehemiah). For example, the "preparation for David's reign" (1 Chr. 1-10) corresponds to the "preparation for Jesus' Davidic reign" (Lk. 1:1-25). Brodie has outlined the history of the Chronicler and Lk. 1-4 in such a way that temple passages in each correspond to one another. "The census and the origin of the Temple" (1 Chr. 21-22) corresponds to the "census and the birth of Jesus" (Lk. 2:1-10). The "building of the Temple" (2 Chr. 1:1-5:1) corresponds to "Jesus growing up" (Lk. 2:39-40). The "Lord takes possession of his Temple" in 2 Chr. 5:2-9:31 corresponds to "Jesus in the Temple" in Lk. 2:41-52. Brodie concludes that Luke has patterned his story of Jesus on the Chronicler's history in order to move "the focus from the Temple of stone to a boy who is the living Temple of God."[19]

Brodie's exegesis is as artificial as Reitzel's. In order to make Luke's narrative correspond with that of the Chronicler, Brodie had to do at least three things. First, he left a great block of the Chronicler's history (2 Chr. 10–36) without any correspondence to Luke. Second, he left two texts in Luke with no correspondence to the Chronicler's history (Lk. 3:7-9; 4:1-13). Third, he had to rearrange radically portions of the Chronicler's history, especially within Ezra and Nehemiah, so that it might correspond with Lukan events. The textual confusion of Ezra-Nehemiah is well known, yet that is not a license to launch into an arbitrary rearrangement of the narrative. Blatant attempts at a christologized interpretation of the temple in Luke are not convincing.

K. Baltzer[20] has also argued that Luke offers a christological interpretation of the temple. Baltzer's exegesis is more sober and deserves serious consideration. Baltzer begins his argument by observing that Ezekiel betrays a close association between the temple and the "glory of Yahweh" (Ezek. 8-11), in which relationship the "glory" denotes an almost hypostatic entity that moves about within the temple (10:18), or can even leave the temple (11:23). Baltzer notes that in Ezekiel God dwelt within the temple when the "glory" was there (Ezek. 43:4-7). Second, he observes that

---

[18]"A New Temple and a New Law," JSNT 5 (1979): 21-45.

[19]Ibid., 43.

[20]"The Meaning of the Temple in the Lukan Writings," HTR 58 (1965): 263-77.

in the intertestamental period there developed an explicit connection between the "divine presence" (שכינה) of the Lord in the temple and the presence of salvation (see 1 En. 90:28-29, 33, 35). Third, the rabbinic literature could equate this "divine presence" with the "glory." Fourth, there exists within the Targumim of Ezekiel the idea that the "divine presence" left the temple and dwelt on the Mount of Olives in order to induce repentance. On the basis of these observations, Baltzer concludes that within Judaism there was a dynamic interaction between the motifs of the temple, the "divine presence," the "glory," the actual presence of salvation, and the temporary habitation of the "glory" and "presence" on the Mount of Olives.

Baltzer relates this to Luke first by noting Luke's association of "glory" with Jesus (see Lk. 2:32; 19:38; 24:26, all of which consist of material peculiar to Luke). Second, he notes the commonly accepted view that for Luke Jesus represents the presence of God's salvation (see Lk. 2:30). Third, he observes that prior to the triumphal entry Luke adds to Mark the detail concerning Jesus' descent from the Mount of Olives (19:37). When these are combined with the motif of Jesus' taking possession of the temple, Baltzer concludes that for Luke Jesus is the "glory" and "divine presence" which legitimate the temple. In short, when Jesus is in the temple, "the temple is really the Temple."[21]

Baltzer does not attempt to equate Jesus with the a temple, but clearly he believes that for Luke the "meaning of the temple" is to be found in its christological associations. Some observations, however, caution against our accepting Baltzer's interpretation. First, much of Baltzer's understanding of the close association of temple, salvation, and "glory" and "presence" was based on Ezekiel and the Targumim of Ezekiel. Yet Luke was relatively uninfluenced by the writings associated with this prophet.[22] Second, had Luke wished to establish a clearly recognizable link between Jesus as the glory of God descending from the Mount of Olives (19:37-38) into the temple to possess it (19:45-46), it is curious that he allowed intervening material (Lk. 19:39-44) to stand between the pertinent texts. Third, while Luke does not hesitate to show the associations of Jesus with the temple, one goes too far to argue that Jesus *validates* the cult. There is no

---

[21]Ibid., 275.

[22]Even a casual reading of Luke-Acts betrays Luke's preference for the Deuteronomic books, Isaiah, and the Psalms. Secondary investigations bear this out, e.g., John Drury, *Tradition and Design in Luke's Gospel: A Study in Early Christian Historiography* (London: Darton, Longman & Todd, 1976; Atlanta: John Knox Press, 1977) 46-81, and Dupont, "Apologetic Use of the Old Testament," in *Salvation of the Gentiles.*

question that the temple cult continues to be valid in Acts, long after Jesus had been rejected by the Jewish leaders and his physical presence had departed from the holy place. Hence, Baltzer's observations are interesting and insightful, yet not persuasive enough to conclude that Jesus Christ is the validating presence in the temple. Once again, Luke's tendency not to "christologize" the temple is evident.

One specific passage needs to be examined which might affirm that Luke did in some way believe that Jesus was the new, true temple, or at least the foundation stone of the new, true temple (the church). Luke 20:17-18 reads:

> But [Jesus] looked at them and said, "What then is this that is written: 'The very stone which the builders rejected has become the head of the corner'? Every one who falls on that stone will be broken to pieces; but when it falls on any one it will crush him."

A number of factors might lead one to suspect that Luke is asserting here that Jesus is the foundation stone of the new temple. First, as was seen in chapter one, stone imagery was often associated with the temple both in Jewish thought and in the New Testament. Why should it not be so here? Second, this saying is placed in Luke (as in the other Synoptics) in a temple setting, thereby making a temple association implicit. Third, reference is made to "stone" in two sets of passages; one preceding 20:17-18 (19:40, 44) and one following 20:17-18 (21:5-6). Both passages deal with the destruction of the temple or city. Hence, it would appear that Luke has couched the reference to Jesus as the "stone" in between two passages dealing with the destruction of the old temple stones. It would certainly appear that Luke wished to set forth Jesus as the stone of the foundation of the temple which replaced the temple stones destined for destruction.

One should not rush to such a conclusion, however. In the first place, it would be tenuous at best to conclude that use of stone imagery to refer to Jesus thereby equates Jesus with the temple when no other Lukan passages explicitly equate Jesus or the church with the temple. Matthew's (Matt. 21:42) or Mark's (Mk. 12:10-11) version of this saying might justifiably be interpreted as referring to Jesus as the temple foundation stone of the new community temple, for both Matthew and Mark apply temple imagery to the community in a more explicit fashion (Matt. 16:18; Mk. 14:58). Yet Luke himself shys away from such imagery.

In the second place, stone imagery was not used in the early church exclusively in connection with the temple. J. Jeremias has argued[23] that

---

[23] λίθος, λίθινος, TDNT 4:268-80.

while stone imagery could often be used in the New Testament in relation to temple imagery, the "stone" was also used as an image of judgment toward those who stumble over the scandal of the gospel. Examples of this use of stone imagery may be seen in Rom. 9:32 and 1 Pet. 2:7-8. Luke 20:17-18 seems to conform to this latter use of the stone motif. This is evidenced primarily by the allusion to this saying in Acts 4:11-12. " 'This is the stone which was rejected by you builders, but which has become the head of the corner. And there is salvation in no one else.' " Clearly, this allusion to the gospel saying serves as a call to repentance and salvation, with the implicit threat that continued rejection of the stone will lead to judgment. Temple imagery is simply not in focus here.

Luke 20:17-18 does use stone imagery with reference to Jesus, imagery which could, given the proper context, point to temple imagery. Yet Luke in speaking of Jesus as the stone in Lk. 20:17-20 is not portraying Jesus as a "temple stone." For Luke this stone metaphor is used to proclaim the rejected yet exalted Lord as the one in whom one can find either salvation or damnation.

For Luke, therefore, neither Jesus nor the church formed the new eschatological temple. Any significance which Luke vested in Jerusalem and the sanctuary must be found not in a spiritualized transferral of the prerogatives and functions of these places to Jesus or his church; the significance must rest elsewhere.

Jerusalem, the Temple, and the Salvation of Israel

Chapter III

Jerusalem, the Temple, and the Infancy Narrative

The focal point of the Lukan infancy narrative is Jerusalem and the temple. The theme of the fulfillment of God's promises of salvation is also prominent in the narrative. Such fulfillment is *eschatological* and *universal* in character.

Some may question whether it is justifiable to view the infancy narrative as genuinely expressive of Lukan theological concerns. Hans Conzelmann did not take the first two chapters into account because he doubted their authenticity.[1] The validity of this arbitrary methodological procedure has been challenged by many scholars.[2] These critics of Conzelmann are correct on this point, and these two chapters should be given careful consideration in any attempt to elucidate Lukan theology. When these two chapters are taken into account, it is plain that they contain important and clear clues concerning Luke's theological agenda.

---

[1]Hans Conzelmann, *The Theology of Saint Luke,* trans. Geoffrey Buswell (London: Faber and Faber; New York: Harper & Brothers, 1960) 118.

[2]E.g., Paul S. Minear, "Luke's Use of the Birth Stories," in *Studies in Luke-Acts,* ed. Leander Keck and J. Louis Martyn (Nashville: Abingdon, 1966) 120-21; Raymond E. Brown, *The Birth of the Messiah: A Commentary on the Infancy Narratives in Matthew and Luke* (New York: Doubleday, 1977) 239-50; Joseph A. Fitzmyer, *The Gospel According to Luke (I-IX),* Anchor Bible 28 (Garden City NY: Doubleday, 1981) 310.

The Focus on Jerusalem and the Temple. Jerusalem and the temple provide the primary setting for the action of the birth narrative. Omitting the prologue (1:1-4) from consideration, fifty-two of the 128 remaining verses describe activity which is taking place in the temple (Lk. 1:2-25; 2:22-38, 41-51). Thus, almost forty percent of the first two chapters is devoted to the setting of the temple.

The structure of Luke 1 and 2 also indicates that Luke wanted to give a prominent role to the temple. Luke begins and ends the infancy narrative in the temple (see 1:5-23; 2:22-38, 41-51), thereby bracketing all the activity of the narrative between temple scenes. It is likely that Luke would have expected his readers to note this.

It is clear that Luke has focused the attention of the reader on the temple and Jerusalem in these initial chapters. Whatever message Luke was attempting to convey, it would appear that he viewed Jerusalem and the temple as the appropriate setting for such a message.

The Coming of God's Salvation. The primary message of the Lukan infancy narrative was that God's promises of eschatological salvation were coming to fruition. Within these chapters, the narrative style is thoroughly Semitic,[3] giving one a sense of being in the Old Testament world. Many of the important characters such as Zechariah and Elizabeth and Simeon and Anna are modeled after great figures of Old Testament piety.[4] But Luke is not merely telling an Old Testament story. It is more precise to say that he is continuing the story of salvation which began in the Old Testament and is now reaching fruition.[5] While Luke wishes to delineate a continuity

---

[3]Scholars are divided as to whether this Semitic style is due to use of a semitized source by Luke or the conscious adoption of a Septuagintal style by Luke. A helpful survey of opinion up to the 1960s may be found in Harold H. Oliver, "The Lukan Birth Stories and the Purpose of Luke-Acts," NTS 10 (1963–1964): 205-15. Many recent interpreters see Luke's hand as ultimately responsible for the Semitic style. See, e.g., John Drury, *Tradition and Design in Luke's Gospel: A Study in Early Christian Historiography* (London: Darton, Longman & Todd, 1976; Atlanta: John Knox Press, 1977) 46-66. Fitzmyer, *Luke,* 309-10, and Brown, *Birth of the Messiah,* 346-53, attribute the narrative portions of Lk. 1-2 (i.e., material excluding the Canticles) to Luke's composition.

[4]Zechariah and Elizabeth, who are depicted as old, pious, and childless, are reminiscent of such ideal Old Testament figures as Abraham and Sarah (Gen. 21:1-3) and the parents of Samuel, Elkanah and Hannah (1 Sam. 1:19-20). The genuine piety of Simeon and Anna is represented by their age, association with the temple, eschatological expectancy, and their prophetic status. See Brown, *Birth of the Messiah,* 451-54.

[5]See in this regard Nils A. Dahl, "The Story of Abraham in Luke-Acts," in *Studies in Luke-Acts,* ed. Keck and Martyn, 139-58; Richard Glöckner, *Die Verkündigen des Heils beim Evangelisten Lukas,* Walberberger Studien 9 (Mainz: Matthias Grünewald Verlag, 1976) 74-77.

between the Old Testament and the events of the infancy narrative, the reader becomes aware that something decisively new is about to take place. What is more, this decisively new thing is eschatological.

Several features within the birth narrative indicate the narrative's essentially eschatological character. The first is the appearance of the angel Gabriel in the scenes of the temple vision to Zechariah (1:5-23) and the annunciation to Mary (1:26-37). The earliest material concerning Gabriel is to be found in Dan. 8:16-26 and 9:21-27 where he is explicitly associated with end-time visions and events. In Dan. 8:17 Gabriel helps Daniel understand his vision of the end-time. In 9:24-27 Gabriel interprets the vision of the seventy weeks of years for Daniel, a vision which focuses much of its attention on the eschatological significance of Jerusalem and the temple. The eschatological character of Gabriel continues to be evidenced in 1 Enoch where he is described as being a ruler over paradise (40:9) and the executioner of God's avenging wrath upon Satan (54:6). The appearance of the end-time angel Gabriel in the opening scenes of Luke's gospel gives an immediate and clear eschatological ring to the narrative.

The second feature that gives to the infancy narrative an eschatological character is Luke's assignment of Elijah-like characteristics to the figure of John the Baptist. Luke does not ever explicitly identify John with Elijah,[6] but he clearly portrays him in the colors and hues of this prophet in 1:16-17 and 1:76. There it is said specifically that John would go before the Lord in the spirit and power of Elijah. What is more, Luke describes John using allusions from the Old Testament and the Apocrypha which speak of Elijah. The clearest allusion is found in 1:17b where it states that John is "to turn the hearts of the fathers to the children" (my translation). Lk. 1:17b is a literal translation of the Hebrew Text of Mal. 3:24.[7] Lk. 1:17a and 17e may allude to the Elijah tradition of Mal. 3:1. Luke says here that John will go before God (17a) for the purpose of doing preparatory work (17e). To be sure, in 17e it is a people whom John is to prepare, whereas in Mal. 3:1 it is a "way" to be prepared. Yet, 1:76b does refer to John's preparing of the Lord's "ways." What is significant about these allusions is the fact that the return of Elijah was perceived as being thoroughly es-

---

[6]See Walter Wink, *John the Baptist in the Gospel Tradition,* SNTSMS 7 (London: Cambridge University Press, 1968) 42; and Jean-Daniel Dubois, "La Figure D'Elie dans la Perspective Lukanienne," RHPR 53 (1973): 155-76.

[7]Luke here is closer to the Masoretic text of Mal. 3:24 than to the LXX (Mal. 4:5a). The latter is literally translated "who will restore the heart of the father toward the son." Sir 48:10c is translated: "he will turn the heart of the father toward the son."

chatological.[8] While Luke stops short of explicitly identifying the Baptist with Elijah, he does associate John with this important preparatory figure of Jewish eschatology, and thereby he sounds another clear eschatological note to these introductory chapters.

The third eschatological feature to be found in the Lukan infancy narrative is the emphasis on the activity of the Holy Spirit (1:15, 35, 41, 67; 2:25, 26, 27). It would be fruitful at this juncture to address briefly the association between the Spirit and the new age in Jewish thought.

Within Jewish circles there is no monolithic, systematic view with respect to the activity of the Holy Spirit. Nonetheless, there exists a pattern which presupposes that in the present age the Spirit was no longer active in Israel. Some rabbinic statements expressed the view that the Holy Spirit departed from Israel with the destruction of the first temple. "Five things which existed in the first temple were lacking in the second. These were: (a) Fire from on high. (b) Anointing oil. (c) The Ark. (d) The Holy Spirit. (e) Urim and Thummim" (b. Yoma 21b).

A second view associates the end of the activity of the Spirit with the end of prophecy. So close is this relationship that G. F. Moore can say "the holy spirit is specifically the spirit of prophecy." He cites the well-known statement, "When the last prophets, Haggai, Zechariah, and Malachi, died, the holy spirit ceased out of Israel; but nonetheless it was granted them (communication from God) by means of a mysterious voice" (t. Sotah, 13,2).[9] This brief glance at the material appears to indicate that the rabbis did not view the Holy Spirit as active in this age. And yet, on the basis of Joel 2:28 (= 3:1 MT), it was widely believed that in the age to come there would be a renewal of the activity of the Spirit: "And it shall come to pass afterward, that I will pour out my spirit on all flesh; your sons and your daughters shall prophesy, your old men shall dream dreams, and your young men shall see visions."[10]

The belief that the spirit of prophecy was absent from Israel is echoed in the Apocrypha and Pseudepigrapha, though again absolute consistency cannot be demanded from this material.[11] Numerous statements affirm that

---

[8]See the discussion concerning the eschatological associations and functions of Elijah in Joachim Jeremias, Ἡλ(ε)ίας, TDNT 2:933-94. According to Jeremias, the tasks of Elijah would include the preaching of repentance, the purging of Israel, and the announcement of the time of eschatological salvation.

[9]G. F. Moore, *Judaism in the First Centuries of the Christian Era*, 2 vols. (New York: Schocken Books, 1971 [originally published 1927]) 1:421.

[10]See the discussion by Eric Sjoberg, πνεῦμα κτλ. TDNT 6:375-89, esp. 385.

[11]Contrast, e.g., Wis. 9:17 and Sir. 39:6 which allude to the present activity of the Spirit.

many Jews of the period of the second temple viewed the days of the prophets either as past (1 Macc. 9:27) or future (1 Macc. 4:46; 14:41; 2 Bar. 85:1-3; Dan. [LXX] 3:38; cf. Josephus, Ant. 4:118-19), but not as present. A few texts appear to establish a relationship between the arrival of the new age and the endowment with the Spirit (2 Macc. 7:23; 14:46; Sib. Or. 4:46, 189).

Within the Qumranic materials there are numerous statements that clearly indicate that the covenanters viewed the Holy Spirit as presently active in the life of the community. The Qumranic material reveals the assumption on the part of the community that the Holy Spirit was not only active (IQS 9:3-5), but that there was a close relationship between being a member of the covenant and receiving the Spirit (IQH 14:12-13). The Spirit was the power that provided strength for the covenanter in the midst of moral trials (IQH 7:6-7a; 16:11-12), as well as the source of knowledge that only members of the covenant possessed (IQH 4:27-33; 9:31-32; 12:11-12; 16:11-12). It was this knowledge that allowed the members of the sect to understand the scriptures properly (1QpHab), and understanding which allowed these members of the covenant to know that they were living in the dawn of the eschatological age (1QS 8: 12-16). Hence, while it is true that the community at Qumran took very seriously the present experience of the activity of the Spirit, such an experience was coupled with an imminent, if not immanent, eschatological awareness.[12]

The overall eschatological character of the Spirit in much of Jewish thought is established. The question is whether Luke so understood the presence of the Spirit. Luke's emphasis on the activity of the Spirit in the context of a narrative permeated with other eschatological motifs would seem to indicate that Luke interpreted the activity of the Spirit as indicative of the dawn of the eschatological age of salvation.

The fourth eschatological feature is the centrally significant fact that these chapters announce the coming of the Messiah. The first such explicit announcement is found in 1:32-33. This announcement makes three specific assertions about the Messiah: one, his filial relationship with God; two, his descent from David; three, his eternal reign over Israel. These three elements correspond precisely to the messianic "promise tradition" which was widely circulated in Jewish eschatological expectations.[13]

---

[12]See James A. Sanders, "From Isaiah 61 to Luke 4," in *Christianity, Judaism and other Greco-Roman Cults,* part one, ed. Jacob Neusner, Studies in Judaism in Late Antiquity 12 (Leiden: E. J. Brill, 1975) 93-94.

[13]A detailed discussion of the "promise tradition" may be found in Dennis Duling, "The Promises to David and their Entrance into Christianity—Nailing Down a Likely Hypothesis," NTS 20 (1973): 55-77.

The second messianic announcement containing eschatological language is found in 1:35. Raymond Brown has observed that this verse contains a "conglomeration of terms" similar to those found in Rom. 1:3-4.[14] The significant terms are Holy Spirit, Son of God, and power. The Romans passage, which is widely recognized as a pre-Pauline christological formula, views the resurrection of Jesus, an eschatological event by definition, as the exaltation of Jesus to the status of God's Son. Brown believes that Lk. 1:35 may be a reading back into the birth of Jesus a primitive Christian resurrection faith, similar to that which is reflected in Rom. 1: 3-4. In other words, a status originally conferred upon Jesus by the explicitly eschatological event of the resurrection is perceived by Luke as belonging to Jesus from the moment of his conception. If Brown's argument is sound, then Luke has purposefully used eschatological language to announce the birth of the Messiah.

The third messianic announcement is found in 1:69-70. Here the Messiah is spoken of in the militant language of deliverance: God "has raised up a horn of salvation." The most direct scriptural allusion is Ps. 18:3 (‖ 2 Sam. 22:3) where the "horn" refers to God. In other places, however, "horn" appears to have a messianic sense (see Ps. 132:17; Ezek. 29:21; 1 En. 90:37, 39), leading Fitzmyer to conclude that this term was a loose messianic title.[15] That Luke clearly intended such a messianic interpretation is indicated by 1:69b which states that the horn has arisen in the house of God's servant David.

That Luke understands the arrival of this Messiah to be eschatological is evidenced not only by the messianic imagery itself, but the Lukan insertion of verse 70.[16] This insertion by Luke asserts that the coming of the Messiah is to fulfill the promises uttered by the prophets. The close verbal

---

[14]Brown, *Birth of the Messiah*, 312-13. He is followed by Fitzmyer, *Luke*, 340. Even if Brown's thesis of a retrojected christology is "an oversimplification of the christological development" (see Reginald H. Fuller, "The Conception/Birth of Jesus as a Christological Moment," JSNT 1 [1978]: 37-52 [quotation from p. 38]), it still seems significant that language associated with the explicitly eschatological event of the resurrection could easily be employed in the Lukan narrative to describe the significance of Jesus' birth.

[15]Fitzmyer, *Luke*, 383.

[16]On v. 70 as a Lukan insertion see Joachim Jeremias, *Die Sprache des Lukasevangeliums: Redaktion und Tradition in Nichtmarkusstoff des dritten Evangeliums* (Göttingen: Vandenhoeck und Ruprecht, 1980) 73-74.

similarity to Acts 3:21 is obvious.[17] In Acts the "words uttered by the prophets of old" make reference to the "times of refreshing," the sending of the Messiah, and the restoration of all things (see Acts 3:19-21). These all have a decisively eschatological ring to them, indicating that Luke could use the phrase of 1:70 and Acts 3:21 to refer to great eschatological promises. If such is the case, then Luke wants the raising up of the horn of salvation to be understood as the fulfillment of an *eschatological* promise.

A fourth messianic announcement is found in Lk. 1:78 where reference is made to the "visitation" of "the dayspring from on high" (my translation, ἀνατολὴ ἐξ ὕψους). 'Ανατολή is used in Zech. 3:8 and 6:17 (LXX) to denote the messianic branch. The eschatological character of this announcement is enhanced by reference to "visitation" (ἐπισκέψεται), the eschatological dimensions of which will be discussed immediately below. Hence, the fourth eschatological feature of the birth narrative is the emphasis on the coming of the Messiah, the announcement of which is set within the context of eschatological motifs and language.

The fifth eschatological feature is the announcement of the arrival of God's redemption (see 1:68 and 2:38). Such redemption is described in eschatological language and imagery. In the first place, such redemption is juxtaposed with the "visitation" of God in 1:68 ("the Lord God . . . has visited and worked redemption for his people," my translation.) The concept of visitation is not unimportant to Luke. He uses the verb ἐπισκέπτεσθαι seven times (Lk. 1:68, 78; 7:16; Acts 6:3; 7:23; 15:14, 36) and the noun once (Lk. 19:44). The word does not always have an intensely theological meaning (see Acts 6:3; 15:36), but generally it does denote the "visitation" of God, or his agents (see Acts 7:23), for the purpose of helping God's people (Lk. 1:68, 78; 7:16; Acts 15:14).

It is clear that Luke can understand such a visitation eschatologically. What may be a conscious echo of Lk. 1:68b stands in Lk. 7:16: "God has visited (ἐπεσκέψατο) his people." The statement is placed by Luke on the lips of the crowd to note their response to the witnessing of the raising of the widow's son at Nain. The eschatological character of this "visitation" is evidenced in the first place by Jesus' appearing in an Elijah-like role (see 1 Kgs. 17:17-24). This is probably how Luke understood the ex-

---

[17]A comparison of the Greek texts bears out this observation:
Lk. 1:70 καθὼς ἐλάλησεν διὰ στόματος τῶν ἁγίων ἀπ' αἰῶνος προφητῶν αὐτοῦ.
. . .
Acts 3:21 ἐλάλησεν ὁ θεὸς διὰ στόματος τῶν ἁγίων ἀπ' αἰῶνος αὐτοῦ προφητῶν.

clamation of the crowd: "A great prophet has arisen among us."[18] I have already discussed the eschatological nuances of the figure of Elijah. Second, the very act of "raising" is to be understood in the Lukan context as a sign that the age of eschatological fulfillment has come. Clearly, the raising of the widow's son is placed in this position by Luke to prepare the reader for the response of Jesus to the Baptist's doubts regarding Jesus' messianic identity: "Go and tell John what you have seen and heard: the blind receive their sight, . . . the dead are raised up and the poor have the good news preached to them" (7:22; see also 4:18). Hence, Luke can envision God's visitation as bringing eschatological help and deliverance.

In the second place the description of the activity of God in 1:51-53 relates an eschatological understanding of redemption. Reference is made in verse 51 to the showing forth of the strength of God's arm and the scattering of the proud. The phraseology is traditional and reflects language found in eschatological texts.[19] What is more, the motif of the reversal of stations and roles (the putting down of the mighty and the exaltation of the humble; the emptying of the rich and the filling of the hungry) is probably to be understood as expressing the theme of eschatological reversal.[20]

The final indicator of the eschatological flavor of the infancy narrative is the portrayal of the main characters as persons who are living in eschatological expectation. The canticles attributed to Zechariah (1:68-79) and Mary (1:46b-55) indicate their expectation of eschatological deliverance. The two prophetic characters at the conclusion of the narrative, Simeon and Anna, are explicitly described as living in eschatological expectation. Of Simeon it is said that he was looking for the "consolation of Israel" (2:25). Anna is described as awaiting the "redemption of Jerusalem" (2:38).

The two phrases are probably to be understood as virtual synonyms denoting God's end-time salvation.[21] Such is likely, given such references as Isa. 52:9 where God's comforting of his people stands parallel with his redemption of Jerusalem: "the Lord has comforted his people, he has re-

---

[18]I. H. Marshall, *The Gospel of Luke: A Commentary on the Greek Text*, The New International Greek Testament Commentary (Grand Rapids MI: Wm. B. Eerdmans, 1978) 286.

[19]See Brown, *Birth of the Messiah*, 359.

[20]So Walter Grundmann, *Das Evangelium nach Lukas*, Theologischer Handkommentar zum Neuen Testament 3 (Berlin: Evangelische Verlagsanstalt, 1961) 65; cf. Isa. 57:15-21; 61:1-11; 1 En. 92-104.

[21]Brown, *Birth of the Messiah*, 438.

deemed Jerusalem." Numerous passages within the Old Testament, stemming primarily from the second half of Isaiah, speak often of the comfort to come to Jerusalem (Isa. 40:1-2, 49:13-18; 51:3; 57:14-19; 66:12-13) or God's people (Isa. 51:12, compare Ezek. 14:22-23) in the eschatological age. Such references as Isa. 52:9 and 51:6 make clear that the comfort and redemption of the city stand hand-in-hand with the salvation of the nation. The association of "comfort" with the eschatological activity of God continued in the literature of the intertestamental period (see Wis. 3:18; Sir. 48:24-25) and could even be used as a shorthand expression for messianic salvation.[22] Hence, the description of Simeon and Anna as living in expectation of such "consolation" and "redemption" places these examples of Jewish piety in the stream of Jewish eschatological hope. For Luke, the salvation which is coming in the person of Jesus (see 2:30) is thoroughy eschatological, fulfilling the promises of God (see 1:55, 70, 72-73).

Luke does not simply affirm the dawn of end-time salvation in these introductory chapters. He is also careful to emphasize the universal character of such salvation. The infancy narrative begins with Luke's continual emphasis that the salvation that is coming is for Jews. All the characters in these two chapters are Jews; in point of fact they represent the best Jewish piety has to offer. It is emphasized that it is to these Jews and the people they represent, that God's promises of salvation are coming to fruition (Lk. 1:16-17, 33, 54-55, 68-73, 77). These declarations, however, reach their climax with the emphatically universal declaration placed on the lips of Simeon: "for mine eyes have seen thy salvation which thou hast prepared in the presence of all peoples, a light for revelation to the Gentiles, and for glory to thy people Israel" (Lk. 2:30-32). The *Nunc Dimittis* leaves no doubt that what God has offered to the Jews, he has also offered to Gentiles. A more detailed examination of Luke's universalism is to be conducted in the following chapter. But it is clear from this statement that from Luke's perspective God's eschatological salvation is not for Jews only. What is more, while Simeon's words of Lk. 2:34 foreshadow the division that is to befall Israel as a result of the coming of the Messiah, there is no hint here that the offering of salvation to Gentiles consequently annuls the promises of God's salvation for Israel. In point of fact, verse 32 makes clear that the "light of revelation to the Gentiles" stands in a parallel relationship with "glory to thy people Israel." The salvation offered by God in

---

[22]Herman L. Strack and Paul Billerbeck, *Kommentar zum Neuen Testament aus Talmud und Midrash*, 5 vols. (Munich: C. H. Beck, 1926-1963) 2:124-25.

the person of Jesus is for both Jew and Gentile. The salvation of God is for all peoples (2:31).

Conclusion. Luke used the infancy narrative to introduce to the reader important themes and emphases that dominate his gospel's message. Two primary features which are emphasized are the dominant role of Jerusalem and the temple and the announcement of the dawn of the fruition of God's *heilsgeschichtliche* promises of eschatological salvation. This salvation is said to be offered both to Jew and to Gentile. The merger of these two primary features indicates that for Luke the offering of eschatological salvation to Jew and Gentile found its most appropriate setting in the context of Jerusalem and the temple. The bringing together of the great message of God's salvation with this centrally significant religious symbol is a pattern similar to that found in the Old Testament and Judaism where Jerusalem and the temple were perceived to be crucially important centers in God's redemptive work, both as it related to the Jews and to the Gentiles. Luke's placing of his message of universal end-time salvation in the setting of Jerusalem and the temple indicates that Luke may very well have been familiar with the pattern of thought existent in contemporary Judaism and that, indeed, he wished to imitate it.

Jesus at the Temple (Luke 19:45-21:38)

Luke initiates Jesus' temple ministry with an abbreviated version of the cleansing narrative (Lk. 19:45-46 ‖ Mk. 11:15-19). This scene which inaugurates the period of Jesus' presence at the temple is followed by a passage that shows signs of purposeful Lukan editing (19:47-48).

Comparison with Mark's version of the cleansing reveals a number of important Lukan motifs and emphases. In the first place, Mark established a close relationship between the cleansing of the temple and the cursing of the fig tree (cf. Mk. 11:12-25). In so doing he established a definitive link between the rejection of Israel (the cursing of the fig tree) and the cleansing of the temple. This link allows easily for the interpretation that the cleansing of the temple prefigures the temple's destruction. Luke's deletion of the cursing of the fig tree removes from the cleansing narrative any intonation of its *necessary* rejection by God and subsequent destruction.[23]

In the second place, comparison with Mark seems to indicate that Luke is not at all interested in the condemnation of the cult per se. Weinert has noted that Mark makes specific reference to Jesus' violent stopping of the

---

[23]F. D. Weinert, "The Meaning of the Temple in the Gospel of Luke" (Ph.D. diss., Fordham University, 1979) 24-26.

very routine of worship (Mk. 11:15-16). He concludes that in Mark's version of the cleansing the temple cult per se comes under attack.[24] What Jesus condemns in Luke is the *abuse* of the temple by those described as "robbers"; he does not condemn legitimate worship. In short, while Mark portrays Jesus' encounter with the temple virtually as a *cursing,* Luke views it more as an actual *cleansing.*

In the third place, Luke's quotation of Isa. 56:7 (Lk. 19:46), in contrast to Mk. 11:17 (cf. Matt. 21:13), omits the reference to the temple being a place of prayer for all nations. The omission is significant. At the very least it may reflect the historical situation of Luke. As he writes, the temple stands in ruins. It does not appear that the temple would be a place in which the Gentiles would worship God.[25] There may also be some intrinsic theological significance: Despite the importance of Jerusalem and the temple as centers of activity in the dawn of the eschatological age of universal salvation, Luke may want to intimate here that they are not necessary elements in the carrying forth of this universal salvation. With or without the temple, God's word of salvation will reach the nations.

Conzelmann offers a helpful interpretation of the effect of the cleansing by describing it as Jesus' taking "possession" of the temple. In Luke's eyes it becomes a place which Jesus occupies—it now belongs to him. However, Conzelmann interprets such possession quite negatively as it relates to the Jews. They no longer have any legitimate claim on this place due to their rejection of Jesus. The temple is now the sole possession of the "new Israel," the church.[26]

Conzelmann's particular interpretation of the "possession" is defective. The notion of the church as the "new Israel" is open to question, especially in light of J. Jervell's investigations.[27] Also, it is clear from the book of Acts that even decades after the rejection of Jesus the temple was still a valid place of worship (see Acts 21:26). Nonetheless, the idea of "possession" itself may yet be functional. In a very real sense the cleansing does set the stage for the demonstration of Jesus' authority over and against that of the religious leaders. Immediately following the story of the

---

[24]Ibid., 23-41.

[25]Marshall, *Luke,* 721; Eric Franklin, *Christ the Lord: A Study in the Purpose and Theology of Luke-Acts* (Philadelphia: Westminster Press, 1975) 90-91.

[26]Conzelmann, *Theology,* 75-78.

[27]See esp. J. Jervell's essay "The Divided People of God: The Restoration of Israel and Salvation for the Gentiles" in *Luke and the People of God: A New Look at Luke-Acts* (Minneapolis: Augsburg, 1972) 41-74.

cleansing (19:45-46) and the summary announcement of his teaching activity in the temple (19:47-48), Jesus engages in conflict with the religious leaders over the issue of authority (Lk. 20:1-8). Jesus is portrayed in this pericope as the one who is the true, authoritative teacher of Israel.[28] The temple is now *his* place where he is free to teach the people.

Lk. 19:38, which makes reference to Jesus as the King, indicates that it is as Messiah that Jesus takes possession of the temple. The temple, therefore, is the *Messiah's* place. It is the proper place for Jesus to carry out his important messianic work of teaching. Unlike Mark, Luke does not condemn the temple because the Messiah has arrived. Rather, the Messiah *restores* the temple, rendering it fit to fulfill its eschatological role as a decisive center of God's saving work.

Evidence of Lukan redaction in 19:47-48 and 21:37-38 is clear.[29] Most obvious is the fact that the summary passage of 21:37-38 is a Lukan composition, not finding any parallel in Mark. Its function is to bring to explicit conclusion the temple activity of Jesus. The two prominent features of this summary passage are, one, the presence of "all the people . . . in the temple," and, two, Jesus' teaching (διδάσκειν) "in the temple." Both of these features appear in the introductory text of 19:47-48. There Luke reports that "all the people hung upon his words" (v. 48b) and that Jesus "was teaching daily in the temple" (v. 47a). This latter phrase is due entirely to Lukan composition for Mark has no reference to Jesus' teaching activity in this context (Mk. 11:18). The presence of these two identical motifs ("teaching" and "people") in two texts heavily redacted by Luke indicates that in Luke's mind the two pericopes were intended to parallel one other.

Jesus' activity of teaching is clearly an important motif for Luke, for it was a distinctive mark of Jesus' ministry. Through the use of periphrasis Luke indicates the continuous and consistent activity of teaching (Lk. 4:31; 5:17; 13:10).[30] The Lukan emphasis of this feature is indicated, in the second place, by Luke's redaction of his source material. In Lk. 5:17 the Evangelist replaces Mark's "he was speaking the word" (Mk. 2:11, my translation) with "he was teaching," making explicit the didactic char-

---

[28]Jerome Kodell, "Luke's use of LAOS, 'People,' Especially in the Jerusalem Narrative (Lk. 19.28-24.53)," CBQ 31 (1969): 327-43.

[29]See the discussion by Weinert, "Meaning of the Temple," 45-74.

[30]The durative force of the periphrastic participle is discussed by Harvey E. Dana and Julius R. Mantey, *A Manual Grammar of the Greek New Testament,* (Toronto: Macmillan Company, 1927; rpt: New York: Macmillan, 1957) 231-32.

acter of Jesus' work. In Lk. 6:6 the third Evangelist has added to Mk. 3:1 a reference to the teaching activity of Jesus. In 13:22, in what is most likely a Lukan composition serving to introduce some "Q" material,[31] Luke makes reference to the teaching activity of Jesus.

Given that Jesus' teaching activity was such an important dimension of his ministry, it is no surprise that such activity is noted in Lk. 19:47-48 and 21:37-38. If teaching were important throughout Jesus' ministry, it would only be appropriate that it be an essential feature of Jesus' climactic encounter with Israel.

This immediately raises the question of the content of this teaching. Unfortunately, Luke prefers to use διδάσκειν without any specific object of content.[32] The content of this teaching, therefore, must be extrapolated from Lukan hints. M. Bachmann has argued that the law is the focus of Jesus' teaching at the final temple scene of the gospel.[33] It is his belief that Luke saw the terms "teacher" (διδάσκολος, Lk. 2:46) and "teacher of law" (νομοδιδάσκολος, Acts 5:34) as virtually synonymous. This connection makes the attribution of the title διδάσκολος to Jesus significant, for this implies that Jesus' function as teacher is to offer instruction in matters of law. In the final temple scene of Luke's gospel, therefore, Luke wished to portray the temple as the place where the will of God was made known to the people of Israel by way of the Messiah.

Moreover, deeper investigation into the activity of Jesus' teaching the will of God reveals that such teaching had an eschatological thrust for Luke. In Lk. 4:15 the Evangelist transforms Mark's summary of Jesus' proclamation of the imminent arrival of the kingdom into a notification that Jesus' ministry was to be characterized by teaching in the synagogues. Indeed, throughout the gospel Luke is careful to remind his readers of Jesus' teaching activity in Jewish synagogues (see 4:31-32; 6:6; 13:10). Luke 4:15 is not, therefore, a casual reference. It serves to notify the reader that the teaching of the Jews in their places of worship is a keystone of Jesus' ministry.

---

[31]So Jeremias, *Sprache des Lukas*, 231.

[32]See Lk. 4:15, 31; 5:3, 17; 6:6; 13:10, 22, 26; 19:47; 21:37; 23:5. In 11:1 the content of the teaching is prayer. The content of Jesus' teaching in 20:21 is "the way of God." Both are most important. But Luke never implies that either "prayer" or "the way of God" captures in a summary fashion the essence of Jesus' teaching.

[33]Michael Bachmann, *Jerusalem und der Tempel: Die geographisch-theologischen Elemente in der lukanischen Sicht des judischen Kultzentrums*, Beiträge zur Wissenschaft vom Alten und Neuen Testament, Sechste Folge, Heft 9 (Stuttgart: Kohlhammer, 1980) 261-89.

The fact that Luke has substituted "teaching" for the "proclamation of the coming kingdom" has tempted interpreters to view Lk. 4:15 as a deeschatologizing of Mark's summary.[34] This is not the case, however. It cannot be coincidental that the programmatic Nazareth pericope immediately follows Luke's announcement of 4:15 that Jesus was teaching in the Jewish synagogues. Two observations are in order. First, features of the Nazareth pericope are carefully linked to Lk. 4:15, allowing the former to serve as a paradigmatic example of Jesus' teaching ministry. This linkage between Lk. 4:15 and the Nazareth story is evidenced in three ways. First, the two pericopes are linked with the catchword "synagogue" (Lk. 4:15, 16). Second, Luke's comment (which is not found in Mark) that Jesus' visitation of the synagogue was "according to his custom" (4:16), alludes to the use of the imperfect "was teaching" in 4:15 (ἐδίδασκεν), if the imperfect is understood to denote habitual or customary activity.[35] Third, the initially positive reaction of Jesus' audience in 4:22 alludes back to Luke's comment in 4:15 that Jesus was "being glorified by everyone" (my translation). The linkage of the two pericopes indicates that Luke wanted the reader to see the events at Nazareth as exemplifying Jesus' teaching ministry introduced in 4:15.

If this be so, then it is significant that Jesus announces in the Nazareth pericope the fulfillment of Isaiah 61:1-2 (Lk. 4:21). A number of Jews understood this Isaianic text to refer to the eschatological age of salvation.[36] Granted this, Jesus' announcement that the promise found in Isaiah is being fulfilled could only mean that Luke intended to say nothing less than that the new age of salvation had objectively dawned in the person and teaching of Jesus.[37] It is also significant that the conclusion of Jesus' teaching of the people in the temple focuses on the absolute end of the age (21:5-36). Hence, any teaching Jesus offers is to be understood in the larger context of Luke's conviction that Jesus as the Messiah announces the coming of the new age of salvation.

---

[34]Conzelmann, *Theology,* 114; cf. Fitzmyer, *Luke,* 522.

[35]See the discussion of the "iterative imperfect" in Friedrich W. Blass and Albert Debrunner, *A Greek Grammar of the New Testament and Other Early Christian Literature,* tr. R. W. Funk (London: Cambridge University Press; Chicago: University of Chicago Press, 1961) §§318(3) and 325; Dana and Mantey, *Manual Grammar,* 188-89.

[36]See Sanders, "Isaiah 61 to Luke 4," 96-103.

[37]Ulrich Busse, *Das Nazareth-Manifest Jesu: Eine Einfuhrung in das lukanische Jesusbild nach Lk 4,16-30,* Stuttgarter Bibelstudien 91 (Stuttgart: Verlag Katholisches bibelwerk, ca. 1977) 91-92.

The recipients of this eschatological teaching are the "people." Luke's careful and consistent use of λαός to denote this group indicates that he does not intend Jesus' audience to be understood merely as a group of Jews who happened to be congregating around the temple. Rather, "all the people" constitutes a representative group that embodies Israel. In this temple scene, Jesus encounters Israel.

Luke's usage of the word λαός bears out this conclusion. In the first place, Luke consistently uses the term λαός to denote Jews (the only exceptions to this rule are Lk. 2:31, Acts 15:14, and 18:10). Second, Luke can use the term λαός to denote a particular group of Jews at a particular locale of an event (Lk. 6:17; 7:1, 29; 8:47; 9:13; 18:43; Acts 5:37). Third, however, Luke can also use this word to denote Israel as a whole. Unambiguous passages consist of those wherein λαός is used to represent the people of Israel as opposed to the Gentiles (Lk. 2:32; Acts 4:25-27; 26:17, 23). In two instances he can use λαός with "Israel" to denote the entirety of God's people (Lk. 2:32; Acts 4:10). Even when not contrasted with the Gentiles or standing in apposition with Israel, there are places where "people" appears to be used to denote the whole of Israel (Lk. 1:17, 68, 77; 2:10; Acts 7:17, 34; 21:28; 28:17, 26-27). In all likelihood Luke intended "the people" of Lk. 19:48 and 21:38 to be used in such a representative sense, for in both summaries Luke designates the temple congregation as "all the people" (19:48; 21:38).

The preceding discussion allows the following conclusions. From Luke's perspective the essentially important features of Jesus' temple ministry were his activity of teaching and the presence of the people. While Luke does not specifically define the teaching, many clues indicate that it was closely related to the message of the eschatological salvation of God. The recipients of this message are described as "all the people" by which Luke means Israel as a whole. Here Luke portrays the Messiah Jesus as confronting for the last time the people of God with the message of salvation.

It is not unimportant that the Lukan summaries (19:47-48 and 21:37-38) indicate that the location of this final and decisive encounter was the temple. That Luke has consciously focused the action on this location is evidenced by Lukan editing. While the parallel passages in Mark show much interest in the temple, the second Evangelist does not focus and fix the action on this one location the way Luke does. In Mark Jesus is portrayed as coming in and out of the temple throughout the various scenes. In Mk. 11:11 he enters the temple and then goes to Bethany where, on the following day, he cursed the fig tree (11:12-16). In 11:15-17 Jesus reenters the temple and cleanses it. Immediately following this pericope Jesus is once again in Bethany where the withering of the cursed fig tree is confirmed (11:20-26). Between 11:27-13:2 Mark confines Jesus to the temple precincts, but the Evangelist moves him to the Mount of Olives to offer the "little apocalypse" of chapter 13. The temple setting was important for Mark, but he does not confine the action to this locale.

In Luke, once Jesus enters the temple he never leaves its precincts until he finally departs. Luke omits all notifications in Mark which indicate that Jesus left the temple area, such as Mk. 11:11, 11:20-26, and 13:3. Rather than allowing the focus of the action to shift localities, Luke brackets the temple scene with the summaries of 19:47-48 and 21:37-38. This serves to give the temple ministry a definite beginning and ending. Here, and only here, the Messiah of Israel confronts the whole of Israel with the message of eschatological salvation.

The Ascension of Jesus

In dealing with the ascension narrative in Luke-Acts I shall examine in detail two issues: one, the meaning of each of the respective ascension narratives in Lk. 24 and Acts 1; and two, Luke's association of the ascension and related events with Jerusalem. The following investigation does not require detailed discussion of the textual problems involving Lk. 24:51b and 52a. I shall assume, along with numerous interpreters, the authenticity of the longer readings here.[38] Also, I shall not attempt to offer any full explication of the complex relationship between the apparently parallel, yet somewhat contradictory, accounts of the ascension in Luke 24 and Acts 1. Luke has frustrated interpreters before by allowing contradictions to stand in parallel accounts (cf. Acts 9:7 with 22:9). I shall assume, therefore, that Luke 24 and Acts 1 are parallel accounts of one ascension.

The Interpretation of the Ascension. P. A. van Stempvoort describes the ascension in the gospel as a priestly doxology.[39] He observes that verses 50-53 follow the pattern of Sir. 50:20-21. In the latter Simon lifts up his hands (ἐπῆρε χεῖρας) and blesses (εὐλογία) the people. This compares well with Lk. 24:50: "having lifted up his hands (ἐπάρας τὰς χεῖρας) he blessed (εὐλόγησεν) them." In Sirach the announcement of the blessing is followed by a description of the people's worship. Lk. 24:52a speaks of the apostles' worshiping Jesus.

---

[38]See, e.g., Marshall, *Luke*, 908-909; P. A. van Stempvoort, "The Interpretation of the Ascension in Luke and Acts," NTS 5 (1957-58): 30-42; Gerhard Lohfink, *Die Himmelfahrt Jesu: Untersuchungen zu den Himmelfahrts- und Erhohungstexten bei Lukas,* Studien zum Alten und Neuen Testament 26 (Munich: Kosel Verlag, 1971) 13-31.

[39]Ibid.

Luke's description of the incidents surrounding the ascension clearly gives a cultic quality to the event. Grundmann believes that Luke is going so far as to identify Jesus with the priestly messianic figure of some Jewish speculation.[40] While Marshall is correct to observe that Luke does very little with such a motif,[41] it would not be right to conclude that Luke was not interested in giving to Jesus a priestly coloring. Both Raymond Brown and Eduard Schweizer have argued that Jesus' blessing completes Zechariah's inability to bless the congregation (Lk. 1:21-22).[42] The fact that Jesus offered this blessing away from the temple, could indicate that his priesthood was one that displaced the Jerusalem cult.[43] Such a negative interpretation is unlikely. While Luke may very well wish to indicate that the "blessings of Jesus" are not confined to the temple, it would seem that the notification in 24:53 that the disciples "were continually in the temple blessing God" would give a positive affirmation to the priestly portrait of Jesus.

The dominant pattern in non-Lukan Christianity was to associate Jesus with the literal cult only in a *negative* sense, portraying Jesus as replacing the cult with himself or his church. Luke has no such conception. Rather, Luke gives Jesus a distinctively cultic character which does not nullify the temple cult. The joyful presence of the disciples in the temple following Jesus' benediction seems to offer an affirmation of the cult.

Such is consistent with Luke's overall presentation. The temple has been cleansed of the elements which are detrimental to true worship (19:45-46). Jesus has both challenged and displaced the corrupt authority of the Jewish leaders (Lk. 20). In 19:45–21:38 he teaches Israel the eschatological message of God. At this point in Luke's narrative the temple still belongs to Jesus. It is he who offers the blessing to the apostles, who will become the leaders of the restored Israel. Far from nullifying the temple, the priestly benediction of Jesus leaves the impression that there is new hope for the temple, the precise nuances of which await examination later in this chapter. Luke, to be sure, does not relate Jesus here with any specific array of Jewish expectations revolving around the Messiah and the temple. But he does share in the overall expectation that messianic activity would have a

---

[40]Grundmann, *Lukas*, 453-54.

[41]Marshall, *Luke*, 908-909.

[42]Brown, *Birth of the Messiah*, 281-82; Eduard Schweizer, *Das Evangelium nach Lukas*, Das Neue Testament Deutsch, Teilband 3 (Göttingen: Vandenhoeck und Ruprecht, 1982) 251.

[43]So van Stempvoort, "Interpretation of the Ascension," NTS 5 (1958): 30-42.

cultic thrust. Quite important is the observation that this cultic thrust revolves *not* around a spiritualized community-as-temple complex, but around the literal temple and Jerusalem. It is here that the Messiah teaches and blesses his people.

The ascension narrative in Acts offers what van Stempvoort calls "the ecclesiastical and historical interpretation [of the ascension], with the accent on the work of the Spirit in the church."[44] Van Stempvoort sees the ascension in Acts as directing the attention of the reader to the work and mission of the church: until the parousia the church is to busy itself in the task of world mission. Van Stempvoort is correct to see here a different nuance to the meaning of the ascension as compared with the gospel. The focus, however, is not so much on the mission of the church, as important as this surely is (see Acts 1:8), but the exaltation of Jesus to the throne of David.

There is good evidence that primitive Christianity interpreted the "raising up" (in the sense of "resurrection") of Jesus as the fulfillment of the promise that God would "raise up" (in the sense of "rear") a descendant of David to sit upon the Davidic throne.[45] In the earliest kerygma it may have been believed that it was by means of the resurrection that Jesus became the Christ, though this view was quickly displaced by reading Jesus' messianic status back into his pre-Easter life. Once Jesus' messianic status was affirmed prior to the resurrection, the resurrection itself would no longer be considered to be the appointment of Jesus to the status of Messiah. It would, however, still be perceived as the exaltation of Christ to the throne itself at the right hand of God. In other words, the resurrection becomes Jesus' coronation.

According to Gerhard Lohfink, Luke altered this pattern. The third evangelist accepted the presuppositions of the cosmic christology which viewed Jesus as exalted to the right hand of God, but he differentiated between the resurrection and the exaltation. From Luke's perspective Jesus' body was glorified at the resurrection, but he did not assume his station on the throne until the ascension. According to Lohfink, this differentiation between resurrection and ascension/exaltation is peculiarly Lukan.[46]

---

[44]Ibid., 34.

[45]See John H. Hayes, "The Resurrection as Enthronement and the Earliest Church Christology," Int 22 (1968): 333-45; Dennis Duling, "Promises to David," NTS 20 (1973): 55-77.

[46]Lohfink, *Himmelfahrt*, esp. 242-50.

This understanding of the ascension of Jesus as Luke's description of the exaltation to his throne can be accepted. Other features of Lohfink's conclusions need modification, for there is evidence that in terms of the functional meaning Luke did not sharply differentiate between the resurrection and the ascension. This is evidenced by Acts 2:30-31. Here Peter states that "God has sworn with an oath to [David] that he would set one of his descendents upon his throne" (v. 30). This enthronement is explicitly defined in verse 31 as "the resurrection of Christ." For Luke, the meaning of resurrection is equivalent to that of the exaltation; it denotes the enthronement of Jesus.

But what specific emphasis did Luke attach to the ascension? The answer lies in the fact that Luke viewed the apostles' *witnessing* of the resurrection as significant (Lk. 24:48; Acts 1:26; 2:52; 3:15; 10:40-41; 13:30-31). While it is not emphasized in all references to the resurrection, Luke viewed this resurrection/enthronement as the fulfillment of God's promise to the fathers that once again a Davidic descendent would sit on the throne of David (Acts 2:30-36; 13:30-37; cf. Lk. 1:32-33). What Luke wished to indicate was that the apostolic witnesses can legitimately testify to the fulfillment of the eschatological promises of God concerning the Messiah: the son of David now sits upon the messianic throne.

How better to describe the witnessing of the enthronement than to allow the apostles to witness objectively Jesus' coronation through a heavenly ascension? Jesus is said to be taken up "as they were watching" (v. 9, my translation). The cloud carrying Jesus away is described as taking Jesus "from their eyes" (v. 9, my translation). Verse 11 describes the apostles watching the gradual elevation of Jesus into the heavens. The apostles were not merely seeing a vision. Luke discarded this idea in Lk. 24:37-43 where he describes the resurrected Jesus of "flesh and bones" (v. 39) eating with the disciples (vv. 41-42). This Jesus is now exalted to the right hand of God. The apostles are witnesses in an objective sense to the event. They can, therefore, authoritatively testify to Israel that God has fulfilled his promises to Israel by placing the son of David on the throne.

The Centrality of Jerusalem. It is significant that Luke has consciously focused the action geographically on Jerusalem and its environs. In the first place, Luke's redaction of Mark removes any association between Galilee and the manifestations of the resurrected one. Lk. 24:8 alters Mk. 16:7 so as to erase the conception of a resurrection appearance in Galilee. Luke also omits from his gospel the promise of Jesus to Peter that after he is raised he will go before this apostle to Galilee (see Mk. 14:28; Lk. 22:31-34). Second, Luke continually reminds the reader that the resurrection appearances happened in or around Jerusalem. Lk. 24:13 introduces the appearance to the disciples on the road to Emmaus by stating that the location was near Jerusalem.

The notification of 24:33 establishes Jerusalem as the stage for the appearance of 24:36-49. To be noted is the fact that Luke's tradition may have understood the locale of this appearance to be Galilee, for involved in this manifestation is the sharing of a meal. According to Reginald H. Fuller, the meal traditions were associated with Galilean appearances.[47] Hence, Luke may have actually altered the tradition to provide a Jerusalem setting. The ascension at Bethany (24:50) does remove one from Jerusalem per se, but the setting is still in the city's immediate environs, for Luke specifically states that the Mount of Olives (the site of Bethany) was near Jerusalem (Acts 1:12). It is also significant that Luke specifically associates the Messiah's ascension with the Mount of Olives, for Zech. 14:3-9 describes this mount as the place from whence God would inaugurate his eschatological reign.

While Luke does not offer any direct allusions to Jewish statements regarding the importance of the Jerusalem setting for the Messiah, he clearly is rejecting Mark's conscious tendency to dissociate Jesus from the holy city. Luke, quite unlike his Markan source, sees the city of Jerusalem as playing a positive role in the activity of the kingly Messiah. As in Jewish expectation, it is the appropriate place for the manifestation of the Messiah.

The Apostles, Jerusalem, and the Salvation of Israel

Lk. 22:28-30 (‖ Matt. 19:28) presents itself as a crucial text for understanding the role of the apostles in relation to Israel. The text states:

> You are those who have continued with me in my trials; and I assign to you, as my father assigned to me, a kingdom, that you may eat and drink at my table in my kingdom, and sit on thrones judging the twelve tribes of Israel.

The Twelve in Acts. Luke's version of the logion is placed in the context of the Last Supper (22:15-39), where he portrays Jesus as establishing a pattern for leadership and authority: Just as he served, so too are the

---

[47]*The Formation of the Resurrection Narratives,* rev. ed. (London: S.P.C.K., 1980) 36-43.

apostles to exercise their authority by means of service.[48] In the context of this discussion Jesus offers the promise that the apostles will rule over the twelve tribes of Israel.[49]

The *twelve* apostles played a unique role for Luke. The primary importance of the circle of the twelve is evidenced by the election of Matthias (Acts 1:15-26). It is said of Judas in 1:17 that he had been "numbered" among the apostles. Scripture itself dictates that the space vacated by Judas must be filled (1:20). The story concludes with the statement that Matthias "was enrolled with the eleven apostles" (1:26).

Taken as a whole, Acts 1:15-26 implies that it was necessary to have *twelve* persons to function as apostles. It has been argued that the primary function of the apostles in Acts is to serve as concrete historical links between the age of Jesus and the church.[50] But if this be so, would not eleven such links have served the purpose of Luke as well as twelve? Such would appear to be the case. Hence, the fact that Luke *emphasized* the election of a twelfth apostle indicates that there is some significance to this group beyond that of a "historical link."

The importance of twelve apostles is understandable in light of Jesus' promise of Lk. 22:28-30: the apostles who continued with him in his trials would sit and judge the *twelve* tribes of Israel. The twelfth apostle is appointed, therefore, to complete the number of the ruling body of Israel.

The Leaders of the People. The idea that the twelve constituted a body to rule Israel would come as no surprise to Luke's readers. The text that relates most directly to this motif is Lk. 20:9-18. This parable of the vineyard deals with the transfer of authority from the traditional Jewish leaders to another (as of yet unidentified) group.

Luke is not advocating in this parable God's rejection of the *people* of Israel. Luke has already distanced them from their leaders (see Lk. 19:47;

---

[48]Charles Talbert discusses the motif of the disciples' imitation of Jesus in "The Way of the Lukan Jesus: Dimensions of Lukan Spirituality," PRS 9 (1982): 237-50. See also Heinz Schürmann, "Der Abendmahlsbericht Lukas 22, 7:38 als Gottesdienstordnung, Gemeindeordnung, Lebensordung," in *Ursprung und Gestalt: Erörterung und Besinnungen zum Neuen Testament* (Düsseldorf: Patmos-Verlag, 1970) 148-51.

[49]There is a question concerning whether κρίνοντες can be understood as "rule," or whether it must take its narrower meaning of "judge." Jacques Dupont, "Le logion des douze trones (Mat 19,28; Lc 22,28-30)," Bib 45 (1964): 355-92, has argued that κρίνοντες must be limited to the narrower sense of "judge." In the following discussion I shall argue that the larger Lukan context indicates that while apostolic leadership contained an element of "judgment," this logion does find a partial fulfillment in the apostolic *leadership* of the primitive community as described in Acts.

[50]Eduard Schweizer, *Church Order in the New Testament* (London: SCM Press, 1961) 69.

20:1), and he will continue to emphasize the division of the people and the leaders in later chapters. The sole object of the parable's attack is the leaders (20:19). It is because they reject God's Son that God will destroy them (20:16). He will not destroy the vineyard, however. Luke does not precisely define the vineyard, but since it clearly represents the domain of the Jewish leaders (the tenants), it would be safest to conclude that the vineyard alluded to Israel (cf. Isa. 5:1-7).[51] The text asserts, therefore, that while the leaders will be destroyed, the vineyard (Israel) will remain, but it will be under the control of another group. In light of the promise of the apostles' kingdom in Lk. 22:30, it would seem that the apostles are these "others."[52]

The hostile response of the Jewish leaders depicted in the parable is part of a larger Lukan pattern that emphasizes conflict between Jesus and the leaders. The hostility of the leaders toward Jesus often stands in direct contrast to the reaction of the people, resulting in a division between the people and their leaders. Since this division plays an important role in Luke-Acts, it is appropriate to examine Luke's description of the responses of the respective Jewish groups to Jesus and his followers.

Luke emphasizes the guilt of the leaders.[53] In the first place, he incorporates a number of statements from Mark that serve to portray the Jewish leaders as hostile to Jesus. Lk. 19:47-48 notes the desire of the Jewish

---

[51]So E. Earle Ellis, *The Gospel of Luke,* 2nd ed., New Century Bible (London: Oliphants; Greenwood SC: Attic Press, 1974) 185.

[52]L. T. Johnson, *The Literary Function of Possessions in Luke-Acts,* SBLDS 39 (Missoula MT: Scholars Press, 1977) 119-21.

[53]There is debate concerning the precise identity of the "leaders" responsible for the death of Jesus. For examples of the discussion see, on the one hand, Richard J. Cassidy, *Jesus, Politics and Society: A Study of Luke's Gospel* (Maryknoll NY: Orbis Books, 1978) 63-76, and his article "Luke's Audience, the Chief Priests, and the Motive for Jesus' Death" in *Political Issues in Luke-Acts,* ed. Richard J. Cassidy and Philip J. Scharper (Maryknoll NY: Orbis Books, 1983) 146-67. Cassidy views the "leaders" primarily as the chief priests and a group which he broadly defines as their allies. On the other hand, E. Jane Via argues that two groups were held accountable by Luke for the death of Jesus, the "rulers" and the "people." See "According to Luke, Who Put Jesus to Death?" in *Political Issues in Luke-Acts,* 122-45. While she includes the chief priests in the group of the "rulers" Via argues that Luke understands the "rulers" to be a more inclusive group consisting of "the chief priests, the high priest, the scribes, the elders, the Sanhedrin, the soldiers or captains, Pilate, and Herod" (132). Despite the differences between Cassidy and Via, both would agree that in some way Luke holds the leaders of Israel accountable for the death of Jesus. Further, I will argue below that within the passion narrative itself, Luke tends to exonerate the people as much as possible.

leaders to destroy Jesus. He states in Lk. 22:2 that the leaders "were seeking how to put him to death." The leaders joyfully accept Judas's proposal to provide them a way to capture Jesus (22:3-6). The leaders arrest Jesus (22:52), hold him during the night at the house of the high priest (22:54), hold a council (22:66), and eventually lead him to Pilate (23:1).

Second, Luke's desire to incriminate the Jewish leaders is more clearly seen in his alterations of and additions to Mark. One, whereas Mk. 12:12 reads that "they tried to arrest him," Luke has made the subjects specific: "The scribes and the chief priests tried to lay hands on him at that very hour" (Lk. 20:19). Two, Lk. 20:20 indicates that the premeditated intention of the Jewish leaders was to deliver Jesus to the Roman authorities. Three, Luke portrays the Jewish leaders as present at the various hearings putting forth charges against Jesus (23:2, 5, 10). Four, the Jewish leaders continually reject Pilate's claims that Jesus is innocent and demand his crucifixion (23:4-5, 13-15, 22-25).

The third piece of evidence pointing to the central role of the Jewish leaders in the execution of Jesus is Luke's association of these leaders with Satan. Conzelmann has observed that with the initiation of the passion narrative proper Satan plays a most influential role in the action.[54] It is Satan who enters the heart of Judas leading him to the Jewish leaders in order to betray Jesus (22:3-4 [the mentioning of Satan is due to Lukan editing]). Luke viewed the hour of the passion as belonging to the "power of darkness" (22:53), likely a reference to satanic power. Darkness was used as a symbol for Satan, both in Judaism[55] and in Luke-Acts (see Acts 26:18). In 22:53 Luke links the Jewish leaders with this satanic power. Speaking to those who came to arrest him ("the chief priests and the officers of the temple and elders"), Jesus says: "But this is your hour and the power of darkness."

In summation, Luke understood the Jewish leaders to be directly involved in the crucifixion of Jesus. Such involvement was the result of their conscious rejection of the authority of Jesus, leading to a premeditated plan to kill him by handing him over to the Roman authorities. In addition, all of this was done in conjunction with the one to whom the hour of the passion belonged: "the power of darkness."

---

[54]Conzelmann, *Theology,* 199ff.

[55]E.g., darkness equals Beliar in T.Nap. 2:7 and T.Jos. 20:2. In Qumran literature the "sons of darkness" are of the "lot of darkness" which is synonymous with Belial (see Conzelmann, σκότος κτλ. TDNT 7:431-32 for abundant references from the Scrolls). In the same article Conzelmann comments on Lk. 22:53 that "the power of the underworld rules in the passion of Jesus" (439).

To be contrasted with the attitude of the leaders is the attitude of the "people." They are often depicted as listening to Jesus as he teaches in the temple (19:48; 20:1; 21:38). It is the "fear of the people" that detains the leaders from arresting Jesus (20:19; 22:20). There are two scenes unique to Luke where the people mourn the death of Jesus (23:26-32; 23:48).

There is only one reference in the passion narrative that links the "people" with the death of Jesus. Lk. 23:13 reads: "Pilate then called together the chief priests and the rulers and the people. . . . " The text goes on to report that "they all cried out together, 'Away with this man . . . ' " (v. 18). Because this attitude of the people seems to contrast so sharply with the attitude as presented elsewhere in the passion narrative some are inclined to amend the text here. Instead of reading "the rulers and the people" it has been suggested that the text should read "the rulers of the people."[56]

Jerome Kodell provides a helpful alternative. He notes that immediately following the troublesome verse 13 the text reads "and he [Pilate] said to them, 'You brought me this man as one who was perverting the people.' " The attention of the reader is immediately focused once again on the leaders, *not the people*. Hence, the antecedent of the subject of verse 18 ("they all cried out together, 'Away with this man' ") could easily be understood as the leaders.[57] In short, Luke's tradition placed the "people" at the scene of Jesus' trial before Pilate. Luke's redaction, however, has made the people silent bystanders. It was only the leaders who insisted on the death of Jesus.

What Luke is developing in the passion narrative is the division of Israel. There are those who reject Jesus and those who accept him (or who are at least open to his message). Such a division is anticipated in the infancy narrative where Simeon upon seeing Jesus states, "Behold, this child is set for the fall and rising of many in Israel" (Lk. 2:34). The statement is somewhat enigmatic in the context of the birth narrative, but it takes on clearer meaning in light of Acts 3:22-26.

Here reference is made to the raising up of a prophet like Moses. Moses had declared that the people shall heed this prophet or else be "destroyed from the people" (v. 23).[58] If Luke did see the acceptance of Jesus as the

---

[56]Augustine George, "Israel dans l'oeuvre de Luc," RB 75 (1968): 503; Gottfried Rau, "Das Volk in der lukanischen Passionsgeschichte, eine Konjektur zu Lk 23, 13," ZNW 56 (1965): 48.

[57]Kodell, "LAOS," CBQ 31 (1969): 333.

[58]See Jervell, "Divided People," in *Luke and the People*, 41-74.

exclusive criterion for remaining a part of the "people," it would follow that the Jewish leaders' rejection of Jesus would lead to their being cut off from the people of God. This understanding of Acts 3:23 gives clear meaning to the parable of the vineyard (Lk. 20:9-18). Lk. 20:16 states concerning the fate of the tenants of the vineyard that "he [the owner] will come and destroy those tenants, and give the vineyard to others." The Jewish leaders have lost their place of authority because as a group they are for Luke no longer a part of the people of God.

The pattern of division continues in the early chapters of Acts. Luke portrays the people as responding positively to the work of the twelve apostles. They respond with repentance to Peter's sermon (Acts 2:37-42). They praise God as a result of Peter's healing of the lame man (3:1-10). Five thousand men from among the people believed the apostolic preaching (Acts 4:4). Acts 5:12-16 reports that the people held the apostles in high honor, bringing their sick to them for healing. It is said in 4:21 and 5:26 that the people's favorable reaction to the apostles prevents the Jewish leaders from harming the twelve.

In direct contrast to the response of the people, Acts 4:1-3 indicates that "the priests and the captain of the temple" arrested the apostles because the latter group was teaching the people. Acts 4:5-21 offers a detailed account of the Jewish leadership's inquisition of the apostles whom they threaten and would severely punish were it not for fear of adverse reaction from the people. Acts 5:17-40 recounts another narrative wherein the Jewish leaders persecuted the apostles and actually "wanted to kill them" (v. 33). Gamaliel's speech convinces them that a beating would be sufficient punishment (5:40).

In the opening chapters of Acts there evolves a gradual movement of action from open acceptance by the people with no opposition from the leaders (chapter 2), to a mixed response consisting of acceptance by the people and hostility from the Jewish leaders (3:1-5:16), to virtually total opposition from the leaders with little indication of the people's response (5:17-42). It is clearly foreshadowed before the Stephen episode (6:8-7:60) that the followers of Jesus will experience intense rejection at the hands of some of the Jews. At the same time, it is quite clear that a substantial number of Jews have accepted the testimony of the twelve concerning the Christ (2:41; 4:4; 5:14). Israel is being divided on the basis of its response to Jesus. Thousands are finding salvation while others are being "destroyed from the people." The opening chapters of Acts portray the Jewish leaders as most consistently rejecting the apostles. But it is almost a misnomer to call them the leaders of the Jews, for as they have been cut off from the people they no longer have a legitimate claim over Israel. From Luke's perspective the rule of God's people would belong to another group. Logically, that group would be the twelve.

The Leadership of the Twelve. Two specific issues need to be addressed to bear out the premise that Luke viewed the twelve as the new leaders of Israel. First, it needs to be shown that the twelve were actually portrayed by Luke as rulers in the opening chapters of Acts. Second, it needs to be established that the contingency over which the twelve ruled was portrayed by Luke as representing Israel as a whole.

The opening chapters of Acts indicate that it is the twelve apostles who exercise authority over the primitive community that accepts Jesus as the Messiah. In an insightful study, L. T. Johnson has shown how possessions in Luke-Acts function literarily to denote the sincerity of one's response to the gospel. A concrete indication of the sincerity of one's response to the gospel is his response to the authority of the apostles who, for Luke, are men of the Spirit who, like Jesus, speak the authoritative word of God. To reject them and their authority is to reject God himself.[59]

Luke uses possessions as a symbolic device to denote one's acceptance of the apostles' authority. Hence, there stands in close conjunction with one another the notification that the earliest Christians "devoted themselves to the apostles' teaching," that the apostles were men of the Spirit (2:43), and that the believers gave up personal possessions for the sake of the community (2:44). Perhaps the clearest symbolic use of possessions in Acts is found in 4:32-5:11. Acts 4:32-37 provides a description of the community's laying of its possessions at the feet of the apostles, an activity directly inspired by the powerful testimony of the apostles concerning the resurrecton of Jesus. According to Johnson, this laying of one's possessions at the apostles' feet symbolically demonstrates the sincere acceptance of the apostles' testimony and authority.

To be contrasted with such sincere acceptance is the hypocrisy of Ananias and Sapphira who laid only a portion of their possessions at the apostles' feet (5:2). Such an act is interpreted as an attempt to deceive God himself (5:4), for it symbolizes a nonacceptance of the apostles' authority which is manifested through the apostles' performance of powerful signs (5:12). Johnson's thesis is commendable, and allows for the conclusion that Acts offers a description of the apostolic rule over the primitive Christian community.

Did Luke view this primitive community as representing Israel? Clearly, Luke viewed the Jerusalem community as consisting of Jews (Acts 2:22,

---

[59]Johnson, *Literary Function of Possessions*, 29-78.

29, 36, 39). Did Luke see these Jews as somehow representing Israel as a whole? It is likely that he did. This is evidenced, in the first place, by Luke's tendency to see the "people" as representatives of the whole of Israel, a point argued earlier in this chapter. Luke often denotes the audience of the apostles' teaching as λαός (Acts 2:47; 3:9, 11-12; 4:1-2, 8, 10, 17; 5:12, 20, 25). Second, Luke offers a number of explicit references which leave the impression that "all of Israel" is the intended audience of the apostolic preaching. Peter concludes his first sermon with the declaration: "Let all the house of Israel therefore know assuredly that God has made him both Lord and Christ, this Jesus whom you crucified" (Acts 2:36). According to Acts 3:11-12, after "all the people" had run together, Peter addressed them as "men of Israel." Finally, in Acts 4:10 Peter says to the rulers "be it known to you all, and to all the people of Israel, that by the name of Jesus . . . this man is standing before you well."

The most impressive indication that Luke intended the reader to see the primitive Christian community as being drawn from Jews who represent all Israel is Acts 2:5-11. Here, following the reading of certain manuscripts, Luke clearly indicates that the audience who hears and responds to the apostolic preaching consists of worldwide Judaism. According to Alexandrinus and Vaticanus Acts 2:5 reads: "Now there were Jews dwelling in Jerusalem, devout men from every nation under heaven" (my translation). Luke then proceeds to list the numerous nations from which this Jewish audience has come. It would seem that Luke wants the readers to view the recipients of Peter's first sermon as worldwide Jewry.

To be sure, this conclusion depends upon the acceptance of the readings of Alexandrinus and Vaticanus. Sinaiticus omits the reference to the Jews, while a number of other manuscripts transpose the location of the word "Jews." This could lead one to conclude that the reference to "Jews" must be a later gloss. In that case, Acts 2:5-11 portrays Peter's audience not as Jews, but as representatives of the Gentile nations.

Despite the textual problems, it is best to view the audience of 2:5-11 as representing diaspora Judaism. In the first place, it is clear throughout the opening chapters that Luke portrays the apostles as speaking to *Jews*. It is not likely that Luke would have introduced the audience of the Pentecost sermon as Jews and Gentiles, and then consistently ignore the Gentile element in the subsequent preaching. Second, Bruce Metzger believes there to be good reason for the omission of "Jews" from verse 5 by some copyists. He suggests that these copyists might have thought that the idea of "Jews" being "from every race" appeared contradictory.[60] With re-

---

[60]Bruce Metzger, *A Textual Commentary on the Greek New Testament* (London/New York: United Bible Societies, 1971) 290-91.

spect to the transposition of word order, Metzger believes this to be due to stylistic considerations.[61] Hence, "Jews" is to be retained in verse 5, indicating that Luke intends the hearers of the Pentecost sermon to represent Israel from all over the world.

The Eschatological Role of the Twelve. Did Luke understand the apostolic rule over Israel as the fulfillment, or at least the proleptic fulfillment, of the eschatological rule predicted in Lk. 22:28-30? In discussing the eschatological character of the rule of the twelve it is necessary to examine whether it is even possible from Luke's perspective to speak of the realization of the promise of Lk. 22:28-30 before the parousia, or whether within the Lukan frame of mind the realization of the apostolic kingdom is tied to the realization of the messianic kingdom. This requires some examination of Luke's understanding of the time and character of the messianic reign of Jesus.

The first reference to the kingdom of the Messiah is found in the annunciation of Lk. 1:32b-33. Here it is said that "the Lord God will give to him the throne of his father David, and he will reign over the house of Jacob forever; and of his kingdom there will be no end." But there is no indication here concerning the time of the promise's realization.

The parable of the pounds (Lk. 19:11-27 ‖ Matt. 25:14-30) also makes likely reference to the messianic kingdom. The parable in its present form is easily open to allegorical interpretation with the most natural meaning being that the "nobleman" of verse 12 corresponds to Jesus. The purpose of his departure is to receive a kingdom, after which time he will return to assess the work of his servants. If the return of the "nobleman" refers to the parousia of Jesus, which is the most likely allegorical interpretation, then verse 15 ("when he returned, having received [λαβόντα] the kingdom") indicates that the Messiah's receipt of his kingdom *precedes* the parousia—it is not simultaneous with it.

The final reference of Jesus' kingdom, aside from Lk. 22:28-30, is found in 23:42 where the penitent thief asks Jesus to remember him when he comes in(to) his kingdom. A textual problem exists here. A number of good manuscripts read ἐν τῇ βασιλείᾳ σου (א, A), while other good witnesses read εἰς τὴν βασιλείαν σου ($\mathfrak{p}^{75,}$ B). Two different meanings are indicated by the change of case. The latter (with the accusative) probably refers to the exaltation and ascension of Jesus, in which case the thief is asking Jesus to remember him when he assumes his exalted status at the right hand of God (cf. Acts 7:55). The use of the dative may reflect

---

[61]Ibid., 291.

a semitism (bᵉmalkutak), meaning "when you come as king."[62] In this instance, reference would be made to the parousia.

The brief survey of the scant passages available for investigation reveals evidence that Luke viewed the kingdom of Jesus as being realized before the parousia (Lk. 19:11-27; Lk. 23:42 with accusative) in which case it is to be distinguished from the kingdom of God. There is also evidence that Luke viewed the advent of the messianic kingdom as simultaneous with the parousia (Lk. 23:42 with the dative), in which case it would stand virtually synonymous with the kingdom of God. The issue, therefore, deserves further consideration.

There does exist further evidence that the messianic kingdom is closely related to, and perhaps virtually synonymous with, the kingdom of God. In the first place, Conzelmann rightly observes that Luke provides no place for an earthly millennial kingdom such as is found in the Apocalypse.[63] Hence, the kingdom of the Messiah must be synonymous with the kingdom of God.

Second, banquet imagery revolves around both the kingdom of Jesus and the kingdom of God. In two passages Luke uses banquet imagery in relation to the kingdom of God. In Lk. 14:15-24 he uses the banquet as a metaphor for the celebration of the kingdom of God. In Lk. 22:16-18 Jesus twice vows not to eat of the bread or drink the wine until the consummation of the kingdom.

Lk. 22:29 makes it clear that Luke also saw banquet imagery as appropriate to depict Jesus' kingdom. Given that this logion stands in such close proximity to 22:16-18, with its use of banquet imagery to depict the kingdom of God, it is possible that Luke viewed the two logia as quite similar in function. This lends support to Conzelmann's belief that there is no real difference between the kingdom of God and the kingdom of the Messiah. Since Conzelmann views the kingdom of God as a transcendent reality which will manifest itself only in the future, the same would have to be said of the messianic kingdom.[64] And since the disciples' kingdom is coexistent with the Messiah's kingdom, then the apostolic rule over Israel would also be in the future.

---

[62]So Joachim Jeremias, *The Eucharistic Words of Jesus,* trans. Norman Perrin (Philadelphia: Fortress, 1966) 249. The reading of D supports this interpretation: ἐν τῇ ἡμέρα τῆς ἐλεύσεώς σου, "in the day of your [second] coming."

[63]Conzelmann, *Theology,* 116-17.

[64]Ibid., 116-19.

But it is quite possible that Luke could have envisioned a messianic kingdom distinct from the kingdom of God and yet manifested in ways other than an interim millennium. A number of things must be remembered. First, Lk. 19:11-27 indicates that the absent Messiah receives his kingdom *before* the parousia. Second, Luke emphasizes the enthronement of Jesus with his description of the ascension. From Luke's perspective Jesus has indeed been installed upon the messianic throne. He has already received the throne of his father David (see Acts 2:30-32; cf. Lk. 1:32-33). One wonders if Luke could have placed so much emphasis on this motif if he did not in some sense see the messianic kingdom as realized. To be sure, its realization is to be found in the heavenly, transcendent sphere, but this does not fail to make its realization any less effective or "real" with respect to its impact on the life of the community. The thesis of Eric Franklin is helpful here, for it is his view that while Conzelmann is correct to assert the transcendental character of the kingdom, it is incorrect to assert that this kingdom has no real impact on the present life of the church.[65] Franklin argues that all dimensions of the life within the Lukan community, from prayer to eucharistic worship to evangelistic mission, operate under the awareness that God's Messiah has been enthroned upon the seat of David and that it is he who directs the community.

A second indication that Luke had some sense of a realized messianic kingdom is found in his understanding of eucharistic fellowship. According to Lk. 22:28-30, the sharing of table fellowship with the Messiah was coexistent with the messianic kingdom. Is there good reason to believe that Luke saw the eucharist as a fulfillment, or at least a partial fulfillment, of the eschatological meal fellowship with the Messiah in his kingdom? There is good evidence that Luke saw the eucharistic meal as denoting primarily an event of table fellowship with Jesus, the Messiah-King.

Investigations of the eucharistic traditions in the New Testament have led some interpreters to conclude that there existed among the earliest Christians two independent interpretations of the Lord's Supper. Hans Lietzmann argued that some early Christians interpreted the eucharist primarily as a memorial in remembrance of Jesus' death.[66] Others interpreted it primarily as an eschatological meal celebrating the spiritual presence of Jesus and anticipating the full fellowship with him after the parousia. Pursuing this interpretation, Oscar Cullmann has argued that the latter inter-

---

[65]Franklin, *Christ the Lord*, 9-47.

[66]*Messe und Herrenmahl: Eine Studie zur Geschichte der Liturgie* (Bonn: A. Marcus und E. Weber's Verlag, 1926).

pretative strain was the most primitive.[67] Many interpreters agree that the New Testament offers two nuances of interpretation of the Lord's Supper, but they do not all agree that they were independent interpretations, nor that the eschatological interpretation was the most primitive.[68] Nevertheless, there is a consensus that there did exist, in some form, an eschatological interpretation of the eucharist that emphasized the motif of the present fellowship with the risen Jesus at the table.[69]

Luke shared in this eschatological conception of the eucharist. This is evidenced primarily by two factors. Negatively, in the first place, Luke does not emphasize the sacrificial character of Jesus' death as efficacious for the atonement of sins. Second, this is evidenced by the particular way in which Luke presents his material concerning the Lord's Supper.

On a number of occasions Luke has altered Mark in order to downplay the motif of the salvific efficacy of the death of Jesus.[70] First, Luke omitted Mk. 10:45: "For the son of man also came not to be served but to serve and to give his life as ransom for many." Luke does incorporate Mk. 10:42-45 into his story of the last supper (Lk. 22:24-27). Yet in place of Mk. 10:45 Luke has simply "But I am among you as one who serves" (22:27b). Second, Mark's narration of the last supper offers the following interpretation of the cup: "This is my blood of the covenant, which is poured out for many" (14:24). Yet, there is a slight alteration in Lk. 22:20: "This cup which is poured out for you is the new covenant in my blood."[71] It appears that what was for Mark a reference to general atonement for sins, was interpreted by Luke as the means whereby the new covenant was established for the *church*. This is confirmed by Acts 20:28 which reads: "Take heed

---

[67]"The Meaning of the Lord's Supper in Primitive Christianity," in *Essays on the Lord's Supper*, trans. by J. G. Davies, Ecumenical Studies in Worship 1 (Richmond: John Knox Press, 1958) 5-23.

[68]See, e.g., Eduard Schweizer, *The Lord's Supper according to the New Testament*, trans. James M. Davis (Philadelphia: Fortress Press, 1967) 23-28; A. J. B. Higgins, *The Lord's Supper in the New Testament*, Studies in Biblical Theology 6 (London: SCM Press, 1952) 56-63.

[69]See esp. Geoffrey Wainwright, *Eucharist and Eschatology* (London: Epworth Press, 1971) 34-42.

[70]The following discussion is based largely on the essay of Augustine George, "Le Sens de la Mort Jesus pour Luc," RB 80 (1973): 186-217.

[71]Lk. 22:19b-20 is to be considered authentic. See Metzger, *Textual Commentary*, 173-77. If one were to conclude that 22:19b-20 were not authentic, this would only strengthen further the argument that Luke downplayed the atoning character of Jesus' death.

. . . to care for the church of God which he ordained by the blood of his own Son." In short, the salvific efficacy attached to the cross by Luke was not understood in terms of dying "for sins" or "for many," but was understood as the means of establishing the new covenant for the church.

If for Luke the death of Jesus was not viewed primarily as a sacrifice for sins, it would be unlikely that within his community the eucharist would find as its focus a memorial of Jesus' death. The sacrificial motif is present (Lk. 22:19b-20), but the eschatological thrust is emphatic (Lk. 22:16, 18).

A second and more positive reason to conclude that Luke shared primarily in the eschatological conception of the eucharist is that Luke, more so than any New Testament writer, draws the reader's attention to the fact that the fellowship of the disciples with the risen Jesus took place in the context of the meal setting. Luke has four allusions to such meal fellowship with the risen Jesus (Lk. 24:30; 24:41-42; Acts 1:4; 10:41). Other direct references to this type of fellowship in the New Testament are found in pseudo-Mk. 16:14 and the Johannine appendix (21:9-14).

The first Lukan story concerning the reunion of Jesus with his disciples has distinctively eucharistic tones, using language which is reminiscent of the last supper.[72] Luke's account of the last supper states (22:19): "and having taken bread, he gave thanks, then he broke it and gave it to them" (my translation). Luke 24:30 reads similarly: "having taken bread he blessed it and when he had broken it he gave it to them" (my translation).

It is clear from the abundance of references that Luke viewed the meal setting as a most appropriate context for describing the disciples' experience of the presence of the risen Jesus. Furthermore, it is clear from Lk. 24:30 that such a meal setting was associated with the eucharist setting or, to use the Lukan phrase, "the breaking of bread" (cf. Acts 2:42, 46). It would seem that for Luke the primary importance of the eucharist was the experience of the presence of the risen Jesus, an experience which anticipated the perfect fellowship to be shared with him at the parousia.

If indeed the Lukan eucharist was perceived as a time of table fellowship with the risen Jesus, then perhaps the eucharist was viewed as a partial fulfillment of the promise of Lk. 22:28-30. Given Luke's emphasis on the objective enthronement of the risen Jesus as the messianic king, it can only be concluded that the Jesus present during the "breaking of bread" would be Jesus the king. In short, during the breaking of bread the community, together with the apostles who led them, sat at table with the messianic

---

[72]So Jaques Dupont, "The Meal at Emmaus," in *The Eucharist and the New Testament, A Symposium,* trans. E. M. Stewart (London: Geoffrey Chapman, 1964) 105-112.

king, experiencing partially and proleptically the fulfillment of the promise ''that you might eat and drink at my table in my kingdom.'' If the first half of the promise is realized, at least partially, prior to the parousia, might also the second half of the promise (''and you shall sit upon thrones judging the twelve tribes of Israel'') find some realization prior to the parousia? Do the twelve apostles, prior to the parousia, engage in an eschatological rule over Israel? There is reason to conclude that such was the case.

In the first place, Luke portrays the primitive church, representative of Israel, as a community of the Spirit. He makes it clear that the distinctive mark of the primitive congregation was the presence of the Spirit (Acts 1:4-5, 8; 2:4, 17, 38; 4:8, 31; 5:32). Furthermore, there is good reason to believe that the gift of the Spirit marked the church as an eschatological community.

Defense of this thesis begins with Acts 2:17 where Peter declares ''in the last days . . . I will pour out my Spirit upon all flesh'' (Joel 3:1, MT). It seems best to see this as an assertion of the eschatological character of the Spirit. To define these ''last days'' as noneschatological seems totally arbitrary and need not be accepted.[73] This is especially true in light of the eschatological character of Joel's prophecy in Judaism.

Midr. Ps. 14:6 states that Moses's words (''Would that all the Lord's people were prophets,'' Num. 11:29) would not be fulfilled in this world, but only in the world to come. Later in the midrash Joel 3:1 is quoted as the prophecy promising that all the people would be prophets in the age to come. The same idea is found in Num Rab. 15:25:

> The Holy One, blessed by He, said, In this world only individuals are endowed with prophecy, but in the world to come all Israel will be prophets; as it is said: [quote Joel 3:1].[74]

Hence, the important place given Joel 3:1-5b by Luke gives to him a clear affinity with those who interpreted the text eschatologically.

Eduard Schweizer has noted that Luke shares with Judaism the conception that the Spirit is conceived of primarily as the spirit of prophecy.[75]

---

[73]The following statement by Fred Francis is apropos: ''The one passage in which Luke uses the adjective *eschatos* in connection with a significant period of time is Acts 2:17. . . . It would seem that one could hardly do other than take Luke's own language at face value: the manifestation of the spirit at Pentecost was an eschatological event, and one connected with the climactic cosmic drama'' (''Eschatology and History,'' JAAR 37 (1969): 151).

[74]Translation from *Midrash Rabbah*, eds. H. Freedman and M. Simon, 9 vols. (London: Soncino, 1951) vol. 6.

[75]πνεῦμα, TDNT 6:407-408.

Schweizer acknowledges that Luke saw the outpouring of the Holy Spirit as the fulfillment of the Old Testament promise that such would be given to the people of God in the last time. He even offers an impressive list of "eschatological" features of the Pentecost story.[76] He states: "A first inclination is to regard the outpouring of the Spirit as the true eschatological event in Luke."[77] Schweizer, however, then goes on to say: "But this is not eschatological for Luke."[78]

He offers two reasons. One is the *heilsgeschichtliche* scheme of Conzelmann itself. Conzelmann's periodization has been sufficiently criticized by the interpreters to nullify this leg of the argument.[79] The second is the observation that "the Spirit . . . does not totally shape the existence of the believer as a completely new, eschatological existence."[80] For example, faith, salvation, repentence, and obedience are never ascribed to the Spirit. This is true, but does this rob the Spirit of its truly eschatological character? Repentence and obedience in Judaism were conceived of as a means of obtaining the world to come and its blessings, not only as aspects of such a new world (cf. Acts 3:19-21).[81]

Luke did not interpret the Spirit as *the* eschatological event without remainder. The community still awaited the restoration of all things. But such affinities with Jewish eschatological expectations cannot be passed over when assessing Luke's view of the eschatological character of the Spirit in the life of the community. Schweizer recognizes such affinities, but his attempt to make such conform to Conzelmann's scheme appears unsuccessful.

It would seem, therefore, that Luke viewed the primitive church as a community of the Spirit in fulfillment of the eschatological passage of Joel 3:1. If this congregation is representative of Israel, then the primitive com-

---

[76]Ibid., 410-11. Schweizer notes, e.g., the use of the Joel quotation itself, the phenomenon of one language, and the concept of a new covenant, corresponding with the giving of the law at Pentecost to initiate the first covenant.

[77]Ibid., 410.

[78]Ibid.

[79]Paul Minear's statement concerning Conzelmann's pivotal text for his threefold periodization of salvation history (Lk. 16:16) is apropos: "It must be said that rarely has a scholar placed so much weight on so dubious an interpretation of so difficult a logion." See "Luke's Use of the Birth Stories," in *Studies in Luke-Acts*, 122.

[80]πνεῦμα, TDNT 6:412.

[81]Moore, *Judaism*, 2:94-95.

munity represents not only Israel, but the eschatological Israel—the Israel of the new age. The twelve apostles rule this Israel.

In addition to this fact, a number of characteristics of the apostolic rule have a decisively eschatological flavor. The apostles are described as "men of the Spirit."[82] The activity of the apostles by which they demonstrate their authority emulates that of Jesus. Like Jesus, who was empowered by the Spirit (see Lk. 4:18-21), so too are the apostles empowered by the Spirit (Lk. 24:29; Acts 1:4-5, 8; 2:4; 4:8, 31). Jesus is described in Peter's Pentecost sermon as one who did "mighty works and wonders and signs" (Acts 2:22; cf. Lk. 24:19). The apostles are described in similar terms (Acts 2:43; 4:30; 5:12). One of these mighty works of Jesus was that of healing. So too the disciples are portrayed as healers (Acts 3:1-10; 4:22; 5:12-16). Finally, a most important activity of Jesus was that of teaching. The apostles too are often described as being engaged in teaching activity (Acts 2:42; 4:2, 18; 5:21, 25, 28, 42). In short, Luke presents the apostles as imitators of the eschatological ministry of Jesus. Would not their imitative activity be eschatological as well? It would seem so and hence the apostolic rule over eschatological Israel is an eschatological rule.

One further factor supports this conclusion. The first Lukan summary of the apostles' authority over the community is found in Acts 2:42-47. In the context of this summary Luke speaks of the apostles' teaching activity (2:42), the signs and wonders they performed (2:43), and the submission to the authority of the apostles by the community as represented by the giving up of possessions (2:44-45). In the midst of all of these references to apostolic authority two references are made to eucharistic fellowship described as "the breaking of bread" (2:42, 46). Eucharistic fellowship in the context of Luke brings to mind the eschatological meal fellowship with Jesus the Messiah. According to the promise of Lk. 22:28-30 an aspect of this meal fellowship with Jesus would be the eschatological rule of the apostles over Israel.

Teaching, signs and wonders, submission to apostolic rule by the eschatological Israel, and the sharing of table fellowship with Jesus the Messiah all point to an apostolic rule that is eschatological in character. The opening chapters of Acts present, therefore, the fulfillment, or at least a proleptic fulfillment, of the promise of Lk. 22:28-30. The twelve apostles

---

[82]Johnson, *Literary Function of Possessions*, 38-60, uses this term to describe the charismatic and awesomely powerful characteristics of the apostles. The following discussion is drawn from Johnson's insights.

in conjunction with the messianic king, rule the twelve tribes of eschatological Israel.[83]

The significance of Jerusalem and the temple. All of the action described in chapters one through five of Acts is confined to Jerusalem. It is
here and only here that Luke describes the activity of the apostles as they
lead the Israel of the end-time. It is not insignificant either that the temple
is the focal point of attention. It is true that only one extended narrative is
located at the temple (3:1-4:2). But what happens here is by no means unimportant. The apostolic activity is neatly divided by Luke into two sections, healing (3:1-10) and teaching (3:11-4:2). Such activity, which occurs
in imitation of Jesus, is understood by Luke to be eschatological. Hence,
Luke perceives the temple to be the appropriate place where there is offered to Israel the eschatological word and demonstration of salvation.

Luke by no means wants the reader to think of this temple scene as an
isolated incident. Throughout the narrative he continually offers reminders
that the temple was a primary location for apostolic activity (2:46; 5:12,
20, 26, 42). Significantly, the first and last references indicate that such
activity at the temple was a daily affair. Acts 2:46 states that the primitive
community, under the leadership of the apostles (2:42-43), attended the
temple daily. This compares nicely with Lk. 19:47, implying that Luke may
want the reader to discern a comparison between Jesus' temple activity and
that of the apostles. Luke presented Jesus' temple ministry as a meeting of
Israel and the Messiah who proclaims the word of eschatological salvation. This implied comparison is made more explicit in Acts 5:42 where
once again Luke indicates that the apostles were in the temple "each day"
where they "did not cease teaching and preaching Jesus as the Christ."
The acceptance of Jesus as the Christ was the criterion, according to Luke,
whereby the Jew retained his status as one of the people of God (see Acts
3:22-23). In Jerusalem and the temple Israel is confronted with the message of salvation.

Of course, within Jewish eschatological expectation Jerusalem was believed to be the place where the salvation of God would be manifested to
Israel. Jerusalem would be the place of the restored people of God who
would return to the city from all corners of the earth (Isa. 35:8-10; 2 Esdr.
13:12-13, 39-40; Bar. 5:5-9; Ps. Sol. 11:5-7; 4QpPs 37, III:10-11; Pes. de
Rab Kah. 20:7; b. B. Bat. 75b). The eschatologically restored people would
be a holy people renewed by God (Isa. 4:4; 60:21; Zech. 8:8; Ezek. 36:26-
28; Ps. Sol. 17:28-31; Sib. Or. 5:249-50; T. Dan. 5:12; 4QpPs 37, III:10-

---

[83]So Johnson, ibid., 166-67, and Franklin, *Christ the Lord,* 97-99.

11; 4QFlor 1:1-2; 11QTemple 47:14-15; b. B. Bat. 75b). In much of the Jewish tradition Jerusalem was *the* place of the restored people of God.

It is possible to detect in the opening chapters of Acts a positive comparison with such Jewish expectations. Luke has portrayed the audience of the apostolic preaching at Pentecost as Jews from all over the world congregated now in the holy city to hear the message of salvation. Hence the gospel is preached not merely to Israel, but to Israel which has been ingathered at Jerusalem. It is in Jerusalem, and more specifically at the temple, that Israel hears the word of God's eschatological salvation as the apostles bear witness to the enthronement of Israel's Messiah (Acts 2:32-36; 5:31). It is in Jerusalem that Israel is renewed and restored, for it is repentence for the rejection of God's Messiah and the acceptance of God's eschatological act that effects forgiveness and salvation (2:38, 40; 3:19-23, 26; 5:31). The renewed Israel is the eschatological community which bears the end-time mark of the promised Holy Spirit (2:17, 38-39; 5:32). The place of this eschatological community is Jerusalem and the temple (2:46). The community is to be a holy community, as evidenced by the severe punishment of Ananias and Sapphira who did not sincerely submit themselves to the apostles' authority.

Luke does wish to show in the opening chapters of Acts that Jerusalem and the temple are truly the places of the renewed eschatological Israel. He portrays the city and temple as the territory of the apostolic rulers. The false "leaders" of Israel, the temple authorities and Sadducees (4:1; 5:17), may possess the power to arrest these leaders, but their efforts are futile and in no way inhibit the apostolic rule of Israel. For example, Acts 4:1-2 states that while the apostles "were speaking to the people" (4:1) they were arrested by the Jewish leaders. The sheer futility of the attempted opposition to the apostles is immediately noted in 4:4 where Luke reports that "many of those who heard the word believed and the number of the men came to about five thousand."

The same pattern is repeated in 5:17-21, which reports that the authorities arrested the apostles. Yet that very night they were miraculously released and instructed to "go and stand in the temple and speak to the people all the words of life" (5:20). Even the subsequent rearrest of the apostles proves futile (5:21b-40) for despite the command of the Jewish authorities that the apostles not "speak in the name of Jesus" (5:40), the fifth chapter ends with the declaration: "And every day in the temple and at home they did not cease teaching and preaching Jesus as the Christ" (5:42). The true sovereigns over the people and the holy precincts are the apostles, the eschatological rulers of Israel.

Luke does not paint an unrealistic picture as he portrays his theology. He does not describe the encounter of Israel with the saving word of God by merely transplanting glorious scenes from Jewish apocalyptic speculation to his portrait of the primitive Jerusalem community. History does not permit him this luxury. Luke is aware that there reside in the literal city those who are "cut off" from the people in accordance with the principle of Acts 3:22-23. The Jewish authorities still reside in Jerusalem and possess the power to arrest and detain the apostles. Yet, their power is demonic (Lk. 22:53). They have no legitimate authority over Israel or the temple. Luke knows as well that not all Jews are literally to be found in Jerusalem; therefore, he offers no glorious picture of a miraculous second exodus comparable of Isa. 35:8-10.

The picture in the opening chapters of Acts, therefore, is not neat. Yet the untidiness is itself significant, for it arises from the very fact that Luke refused to dismiss the literal Jerusalem from its decisive role in the realization of God's eschatological promises. Had Luke simply dismissed the city and temple and transferred the expectations revolving around them to the church, then the presence of the unredeemed of Israel in Jerusalem would have caused no problems. Had Luke made the church the "place" of ingathered Israel, then the fact that Jews were still literally scattered all over the world would have caused no problems. Luke is limited in his presentation, however, because he will not accept the solution of the rest of early Christianity. Thus, he does the best he can. Despite the power of the unredeemed in Jerusalem, Luke goes to great lengths to show that the apostles were really in control of the city and temple. They moved and preached at will. Despite the fact that Jews still inhabit all the world, Luke emphatically portrayed the Jews of Jerusalem as the embodiment of diaspora Judaism. Within the context of real history, God's promises of salvation were finding concrete fulfillment.

Conclusion: Jerusalem, the Temple, and the Salvation of Israel

Luke focused the attention of the reader on the vicinities of Jerusalem and the temple in a number of places in Luke-Acts. The birth narrative, which announces the coming of God's eschatological salvation, finds its center at Jerusalem and the temple. Jesus' final encounter with the whole people of Israel, confronting them with the message of God's eschatological salvation, happens at the temple. Near the environs of Jerusalem, Messiah Jesus is enthroned in the heavenly sphere. Finally, Luke portrays Israel as restored at Jerusalem, a community of the eschatological Spirit, ruled by the twelve apostles, those destined to rule Israel in conjunction with the reign of the Messiah.

Luke wants his readers to see that in the literal Jerusalem and at the literal temple, God fulfills his promises of salvation to Israel. As Peter says, "For the promise is to you and your children and to all that are far off, every one whom the Lord our God calls to him" (Acts 2:39). The role played by Jerusalem and the temple in fulfilling the promise to those who are far off, the Gentiles, must now be examined.

Jerusalem, the Temple,
and the Salvation of the Gentiles

Chapter IV

The Eschatological Character of the Gentile Mission

An influential strain of Lukan scholarship has denied that Luke viewed the conversion of the Gentiles as having any direct eschatological significance. Two chief representatives of this point of view are Hans Conzelmann and S. J. Wilson. In addition to Conzelmann's general argument that Luke replaced eschatology with salvation history, he discusses three features of Luke-Acts that bring out more specifically the noneschatological character of the mission of the church. The first is the Lukan emphasis on the plan of God. Luke wants to show that the Gentile mission accords with the whole plan of God as contained in the scriptures, thereby legitimizing the mission of the church. But, Conzelmann asserts, there is no concern in such proofs-from-prophecy to establish an eschatological rationale for the mission. Quite the contrary, Luke has interpreted the whole motif of the predetermined plan of God in such a way as to forbid speculation concerning the end. The function of such proofs is only to motivate repentance.[1] Second, Luke's entire emphasis on the delay of the parousia forces him to rob the Gentile mission of any eschatological significance. Conzelmann explains that Luke has removed Mk. 13:10 from his account of the little apocalypse precisely because he wants to sever any connection

---

[1]Hans Conzelmann, *The Theology of Saint Luke,* trans. Geoffrey Buswell (London: Faber and Faber; New York: Harper & Brothers, 1960) esp. 151-54.

between the mission and the eschaton.[2] Third, the power for the church age and the power for its Gentile mission is the Holy Spirit. But for Luke the outpouring of the Holy Spirit is not an eschatological event, but only notes the beginning of the last epoch of salvation history.[3] For Conzelmann, therefore, the Gentile mission is not eschatological.

S. J. Wilson questions Conzelmann's view that Luke believed the parousia to be indefinitely delayed. Rather, Wilson has detected two strands in Luke's eschatological pronouncements, an imminent strand and a delay strand.[4] Yet Wilson stands in basic accord with Conzelmann concerning the implications of "proof-from-prophecy" and the meaning of the Holy Spirit for the noneschatological character of the Gentile mission.

Wilson discusses the motif of proof-from-prophecy under the rubric of promise-fulfillment, and sees this motif as evidence of the noneschatological character of the Gentile mission. For Wilson the whole theme of promise-fulfillment places the discussion exclusively on the historical plane, and hence eschatology does not come seriously into play.[5] Wilson also follows Conzelmann in arguing that the Spirit is for Luke the power of the *historical* work of the church; it is not, however, eschatological.[6] Wilson's own words provide the best summary of his position:

> In consistently [linking] the Gentile mission with the Holy Spirit and the fulfillment of prophecy, Luke betrays his own viewpoint. The Gentile mission, planned for in God's eternal purpose, takes place in ongoing history, the salvation history of the Church. It is neither determined by nor determines the end.[7]

The theses of Conzelmann and Wilson are in need of further discussion and correction.

The Eschatological Character of the Holy Spirit. In the previous chapter I discussed in some detail the eschatological character of the Spirit in Luke-Acts. On the basis of this discussion, one is justified to conclude that while Conzelmann and his followers are correct to assert that the Spirit

---

[2]Ibid., 214n1.

[3]Ibid., 95.

[4]*The Gentiles and the Gentile Mission in Luke-Acts,* SNTSMS 23 (London: Cambridge University Press, 1973) 59-87.

[5]Ibid., 54.

[6]Ibid., 56-57.

[7]Ibid., 57.

provided the guidance and power for the Gentile mission, one should add that this power and guidance were eschatological. Luke does not believe that the Spirit is the eschatological event without remainder, but it is eschatological. Hence, the mission which it inspires may be seen as eschatological as well.

The Pattern of Prophecy and Fulfillment. The second argument in favor of the noneschatological character of the Gentile mission was that such a mission was seen by Luke as the fulfillment within *history* of the promises of God. This argument presupposes that history and eschatology are mutually exclusive categories. But the entire dichotomy established between history and eschatology is unnecessary. Within Jewish speculation the "days of the Messiah" were clearly eschatological. Yet these days took place on the plane of history, as a transitional period to the fully transcendent age to come. The very fact that the Rabbis could use the term עולם הבה to denote both the messianic age and the world to come attests to the fluid relationship that existed between history and eschatology. Thus, the entire assumption that history and eschatology are mutually exclusive is unfounded.

Furthermore, the very motif of promise in the Lukan writings appears to point to eschatological phenomena. He uses the word often, especially in Acts, and save for one reference (Acts 23:21), all references to ἐπαγγελία are theological in content. Luke can use the word "promise" to denote noneschatological phenomena, such as the promise of the land given to Abraham in Acts 7:5, 17. Yet Luke here is clearly discussing an event of past time, the fulfillment of which has already come to pass (see Acts 7:5). Interestingly, all other concrete references to "promise" appear to point to eschatological phenomena: the Holy Spirit (Lk. 24:49; Acts 1:4-5; 2:33, 39), the bringing forth of the Messiah-Savior to Israel (Acts 13:23, 32), through whom Israel secures salvation (Acts 13:26), and the future resurrection from the dead (Acts 26:6). It is clear that Luke associates the motif of promise with eschatological phenomena. Hence, placing the Gentile mission under the rubric of promise-fulfillment does not necessarily lead to the conclusion that such a mission was noneschatological.

It is significant that the whole motif of promise often had an eschatological flavor in Judaism contemporary with Luke. Of particular interest is the phenomenon that D. Duling refers to as the "promise tradition" which related to David.[8] Duling argues that there developed within Judaism a

---

[8]"Promises to David" NTS 20 (1973): 55-77; cf. John H. Hayes, "Resurrection as Enthronement" Int 22 (1968): 333-45.

"promise tradition" originating in 2 Sam. 7:5b-16 and consisting of three elements. First, the tradition stated that God would raise up a Davidic descendent as king. Second, there would exist a filial relationship between God and this king. Third, the kingdom of this king would be established forever.

Duling traces the development of the tradition showing that it continued to thrive, especially in prophetic circles. His own words summarize well the eschatological significance of this "promise tradition":

> With the removal of the political foundation of the monarchy after the exile, the future orientation implied in many of the preexilic and exilic statements about the Davidic descendent became even more explicit in the redaction of these traditions, while the metaphors for the Davidic descendent persist *and become focal in Jewish eschatological hopes*. . . . In the Jewish texts there is an observable tendency to draw out and focus on the metaphors for the Davidic descendent in the promise tradition, but now in a gradually unfolding eschatological context.[9]

Duling hypothesizes that it was Easter faith that led the Christians to associate Jesus with this Davidic descendent. An important phrase in the promise tradition was the reference to the "raising up" ("rearing") of this descendent (see 2 Sam. 7:12). This motif embedded itself within the tradition and became a permanent fixture.[10] While this tradition did not interpret such "raising up" as the resurrection of the descendent, the Christians, in the light of Easter faith, could easily offer such an interpretation. Thus, the Christians understood the raising up of Jesus from the dead by God in the context of the promise tradition and thereby made explicit the association of Jesus with this descendent.

There is good reason to believe that Luke embraced this promise tradition. He shows specific awareness of such a tradition in places such as Acts 13:32-33 where Paul states that the "promise" God made to the fathers was fulfilled in the "raising" of Jesus. What is more, Luke embraced the specific features of this tradition. He affirms the Davidic descent of Jesus (Lk. 1:27, 32; 2:4; Acts 2:30; 3:23). He affirms the filial relation to God (Lk. 1:32, 35; 2:49, 3:22). And Luke emphasizes the element of the eternal kingship of this descendent. Only Luke records the ascension depicting the enthronement of Jesus. The eternal character of this kingdom

---

[9]Ibid., 60; italics added.

[10]Ibid., 75-77. Duling here offers a list of references from numerous Jewish circles showing the pervasiveness of the "raising" motif in the promise tradition.

is affirmed in Lk. 1:33. In fact, it would appear to be no coincidence that the first christological affirmation in the Lukan writings consists of a formula which contains precisely the three elements of the promise tradition:

> He will be great, and will be called the Son of the Most High; and the Lord
> God will give to him the throne of his father David, and he will reign over
> the house of Jacob for ever; and of his kingdom there will be no end. (Lk.
> 1:32-33)

Luke's embrace of this eschatological promise tradition, combined with his assumption that such was "fulfilled" by the raising of Jesus (Acts 13:32-33), casts immense doubt over any view that would argue that the employment of the promise-fulfillment paradigm serves as a tool in Luke's mind for the de-eschatologizing of events. Luke's use of this eschatological promise tradition would seem to indicate that the fulfillment of promises points to the fulfillment of *eschatological* hopes. Coming under the purview of such fulfillment is the mission of the church. Thus, one may not legitimately argue that Luke's use of a scheme of promise and fulfillment detracts from the eschatological character of the Gentile mission.

Eschatological Imminence in Luke-Acts. The third objection to the eschatological character of the Gentile mission, emphasized by Conzelmann, is the idea that Luke envisioned a delay of the parousia. Given this, Luke was forced to rob the Gentile mission of its eschatological flavor. But a number of Lukan texts provide good evidence that Luke did not embrace a notion of a far-off and distant parousia.

The first text is Lk. 9:27. Here Luke records the saying of Jesus from Mark, "But I tell you truly, there are some standing here who will not taste death, before they see the kingdom of God." If the reference to "seeing the kingdom of God" is a reference to the parousia, then there must be sounded here a note of imminent expectation, for the text clearly states that some (whether the apostles or onlookers, Luke is ambiguous) who lived when Jesus taught in Galilee would not die before seeing of this kingdom.

It may be objected against this interpretation that Luke does not understand the seeing of the kingdom as a reference to the parousia. To be noted especially is the fact that Luke omits from Mk. 9:1 the phrase ἐληλυθυῖαν ἐν δυνάμει. Hence, the "kingdom" that Luke envisions the "some" as seeing is not to be understood as the final glorious coming of the reign of God. Rather, Luke is making reference to some who will acquire the insight to witness the present reality of God's rule. This experience may be understood as the transfiguration which immediately follows, the resurrection, the coming of the Holy Spirit, or the mission of the church.[11] But is Luke advocating a type of realized eschatology in Lk. 9:27?

Such does not seem to be the case. Since the logion in question clearly indicates that only "some" hearers will "see the kingdom," the implication is that "most" will not. Therefore, some time will pass between the utterance of this logion and the "seeing of the kingdom." This hardly makes events in the near future, such as the transfiguration or even the resurrection and the events following it, the probable referents of the kingdom.

Furthermore, while Luke could use the various words for "see" to denote the present experience of eschatological realities, he could use the words also to describe the objective witnessing of future eschatological events. Evil people (Lk. 13:27) will "see Abraham and Isaac and Jacob and all the prophets in the kingdom of God" (v. 28). Men will "see the Son of man coming in a cloud with power and great glory" (Lk. 21:27). People will see signs which indicate that "redemption is drawing near" (Lk. 21:28). The apostles are told in Acts 1:11 that they will "see" Jesus return just as they saw him ascend. It cannot be shown beyond any doubt that Lk. 9:27 makes reference to the witnessing of the parousia, but such an interpretation is quite possible.

A second passage is Lk. 10:9,11. Here Jesus instructs the seventy (-two) to announce that "the kingdom of God has drawn near" (ἤγγι-κεν). Persons sent out to preach during the days of Jesus' ministry proclaimed the "nearness" of the kingdom. The precise meaning of ἐγγίζειν and its adverbial cognate has been debated since C. H. Dodd put forth his thesis that Jesus proclaimed a thoroughly realized eschatology.[12] A key text for Dodd was Mk. 1:15 where Jesus says "The time is fulfilled and the kingdom of God has drawn near" (ἤγγικεν, my translation). Dodd argues: "In the LXX ἐγγίζειν is sometimes used (chiefly in past tenses) to translate the Hebrew verb naga' and the Aramaic verb m'ta, both of which mean 'to reach' or 'to arrive'."[13] Thus, Mk. 1:15 should be translated "the kingdom of God has come." He then understands Lk. 10:9, 11 as sharing in such realized eschatology.[14] As a result, Lk. 10:9, 11 advocates not imminent eschatology but realized eschatology.

---

[11]A. J. Mattill, Jr., *Luke and the Last Things: A Perspective for Understanding Lukan Thought* (Dillsboro NC: Western North Carolina Press; Macon GA: Mercer University Press, 1979) discusses these and other options, 58-70.

[12]*The Parables of the Kingdom,* 3rd ed. (London: James Nisbet; New York: Charles Scribner's Sons, 1936).

[13]Ibid., 44.

[14]Ibid., 45.

Dodd's analysis of ἐγγίζειν has not gone unchallenged. Kümmel has argued that ἐγγίζειν and its cognates contained the idea that something was quite near, but not yet arrived.[15] Detailed examination of Luke's use of the words bears out Kümmel's conclusions. Luke can use ἐγγίζειν and ἐγγύς both spatially and temporally. The verb form is used seventeen times while the adverbial form is used four times to denote spatial proximity.[16] In none of these instances does Luke unambiguously use either of these words to denote *arrival* at a place. On the other hand, the context of a number of passages makes clear that Luke did use the words in question specifically to denote *nearness,* as opposed to arrival.[17]

Luke employs ἐγγίζειν seven times and ἐγγύς twice in a temporal sense.[18] As in the case of the spatial use of these words, no reference refers unambiguously to the *arrival* of an event. However, numerous texts indicate that Luke used the words to denote the *nearness* of an event. This is evidenced most clearly by the use of these words in relation to events other than the reign of God.

Lk. 21:20 reads, "But when you see Jerusalem surrounded by armies, then know that its desolation has drawn near" (my translation). Luke plainly does not intend to say that the city's desolation has arrived, for verse 21 indicates that inhabitants of the city still have time to flee. Lk. 22:1 reads "the feast of unleavened bread was drawing near . . . " (my translation). That Luke does not intend to say that the Feast had arrived is indicated by 22:7, for only then is it stated that "the day of unleavened bread had come." Acts 7:17 introduces the story of the birth of Moses and his subsequent leadership over Israel with the phrase "the time of the promise which God swore drew near" (my translation). The promise is the possession of the land wherein Israel might worship God (Acts 7:5-8). The birth of Moses is hardly the arrival of the fulfillment of this promise, but it does mark the beginning of events that would soon lead to its fulfillment. Finally, Lk. 21:29-30 says that the budding of the tree means that summer is ἐγγύς . Clearly ἐγγύς means "near," for the first buds hardly denote the "ar-

---

[15]Werner Georg Kümmel, *Promise and Fulfillment: The Eschatological Message of Jesus,* Studies in Biblical Theology 23, trans. Dorothea M. Barton (London: SCM Press, 1957); cf. also Mattill, *Luke and the Last Things,* 71-76.

[16]ἐγγίζειν: Lk. 7:12; 12:33; 15:1, 25; 18:35, 40; 19:29, 37, 41; 22:47; 24:15, 28; Acts 9:3; 10:9; 21:33; 23:15. ἐγγύς: Lk. 19:11; Acts 1:12; 9:38; 27:8.

[17]ἐγγίζειν: Lk. 7:12; 15:25, cf. v. 28; 18:35; 19:29, 37; Acts 9:3, cf. v. 9; 22:6, cf. v. 10. ἐγγύς: Lk. 19:11; Acts 1:12; 9:38.

[18]ἐγγίζειν: Lk. 10: 9, 11; 21:8, 20, 28; 22:1; Acts 7:17. ἐγγύς: Lk. 21:30, 31.

rival'' of the summer season. If Luke consistently employs ἐγγύς and its cognates in non-kingdom sayings to denote temporal *nearness*, it is highly unlikely that when referring to the eschaton he would use the word to denote arrival.

It is safe to conclude that references that relate ἐγγίζειν and its cognates with the kingdom of God (such as 10:9, 11) or the redemption that accompanies the arrival of the kingdom (Lk. 21:28) denote the temporal nearness of that kingdom, not its arrival. Lk. 10:9, 11, the immediate text in question, does not command the seventy(-two) to preach the arrival of the kingdom, rather they are to preach its temporal nearness.

A most important passage is Lk. 18:1-8, especially verses 7-8. C. E. B. Cranfield observes that verse 8b is a reference to the parousia and, hence, the whole parable deals with eschatological expectation.[19] The phrase ἐν τάχει in verse 8a contains the idea of temporal nearness, a sense captured by the RSV translation: ''I tell you, he will vindicate them speedily.'' Cranfield acknowledges that such nearness need not be limited to temporal *immediacy*, but it plainly rules out any notion of temporal distancing.

A fourth passage is Lk. 21:32. Luke retains from his tradition the saying that ''this generation will not pass away till all has taken place.'' This logion serves to conclude Luke's discussion regarding the parousia. In order to maintain his thesis of a far-off parousia, Conzelmann has tried to interpret ''generation'' to mean ''human race.''[20] The commentators have consistently rejected this interpretation.[21] Granted that Luke may have understood ''this generation'' to refer to his readers and not Jesus' original generation, a far-distant parousia is still out of the question.

Fifth, there is Acts 3:19-21. This passage reflects to a great extent typical Jewish expectations that the repentance of the nation assists in the arrival of the end.[22] According to this text repentance leads directly to the

---

[19]''The Parable of the Unjust Judge and the Eschatology of Luke-Acts,'' SJT 16 (1963): 297-301.

[20]Conzelmann, *Theology*, 105.

[21]See, e.g., Richard Hiers, ''The Problem of the Delay of the Parousia in Luke-Acts,'' NTS 20 (1974): 152; and S. G. Wilson, ''Lukan Eschatology,'' NTS 16 (1969-70): 343-44; Mattill, *Luke and the Last Things*, 97-104, offers a detailed discussion of the various attempts to understand ''generation'' in ways other than the generation of Jesus' hearers, or at least Luke's readers.

[22]See b. Sanh. 97b for a number of examples. For further discussion see Richard F. Zehnle, *Peter's Pentecost Discourse: Tradition and Lukan Reinterpretation in Peter's Speeches of Acts 2 and 3*, SBLMS 15 (Nashville: Abingdon, 1971) 71-73.

"times of refreshing" (3:20).[23] It would be possible to understand the καί of verse 20b, which introduces the sending of Christ, in an epexegetical fashion. Such would render the following understanding of Acts 3:19-20: "Repent . . . that the times of refreshing may come from the presence of the Lord, that is that he may send the Christ." If Luke could portray Peter as preaching at least five decades earlier the direct linkage between Jewish repentance and the coming of Christ, it is reasonable to conclude that Luke envisioned the real possibility of an imminent parousia.

In light of the above investigation there is good evidence for assuming that Luke did not view the end as a far-distant phenomenon. Hence, any necessity of robbing the Gentile mission of its eschatological significance because of an assumed delay of the parousia is removed.

It may be objected, however, that there is no good reason to explain the omission of Mk. 13:10 from Lk. 21 if, indeed, Luke wished to advocate an imminent parousia.[24] Mk. 13:10 asserts that the mission to the nations must be accomplished before the parousia. If Luke wished to maintain an imminent parousia, it would seem that he would have retained this verse which so closely associated the accomplishment of the universal mission with the coming of the kingdom. On closer examination, however, it is clear that the retention of this logion would not have served Luke's purposes.

E. Schweizer has argued that Mk. 13:10 serves as an attempt to *delay* eschatological expectation: before the end can come the gospel must first be preached to all nations.[25] This could lead to an understanding that with the fulfillment of the mission the end would come. Matthew seems to have interpreted the Gentile mission in this way (see Matt. 24:14). Luke, however, clearly could not retain such a saying of Jesus, since from his perspective this activity of world mission had already been accomplished, as attested by the book of Acts itself. Yet the end had not come. To retain such a saying of Jesus might have made *Jesus* look wrong, and, hence, it was best left unsaid.[26]

---

[23]Cf. 2 Esdr. 11:41-46. See also the discussion by Eduard Schweizer, ἀνάψυξις, TDNT 9:664-65.

[24]So Conzelmann, *Theology,* 214n1.

[25]Eduard Schweizer, *The Good News According to Mark,* trans. Donald H. Madvig (Richmond: John Knox Press, 1970) 221.

[26]Hiers, "Problem of Delay," 147, argues that it was a concern of Luke to remove from the tradition material which made Jesus appear to be in error.

The Eschatological Character of the Gentile Mission. In addition to the critiques presented above against arguments advocating that Luke believed the Gentile mission to be noneschatological, there is additional positive evidence that Luke believed the conversion of the nations to be an event of the end of the age. In the first place, there is evidence that Luke did view the Gentile mission as part of the chronology of events that were tied to the arrival of the eschaton. Both Talbert and Mattill have noted that according to Conzelmann's own interpretation of Lk. 21, the chronology of events preceding the end betrays a sense of imminence. According to Conzelmann, Lk. 21 predicts that three things will happen before the arrival of the end: one, a period of persecution and the offering of testimony; two, a period of political dissolution (which includes the destruction of Jerusalem); and three, cosmic disturbances.[27]

Assuming Luke and Acts to be post 70 C.E. documents, the first two prerequisites for the parousia would already have been fulfilled: the period of persecution and testimony and the destruction of Jerusalem. This would leave only the fulfillment of the cosmic signs. There is nothing in the text to lead to the conclusion that Luke viewed such disturbances as laying far out in the distant future. Hence, according to Conzelmann's own interpretation of the Lukan chronology of the last things, there can be detected a note of imminence associated with the advancement of the gospel.

The Gentile mission takes place under the reign of Jesus, the messianic king. This also indicates that Luke saw the Gentile mission as eschatological in nature. Luke closely associates the Gentile mission with the leadership and direction of Jesus the Messiah. It is the resurrected Jesus who commands the apostles to preach the gospel to all nations (Lk. 24:46-47; Acts 1:8). This preaching is to be done "in his [Christ's] name" according to Lk. 24:47, by which Luke may mean under the Christ's direction and power.[28] This seems to be affirmed by Acts 26:22-23, which bears a resemblance to Lk. 24:46-47.[29] Whereas Lk. 24:47 indicates that the preach-

---

[27]See Conzelmann, *Theology,* 129; Charles H. Talbert, "The Redaction Critical Quest for Luke the Theologian" in "Jesus and Man's Hope," special edition of *Perspective* 11 (1970): 181-84; Mattill's summary and critique may be found in *Luke and the Last Things,* 133.

[28]Hans Bietenhard, ὄνομα, κτλ., TDNT 5:277.

[29]The parallelism of the two passages is seen in the fact that both refer to (1) the necessity of Jesus' suffering, (2) his resurrection from the dead, and (3) the mission of the church. See Jacques Dupont, "Salvation of the Gentiles" in *The Salvation of the Gentiles: Essays in the Acts of the Apostles,* trans. John R. Keating (New York: Paulist, 1979) 29, for further discussion of the relationship between the two texts.

ing to the nations is to be accomplished in the *name* of the Messiah, Acts 26:23 actually affirms that it is the Messiah himself who "proclaim[s] light both to the people and to the Gentiles."

From Luke's perspective, Paul is a most important instrument for the Gentile mission. Yet Luke is emphatic that it is *Jesus* who calls Paul to this task. The three accounts of Paul's call all affirm that Paul had an encounter with Jesus (see 9:1-9; 22:6-11; 26:12-18). The risen Jesus speaks of Paul in Acts 9:15 saying "he is a chosen instrument of mine to carry my name before the Gentiles." In Acts 26:17 it is explicitly said that Jesus sends Paul to the Gentiles "to open their eyes, that they may turn from darkness to light." It is clear that the mission to the Gentiles is conducted under the direction and authority of the one who reigns from the messianic throne.

The association of the Gentile mission with the rule of the Messiah certainly colors the mission in eschatological hues. The colors become even bolder against the backdrop of the Jewish idea that the conversion of the nations was occasionally associated with messianic rule. T. Jud. 24:5-6 describes to the sons of Judah a messianic figure saying:[30]

> Then shall the sceptre of my kingdom shine forth;
> And from your root shall arise a stem
> And from it shall grow a rod of righteousness to the Gentiles
> To judge and to save all that call upon the Lord.

A similar view is expressed in the messianic hymn of T. Levi 18:9.

> God will raise up a new priest
> And in his priesthood the Gentiles shall be multiplied
>   in knowledge upon the earth,
> And enlightened through the grace of the Lord; . . .

At the head of the Gentile mission marches the messianic king. It would seem, therefore, that Luke saw this mission as possessing an eschatological character.

---

[30]This text and others from the *Testaments* need to be quoted with some caution. M. de Jonge believes the *Testaments of the Twelve Patriarchs* to be thoroughly reworked by a later Christian redactor. Concerning T. Jud. 24 he states: "The [Christian] redaction of T. Jud XXIV has been so thorough, however, that it is impossible to reconstruct the pre-Christian text of the passage" ("Christian Influence in the Testaments of the Twelve Patriarchs," NovT 4 [1960]: 205). His skepticism is not universally shared. Howard Clark Kee believes there to be no more than twelve Christian interpolations in the whole of the *Testaments*. Regarding de Jonge's overall thesis he states: "His theory . . . seems both unwarranted and unnecessary." See *The Old Testament Pseudepigrapha,* vol. 1: *Apocalyptic Literature and Testaments,* ed. James H. Charlesworth (Garden City NY: Doubleday, 1983) 777.

A third indicator of the eschatological character of the Gentile mission is found in Acts 15:14 where it is reported that James said, "Simeon has related how God first visited the Gentiles to take out of them a people for his name." Two specific features of the statement point to the eschatological character of the conversion of the Gentiles.

In the first place, Luke describes God's activity toward the Gentiles as "visitation" (ἐπισκέπτεσθαι). I have shown in the preceding chapter that Luke understood God's visitation of his people to be an eschatological act (cf. Lk. 1:68b; 7:16). Dupont has argued that Acts 15:14 makes a conscious allusion to Lk. 1:68.[31] This is likely since in both verses the words "God," "to visit," and "people" are key words. Given that Luke viewed God's visitation of his people as eschatological, it would seem that he would have also understood the divine visitation of the Gentiles as eschatological.

The very description of the Gentiles as "people" also gives an eschatological thrust to the statement. James's assertion alludes back to Peter's report in 15:7-9 which itself alludes back to the Cornelius episode of Acts 10. Peter's words of verses 7-9, therefore, provide the interpretative key:

> Peter rose and said to them, "Brethren, you know that in the early days God made choice among you that by my mouth the Gentiles should hear the word of the gospel and believe. And God who knows the heart bore witness to them, giving them the Holy Spirit just as he did to us; and he made no distinction between us and them, but cleansed their hearts by faith."

The decisive point is found in the declaration that God gave to the Gentiles "the Holy Spirit just as he did to us," and that God makes "no distinction between us and them." What is being affirmed here is nothing less than the full incorporation of the Gentiles to the people of God. As such, the promises of salvation are intended for them just as much as for the Jews (see Acts 2:39). They are offered the same release from sins as the Jews (Acts 26:18b), with the result that they too receive "a place among those who are sanctified by [God]" (Acts 26:18c). Most importantly, the Gentiles receive the same gift of the Holy Spirit just as the Jewish believers did (Acts 15:8).

Luke emphasizes this fact. Acts 10:47 states: "Can anyone forbid water for baptizing these people who have received the Holy Spirit just as we have?" And in Acts 11:17 Peter is said to declare: "If then God gave the same gift to them as he gave to us when we believed in the Lord Jesus

---

[31]Jacques Dupont, "ΛΑΟΣ 'ΕΞ 'ΕΘΝΩΝ (Acts xv. 14)," NTS 3 (1956-57): 48.

Christ, who was I that I could withstand God?'' Luke emphatically affirms in Peter's summary of Acts 15:7-9 not only the incorporation of the Gentiles into the people of God but, further, their incorporation into the *eschatological* people of God. This is evidenced by the Gentiles' reception of the Holy Spirit, the mark of the new age. It would be consistent to affirm that the *mission* which brings the Gentiles into the eschatological community is nothing less than thoroughly eschatological in character.

The preceding discussion has endeavored to show that Luke did view the Gentile mission as eschatological. Summarized and criticized were arguments that serve to deny the eschatological character to this mission. In addition, evidence that lends support to the notion that Luke did view the Gentile mission as eschatological was offered. Luke did, therefore, view the present time of mission, as well as the mission itself, as related to the dawning new age.

Jerusalem, the Temple, and the Salvation of the Gentiles

The tributaries of tradition that flowed into the Lukan stream both from Jewish and Christian sources reserved for ''Jerusalem'' and the ''temple'' a significant role in the nations' conversion. Judaism held these literal places to be significant, while Luke's Christian contemporaries spiritualized these entities. It would seem, therefore, that Luke would have felt compelled to deal with such conceptions.

Scholars have long noted that both Jerusalem and the temple do play some role in Luke's conception of mission. The numerous references to the city and sanctuary in Luke's second volume attest to this fact. Many interpreters who have acknowledged the important place of Jerusalem give the city and its temple primarily a transitional role. For such interpreters, Luke's ultimate purpose is to *dissociate* Christianity from these hallowed places.

Conzelmann believes that Luke has focused attention on Jerusalem and the temple in order to give continuity to salvation history. As Luke writes, Christianity is a Gentile phenomenon, free of both Law and temple. The importance of Jerusalem and the temple is confined in Luke's scheme of things to the past. Christianity has now outgrown these places; yet because her growth passed through them, the church can claim to be the legitimate heir of Israel.[32]

W. C. Robinson disagrees with many specific features of Conzelmann's interpretation of Lukan theology. Yet he too sees salvation history

---

[32]Conzelmann, *Theology*, 209-13.

as the decisive feature of Luke's understanding of the church. Luke presents salvation history as a "way" or march toward the salvation of the Gentiles. The church in which the Gentiles find salvation is understood by Luke to be the new Israel. This "way" of salvation in the Lukan documents moves progressively from Galilee to Jerusalem to Rome. As in Conzelmann's scheme, Jerusalem marks only a step along the way. At this juncture of the way, however, the gospel finds rejection and, hence, Jerusalem and her destruction come to represent for Luke the fate of those who reject the message of the kingdom. As for Jerusalem, she has been left behind as the new Israel marches forward.[33]

J. C. O'Neill argues that the primary concern of Luke is to offer an apologetic that portrays Christianity as a religion totally independent of Judaism. The independence of Christianity is represented in Luke by Christianity's break with Jerusalem and the temple. Luke portrays the temple as an institution that inhibits God's outward reach of salvation, and hence Luke offers a portrait of God "driving Christians out of the Temple."[34] Once again, while Jerusalem played an important role in the church's outward growth, it is a place that has now been forever left behind.

W. D. Davies, while he rightly emphasizes Luke's desire to portray the mission to the Gentiles as having a strong connection with Jerusalem,[35] argues along lines very similar to the above interpreters. Luke's interest in Jerusalem and the temple was not grounded in an intrinsic theological appreciation of the importance of these places in the eschatological age. In fact, Davies argues, Luke was aware of such a "mystique" in Judaism and primitive Christianity, and was writing in part to combat it.[36] Rather, Luke's emphasis on Jerusalem had the apologetic function of showing forth the religious and historical continuity of Christianity with Judaism, with the latter being symbolically embodied in Jerusalem and the temple.[37] In this regard, there is little difference between Davies and other interpreters of

---

[33]W. C. Robinson, *The Way of the Lord: A Study of History and Eschatology in the Gospel of Luke* (Ph.D. diss., University of Basel; privately published, 1962) 61-65; 97-98. Cf. similarly C. H. Giblin, *The Destruction of Jerusalem according to Luke's Gospel: A Historical-Typological Moral*, Analecta Biblica 107 (Rome: Biblical Institute Press, 1985).

[34]O'Neill's view of Jerusalem may be found in *The Theology of Acts in Its Historical Setting*, rev. ed. (London: SPCK, 1970) 59-66; 81-84; 96-97.

[35]W. D. Davies, *The Gospel and the Land: Early Christianity and Jewish Territorial Doctrine* (Berkeley: University of California Press, 1974) 275-78.

[36]Ibid., 260-72.

[37]Ibid., 275-78.

Luke's view of Jerusalem and the temple as they relate to the conversion of the nations.

This tendency to view Luke as portraying Christianity as a religion straining to sever its ties with Jerusalem warrants challenging. Such a view operates under the assumption that Luke wants ultimately to dissociate the church from Judaism. Former ties with Israel belong exclusively to the past and serve an apologetic function to justify and legitimate the church's existence. Recently, however, Lukan scholarship has challenged this very assumption. Interestingly, Luke's affinities with Judaism are noted and emphasized, not ignored or diminished.[38] If Luke did indeed view the church as tied in some decisive way to historic Israel, then he might have been more inclined to view her institutions, such as Jerusalem and the temple, as possessing more of a permanent as opposed to merely transitional significance.

Indeed, one may legitimately question whether the literary flow of Acts even supports the claim that the church is portrayed by Luke as moving *away* from Jerusalem. Even a cursory reading of Acts could easily render the opposite conclusion: Luke is continually bringing the church back to Jerusalem. As late as Acts 21 Paul finds himself in Jerusalem worshiping in the temple! The very presence of this preacher to the Gentiles in the holy space of Judaism toward the end of Acts calls into question any notion that Acts pictures Christianity as marching continually away from this Jewish center. While there is no debate that the Gentile mission moves centrifugally from Jerusalem, it is doubtful that Luke saw the church as severing its ties with this hub. Rather, Luke viewed the Gentile mission as comparable to the spokes of a wheel, extending beyond the central hub, but supported by it and linked to it. Further investigation will bear out this impression.

In the first place, Jerusalem and the temple form the appropriate setting whence the declarations of God's universal salvation are sounded. I have already examined the birth narrative and there found that Luke focused the attention of the reader on the motif of the dawn of God's universal, escha-

---

[38]See, e.g., Jacob Jervell's essays in *Luke and the People of God: A New Look at Luke-Acts* (Minneapolis: Augsburg, 1972); David L. Tiede, *Prophecy and History in Luke-Acts* (Philadelphia: Fortress, 1980); Eric Franklin, *Christ the Lord: A Study in the Purpose and Theology of Luke-Acts* (Philadelphia: Westminster Press, 1975); John Drury, *Tradition and Design in Luke's Gospel: A Study in Early Christian Historiography* (Atlanta: John Knox Press, 1977); Mattill, *Luke and the Last Things;* Donald Juel, *Luke-Acts: The Promise of History* (Atlanta: John Knox, 1983); R. C. Tannehill, "Israel in Luke-Acts: A Tragic Story," *JBL* 104 (1985): 69-85. Even O'Neill, *Theology of Acts,* wants to view the author of Luke-Acts as a second century hellenistic Jew.

tological salvation. The setting for the announcement of this universal salvation was Jerusalem and the temple. It is not coincidental that as the gospel of Luke begins in the environs of Jerusalem and the temple, so too does the book of Acts.[39] Here, in the context of apostolic preaching, Jerusalem and the temple provide the setting for the announcement of God's universal salvation.

The first affirmation of the universal mission in Peter's preaching is found in 2:17 where Peter quotes Joel 2:28 (3:1 in Hebrew): "I will pour out my Spirit on all flesh." The universalistic thrust is echoed further in 2:21, where again Joel is quoted: "Whoever calls on the name of the Lord shall be saved." In and of themselves, the passages do not explicitly affirm a mission to Gentiles. In the larger Lukan context, however, a universalistic thrust is probably intended. Luke 3:6, quoting Isa. 40:3-5, is the only other place where Luke uses the phrase "all flesh." The Markan parallel to Luke quotes only Isa. 40:3. In all likelihood Luke extended the quotation through verse 5 because he found in this verse the explicit reference to "all flesh" and felt that it served his universalistic purposes.[40] "All flesh," in Acts 2:17 may, therefore, denote in Luke's mind the universal implications of the coming of the Spirit.

Luke also intended the phrase "whoever calls upon the name of the Lord shall be saved" (Acts 2:21), to refer to the salvation of the Gentiles. In the account of the conversion of Cornelius Peter made general reference to "all" and "everyone" in similar formulaic statements. Acts 10:34 reads "in every nation anyone who fears him and does what is right is acceptable to him." Acts 10:43 states: "To him all the prophets bear witness that everyone who believes in him receives forgiveness of sins through his name." Here, the context makes clear that the general reference to "all" and "everyone" is intended by Luke to denote the inclusion of the Gentiles. While Acts 2:21 does not explicitly speak of Gentile salvation, the all-embracing language used in the passage is used elsewhere by Luke to

---

[39]So Michael Bachmann, *Jerusalem und der Tempel: Die geographisch-theologischen Elemente in der lukanischen Sicht des judischen Kultzentrums,* Beitrage zur Wissenschaft vom Alten und Neuen Testament, Sechste Folge, Heft 9 (Stuttgart: Kohlhammer, 1980) 132-70.

[40]So, e.g., Conzelmann, *Theology,* 161; I. H. Marshall, *The Gospel of Luke: A Commentary on the Greek Text,* The New International Greek Testament Commentary (Grand Rapids MI: Eerdmans, 1978) 137; Walter Grundmann, *Das Evangelium nach Lukas,* Theologischer Handkommentar zum Neuen Testament 3 (Berlin: Evangelische Verlagsanstalt, 1961) 102; Eduard Schweizer, *Das Evangelium nach Lukas* (Göttingen: Vandenhoeck und Ruprecht, 1984) 46.

point to the salvation of the nations. Acts 2:21 may very well be an early allusion to the universal salvation announced from Jerusalem.

The second announcement of universal salvation from Peter is found in 2:39: "For the promise is to you and to your children and to all that are far off, everyone whom the Lord our God calls to him." The universal character of this announcement is found in the expression which affirms that the promise is for those who are far off (εἰς μακράν). Read in the larger context of Luke-Acts, the phrase "those who are far off" is probably a designation for the Gentiles. The author of Ephesians certainly used οἱ μακράν to denote the Gentiles (Eph. 2:13, 17).[41] Luke too closely associated μακράν with the Gentiles, as Acts 22:21 shows unambiguously. Here the risen Jesus says to Paul: "Depart; for I will send you far away (μακράν) to the Gentiles." The affirmation that the promises of salvation are to οἱ μακράν is an affirmation of the universal reach of the gospel.

The third universalistic announcement of the gospel is found in Acts 3:21. Here reference is made to "establishing all that God spoke by the mouth of his holy prophets from of old." Peter is affirming that the restoration of all things spoken of by the prophets is in the process of finding fulfillment. To Luke's way of thinking, the conversion of the Gentiles stands among those things "spoken of by the prophets."[42] In a number of places Luke simply asserts that the conversion of the nations stands in accordance with the utterances of the prophets (Lk. 24:46-47; Acts 10:43; 26:22-23). In other places Luke will make the assertion and then support it with a specific text (Acts 15:15-18). In still other places Luke will quote or allude to the Old Testament texts to give scriptural support to the Gentile mission (Acts 13:47; 26:18; see Isa. 49:6; 42:6-7). It is clear that Luke intended to leave the impression that the conversion of the Gentiles happens in accordance with the will of God as expressed in prophetic expectation. Jerusalem, more specifically the temple, was the place whence this plan of God is announced.

The final passage from Peter's sermon coming from within the temple precincts is found in Acts 3:25. Speaking to Jews Peter quotes Gen. 22:18: "In your [Abraham's] posterity shall all the families of the earth be blessed." It is doubtful that Luke understood "Abraham's seed" as a reference to Christ as Paul did in Gal. 3:16. Luke understood the seed of Abraham to be Israel. The gospel has been offered to them first (3:26) that

[41]Marcus Barth, *Ephesians: Introduction, Translation and Commentary on Chapters 1-3*, Anchor Bible, vol. 34 (Garden City NY: Doubleday, 1974) 260, 267, 276-79.

[42]So Dupont, "Salvation of the Gentiles," in *Salvation of the Gentiles*, 11-33; Franklin, *Christ the Lord*, 121-27.

through them, penitent Israel, the same blessings may be offered to the nations.[43]

One way, therefore, that Luke associates the conversion of the nations to Jerusalem and the temple is to make these sacred sites the location whence the offering of salvation to the Gentiles is announced. In the corresponding introductions to each respective volume of Luke's work, the birth narrative and the opening of Acts, the conversion of the nations is proclaimed from Jerusalem and/or the temple.

The second way that Luke associates the conversion of the nations with Jerusalem and the temple is to make these sacred locations the starting point of the mission. This is seen most readily in the expression of the risen Jesus found in Lk. 24:47-49 and Acts 1:8. In Lk. 24:47 Jesus announces that "repentance and forgiveness of sins should be preached in his name to all nations, beginning from Jerusalem." Explicit instructions are given that the disciples are to "stay in the city until you are clothed with power from on high" (Lk. 24:49). Acts 1:8, the programmatic passage of Acts, contains the same idea. "But you shall receive power when the Holy Spirit has come upon you; and you shall be my witnesses in Jerusalem and in all Judea and Samaria and to the end of the earth." Jerusalem is the place where the apostles receive the power and the place whence the mission ensues.

The third way in which Luke links the Gentile mission to Jerusalem is through the sanctioning of such a mission by the leaders of the Jerusalem church. I discussed in the previous chapter how Luke established a close association between the leadership of the primitive church and the city of Jerusalem. To some extent, therefore, Luke makes this leadership an extension of the city. Their sanction of the mission represents the sanction of Jerusalem, the city which they rule.

There are four major passages where the Jerusalem leadership, or one of their official representatives, gives sanction to the conversion of non-Jews. The first passage is Acts 8:14-17 where it is reported that following the Samaritans' reception of the gospel the "apostles at Jerusalem heard that Samaria had received the word of God" (8:14). Upon hearing of the Samaritan mission Peter and John sanction the mission by praying "for them that they might receive the Holy Spirit, for it had not yet fallen on any of them, but they had only been baptized in the name of the Lord Jesus" (8:15-16). It is significant that through the activity of the Jerusalem apostles the Samaritans receive the Spirit (8:17), making them members

---

[43]See the discussion by Jervell, "Divided People," in *Luke and the People*, 58-60; Dupont, "Salvation of the Gentiles," in *Salvation of the Gentiles*, 23.

of the eschatological people of God. The Samaritan believers are now part of this community and it is the activity of the apostles from Jerusalem which brings this to pass. Through Peter and John the phase of mission announced in Acts 1:8 and extending to Samaria finds the sanction of Jerusalem.

The second major passage concerns the conversion of Cornelius under the preaching of Peter. Peter first had to be convinced by God that he was to accept the full inclusion of the Gentiles into the people of God (Acts 10:9-16, 34-35; 11:9).[44] Being convinced by God, Peter strongly advocates God's desire that the Gentiles be admitted into the people of God. He states in Acts 10:47: "Can any one forbid water for baptizing these people who have received the Holy Spirit just as we have?" Peter also defends before the Jerusalem church the offering of the gospel to Gentiles (11:1-18), leading the Jerusalem brethren to conclude that "to the Gentiles also God has granted repentance unto life" (Acts 11:18). With this declaration of the Jerusalem church, induced by Peter, the chief of the Jerusalem apostles, Jerusalem affirmatively sanctions the mission to the Gentiles.

The third passage portraying the sanctioning of the Gentile mission by Jerusalem is found in Acts 11:19-26. The gospel has been introduced to non-Jews in Antioch by Hellenists. Luke has paved the way for this progression by being careful to recount the conversion of Cornelius *prior* to the notification of the Antioch mission. In principle, therefore, the reader knows this advancement of the gospel to be in accordance with the will of God. Yet Luke is careful not to sever the "Jerusalem connection," for Luke indicates that "news of this came to the ears of the church in Jerusalem, and they sent Barnabas to Antioch" (11:22). Luke states that "when he [Barnabas] came and saw the grace of God, he was glad; and he exhorted them all to remain faithful to the Lord with steadfast purpose" (Acts 11:23).

Luke has already introduced the reader to Barnabas, and has shown him to be totally loyal to the Jerusalem church. In Acts 5:37 Luke reports that Barnabas "sold a field which belonged to him, and brought the money and laid it at the apostles' feet." L. T. Johnson has convincingly shown that such disposal of personal property to the care of the apostles functions literarily in Luke to describe one's submission to apostolic authority and leadership.[45] Barnabas's legitimacy as a trusted member of the Jerusalem

---

[44]See Dibelius, "Conversion of Cornelius," in *Studies in the Acts of the Apostles,* trans. Mary Ling (London: SCM Press, 1956) 109-122.

[45]L. T. Johnson, *The Literary Function of Possessions in Luke-Acts,* SBLDS 39 (Missoula MT: Scholars Press, 1977) 29-78.

church is affirmed further in 9:27 where his endorsement of Paul is sufficient to confirm him to the Jerusalem church. Hence, Barnabas stands in the text of Acts as a trustworthy representative of the Jerusalem leadership. His sanction and affirmation of the Gentile church in Antioch (Acts 11:23) represent the favor of the Jerusalem church.

The fourth passage depicting Jerusalem's endorsement of the Gentile mission is founded in Acts 15. The setting of the story is Jerusalem (15:1-24). At this city the Jerusalem leadership leaves no ambiguity regarding the fate of the Gentiles. Peter affirms their inclusion with the people of faith by recounting the Cornelius episode (15:7-11). James, who from this point on assumes the leadership role at Jerusalem, explicitly sanctions the Gentile mission by affirming that this is in accordance with the will of God as declared by the prophets (Acts 15:14-19). Jerusalem endorses the conversion of the Gentiles.

The fifth way that Luke ties the Gentile mission to Jerusalem is by portraying the Hellenists, primary agents of the Gentiles' conversion, as legitimate extensions of the Jerusalem church. The precise identity of the Hellenists is something of an enigma to the critics.[46] This is due partially to the fact that Luke does not portray them as a monolithic block. Some Hellenists, such as Stephen and Philip, are portrayed as trailblazers who are skeptical of revered Jewish traditions, or who are anxious to break down the barriers between Jew and Gentile. On the other hand, some Hellenists are portrayed as violently opposed to the Christians (Acts 6:9-11; 9:24). It is generally believed that the term denotes Jews who, at the very least, spoke Greek as their mother tongue, implying that these were Jews of the diaspora who settled in Palestine.[47] Luke reports that many Hellenists who were persecuted and scattered (8:1; 11:19) preached the gospel to non-Jews (11:20; cf. 8:5-6, 26-40). This probably stands in accordance with historical fact,[48] a fact of which Luke is well aware. He knows that the Hellenists played an important role in the centrifugal spread of the gospel. Apparently, such a fact does not bother Luke. He must, however, show the close association between this group called the Hellenists and Jerusalem if the mission to the Gentiles is to retain its Jerusalem connection.

---

[46]A convenient survey of options is offered by Ralph Martin, *New Testament Foundations: A Guide for Christian Students,* 2 vols. (Grand Rapids MI: Eerdmans, 1978) 2:85.

[47]So Martin Hengel, *Acts and the History of Earliest Christianity,* trans. John Bowden (Philadelphia: Fortress, 1980) 71-80; Hans Conzelmann, *Die Apostelgeschichte* (Tübingen: J. C. B. Mohr, 1963) 43.

[48]Hengel, *Acts and the History of Earliest Christianity;* Hans Conzelmann, *History of Primitive Christianity,* trans. John Steely (Nashville: Abingdon Press, 1973) 59.

Luke offers such an association in a number of ways. In the first place, the Hellenists' leadership finds its origin in Jerusalem itself (Acts 6:1-6). The Hellenists' invasion of the Gentile world did not, therefore, spring from dissidents who had no connection with the mother church and its city.

The second and most decisive way by which Luke affirms the Hellenists' Jerusalem connection is to associate the group with the apostles, the leaders of the eschatological community.[49] First, key words used by Luke to denote the activity of seven Hellenists are διακονεῖν and διακονία (Acts 6:1-2), terminology which he also uses to describe apostolic activity (διακονία τοῦ λόγου, Acts 6:3). Furthermore, Luke appears to use the word διακονία to denote authoritative rule. In the previous chapter I argued that Lk. 22:28-30 was a key text for describing apostolic rule in the context of "table fellowship."

Immediately preceding the logion of Lk. 22:28-30 Luke provides another text that describes the spirit of this apostolic rule (Lk. 22:25-27):

> And he said to them, "The kings of the Gentiles exercise lordship over them; and those in authority over them are called benefactors. But not so with you; rather let the greatest among you become as the youngest, and the leader as the one who serves (διακονῶν). For which is the greater, one who sits at table, or one who serves (διακονῶν)? Is it not the one who sits at table? But I am among you as one who serves (διακονῶν).

Not only is the word διακονεῖν used to describe apostolic leadership, but the portrait of service is conveyed through the imagery of table service.

Table service is precisely the term used to describe the activity of the seven. They share in the same "service" as the apostles. Indeed, the implication of Acts 6:2 might very well be that henceforth, the seven will assume this important dimension of authoritative rule. Luke makes no mention of any literal "table service" on the part of the seven following their selection in Acts 6, implying that the "table service" denoted for Luke something symbolic. Given the use of διακονεῖν in other Lukan contexts, such service would symbolize power and authority comparable to that of the apostles themselves.

The second way in which Luke associates the Hellenist leadership with the twelve is by placing the former group in the same category as the latter: that of "men of the Spirit."[50] As men of the Spirit the apostles' message could be received as the authoritative word of God. The seven are de-

---

[49]See Johnson, *Literary Function of Possessions*, 211-13.

[50]Ibid.

scribed in similar terms by Luke. The seven are said to be "full of the Spirit and of wisdom" (6:3). It is explicitly said of Stephen that he was full of the Holy Spirit (6:5). Stephen's spiritual character is affirmed by his vision of the risen Jesus (7:55-56). Luke reports that Philip performed signs and exorcisms (8:6-7). He is guided by the Spirit of God (8:29, 39). Even the daughters of Philip are prophets (21:8). By describing the Hellenists in the same charismatic terms of the twelve, Luke establishes a solid affinity between these preachers to Gentiles and the Jerusalem apostolate.

The final, and perhaps most decisive way that Luke ties the Gentile mission to Jerusalem is by linking, and even subjugating, Paul to this holy center. In Acts Paul is an extension of the Jerusalem church.[51] Contrary to arguments that Paul's mission ultimately separates the gospel from its Jewish center, Luke emphasizes the connection between Paul and Jerusalem and even the temple.

Paul's first introduction to Jerusalem following his calling clearly indicates Luke's concern to establish a clear link between Paul and the holy city. The Lukan chronology of Paul's early days following his call indicates that Paul spent considerable time in Damascus (Acts 9:10-23). Discovering a plot against his life Paul escaped from this city (Acts 9:24-25, cf. 2 Cor. 11:32-33). Luke then informs his readers that Paul went to Jerusalem where Barnabas presented him to the apostles (9:26-30).

Luke's editorial hand is very active in this passage, for the thrust of his narrative does not conform to Paul's own account of his early Christian years (see Gal. 1:16-18). Paul emphatically *dissociates* himself from the Jerusalem apostles: "I did not confer with flesh and blood, nor did I go up to Jerusalem to those who were apostles before me, but I went away into Arabia, and again I returned to Damascus" (Gal. 1:16b-17). It was only "after three years" (at least two years even assuming that Paul is reckoning time inclusively) that Paul went up to Jerusalem. He is quite explicit that he saw none of the apostles, save for Peter and James, Jesus' brother. There is no mention of Barnabas as a mediator between Paul and the apostles.

It can hardly be coincidental that the differences of the two accounts render two entirely different perceptions precisely with respect to Paul's association with Jerusalem. Luke's omission of the "Arabian period"

---

[51]This is even recognized by scholars who generally ascribe this pattern in Luke to what might be called an "early catholic" tendency. See, e.g., Ernst Käsemann, "Ministry and Community in the New Testament," in *Essays on New Testament Themes,* trans. W. J. Montague, Studies in Biblical Theology 41 (London: SCM Press, 1964; Philadelphia: Fortress Press, 1982) 63-94; cf. Talbert, "Critical Quest," 171-222.

serves to establish an immediate Pauline connection with Jerusalem. Luke reports that Paul was presented to the "apostles," the implication being that he was presented to all the apostles, the rulers of Jerusalem. Even the intermediary role of Barnabas heightens Paul's Jerusalem connection, for Luke had already presented Barnabas as a loyal and devoted follower of the apostolic teaching and authority (Acts 5:36-37). Acts 9 by itself clearly gives the reader the impression that there was a quick and almost immediate linkage of Paul to the apostles and the center of the Gentile mission, the city of Jerusalem.

Luke is aware that an important center for Paul's Gentile mission was the city of Antioch. Historically, neither Paul's early association with this city nor the important role of the city in the Gentile mission is to be doubted.[52] As interested as Luke may be in theology, his role as a historian will not allow him to ignore this city and its association with Paul. But Luke is careful to establish a solid connection between Antioch and Jerusalem, portraying Antioch as a loyal and even subservient arm of Jerusalem.

Such a portrayal is offered in a number of ways. In the first place, the gospel is preached in Antioch by persons associated with the Hellenist Stephen (11:19-21). Luke has shown the Hellenists to be legitimate extensions of the Jerusalem twelve. Second, Barnabas, representing the Jerusalem church, sanctions the mission on behalf of the holy city (Acts 11:22-23). Third, the submission of Antioch to Jerusalem is represented by the financial relief that the Gentile church sent to Judea (11:27-30). Luke has consistently portrayed the delivery of one's possessions to the apostles as symbolic of one's submission to a higher authority (Acts 2:43-45; 4:32-37; cf. 5:1-11).

It is significant that Luke relates that Paul and Barnabas were the ones to deliver this gift to Jerusalem. One suspects that Luke is surely making an emphatic statement concerning Paul's relationship with Jerusalem. The fact that Paul delivers the gift to the church is a statement of Paul's loyalty and even submission to this Jerusalem center. Luke's portrayal of the apostle as subservient to the Jerusalem church comes forth even more clearly when the historical problems revolving around this second visit of Paul's to Jerusalem are considered.

Paul himself speaks of a second trip to Jerusalem in Gal. 2:1-10. The complex debate concerning the possibility of reconciling Gal. 2 with Acts

---

[52]See Hengel, *Acts and the History of Earliest Christianity,* 99-110.

need not be rehearsed.[53] Many interpreters think that Gal. 2 sounds more like Acts 15 than Acts 11:12, in which case one is forced to conclude that Paul's second trip to Jerusalem did not occur until the apostolic council of Acts 15. Hence, the trip recorded by Luke in Acts 11 did not involve Paul.[54] Nonetheless, as Luke has presented the story, Paul is portrayed as a loyal servant of Jerusalem.

This portrait of Paul is reinforced by Luke in 12:25. Here, in a rather clumsy editorial comment, Luke informs the reader that Barnabas and Paul returned (to Antioch) from Jerusalem. It would seem that Luke is being careful to remind the reader of Paul's Jerusalem connection before he relates the story of the sending forth of Paul on the so-called first missionary journey (13:1-3). It is Antioch that stands behind this mission; it is Paul and Barnabas who are sent out on this mission. But Luke has been careful to show that both Antioch and the two missionaries are loyal and even subservient to Jerusalem.

Paul's Jerusalem connection is reiterated in Acts 15. Once again, comparison with Paul's own account of events throws into sharp focus Luke's concern to portray Paul as a loyal extension of the Jerusalem church. Even allowing for Paul's apologetic motives in the writing of Galatians,[55] one gets a totally different picture of events. According to Gal. 2 Paul plays an active role in the proceedings. Paul's role in Acts 15 is reduced to one sentence (15:4b). The active participants according to Luke are the *Jerusalem leaders,* the decisions of whom Paul passively accepts. Furthermore, while Paul himself makes no mention of any apostolic decree, Luke portrays Paul as an emissary of Jerusalem through whom the decree was actually delivered (15:30; 16:4). Luke's Paul is hardly the independent missionary of Gal. 2.

Finally, Paul's Jerusalem connection is evidenced by Luke's portrayal of Paul's second and third missionary journeys as being linked with the

---

[53]One must conclude that Gal. 2 = Acts 11-12 if the texts are to be reconciled. See I. H. Marshall, *The Acts of the Apostles: An Introduction and Commentary,* Tyndale New Testament Commentaries (Grand Rapids MI: Eerdmans, 1980) 204-205; 244-46 for good arguments in favor of this explanation.

[54]Hengel, *Acts and the History of Earliest Christianity,* 112, suggests that Barnabas made this trip alone. The traditional association of Paul with Barnabas led Luke to indicate that Paul made the trip. Given Luke's desire to show the close association between Paul and Jerusalem, he may have been inclined to presume that Paul did make this trip.

[55]On Galatians as a formal apology see Hans Dieter Betz, "In Defense of the Spirit: Paul's Letter to the Galatians as a Document of Early Christian Apologetics," in *Aspects of Religious Propaganda in Judaism and Early Christianity,* ed. E. S. Fiorenza (Notre Dame IN: University of Notre Dame Press, 1976) 99-114.

city of Jerusalem. E. Franklin asserts that Acts 15:30 and 21:15 serve as the respective points of initiation and termination for the missionary journeys of Paul.[56] He argues that Acts 21:25, which summarizes the content of the apostolic decree, functions literarily to link Paul's final Jerusalem visit with that of Acts 15. This would appear to be the case, for the summary of 21:25 is surely for the reader's benefit. Paul hardly needs to be told that the apostles sent out such a decree when, according to Luke, Paul himself delivered the letter. By reminding the reader of this decree, Luke simultaneously reminds the reader of Paul's subservient role to Jerusalem and his function as an emissary of that decree. Hence, Luke has structured his narrative so that the missionary journeys of Paul are bracketed by affirmations of Paul's association with Jerusalem.

Two other features support this argument. First, Acts 15:30 indicates that Paul and his companions were "sent off" (ἀπολύειν) by the Jerusalem leadership. 'Απολύειν is often used to denote the letting go of an inferior by a superior, such as the release of a prisoner (Matt. 27:15-26 ‖ Mk. 15:6-15; Lk. 23:16-25; Acts 3:13; 5:40; 16:35f.; 26:32; 28:18) or a debtor (Matt. 18:27). It can be used to describe a general's dismissal of his troops (1 Macc. 11:38) or the dispersion of a crowd (Jos. Ant. 11:337; Acts 19:40). The sending out of Paul by the Jerusalem church in Acts 15:30 has the ring, therefore, of an official, authoritative, sending forth.

The second feature is found in Acts 18:22. During a transitional period between the second and third missionary journeys, it is reported that "when Paul landed at Caesarea, he went up and greeted the church, and then went down to Antioch." There is no explicit mention of Jerusalem, but the reference to "went up" and "went down" could very well serve to notify the reader that Paul touched bases with Jerusalem.[57] Luke was not unfamiliar with the traditional terminology which described one as going "up" to Jerusalem and "down" from Jerusalem.[58] With this notification Luke reminds his readers of Paul's Jerusalem connection.

---

[56]Franklin, *Christ the Lord,* 129. Acts 15:30 reads: "And when they were sent off [from Jerusalem], they went down to Antioch; and having gathered the congregation together, they delivered the letter." Acts 21:15 reads: "After these days we made ready and went up to Jerusalem."

[57]So, e.g., Ernst Haenchen, *The Acts of the Apostles: A Commentary,* trans. Bernard Noble and Gerald Shinn with Hugh Anderson, rev. trans. R. McLeod Wilson (Philadelphia: Westminster, 1971) 544n5; Marshall, *Acts* 301-302; Conzelmann, *Apostelgeschichte,* 108.

[58]Luke refers to "going (or coming) down" from Jerusalem in Acts 8:5; 9:32; 11:27;

Paul's loyalty to the city, its leadership and the temple is affirmed one final time by Luke in Acts 21:15-26. There Paul follows the instructions of James and the Jerusalem elders to make the necessary temple offering for the Nazarites (21:23-26). Here, once again, Luke is careful to note Paul's reverent feelings for the holy sanctuary (21:27-29).

Paul is portrayed by Luke as an important instrument in the mission to the Gentiles, who are a primary object of his call (Acts 9:15; 13:47). Luke, however, goes to great lengths *not* to portray Paul as an independent maverick, working without any solid association with Jerusalem and its leadership. He has consistently portrayed Paul's mission as an extension of Jerusalem. Through Paul Jerusalem reaches out to the nations. He is the link between the Gentiles and the place of eschatological salvation. Lest there be any doubt in the reader's mind of the important role of Israel's holy places in the conversion of the nations, Luke relates in Acts 22:21 that it was from the temple of Jerusalem that Paul received the command of Jesus: "Depart, for I will send you far away to the Gentiles."

Conclusion

For Luke, the mission to the Gentiles is wrought with eschatological significance. Contemporary Judaism and contemporary Christianity were immersed in the conception that Judaism and Jerusalem and/or the temple, whether literal (so Judaism) or spiritual (so Christianity) entities, would play significant roles in the end-time conversion of the nations. Luke rejects the spiritualistic conception of the city and temple followed by his Christian contemporaries. Therefore, if from Luke's perspective Jerusalem and the temple were to play any significant role in the conversion of the nations, such significance would have to be associated with the literal holy places. The facts of history did not allow Luke to paint any grand pictures of the massive pilgrimage of the nations to Jerusalem. The fact was that salvation went out to the Gentiles; they did not come to the place of salvation. But Luke can paint a picture that, despite the uncooperative facts of history, allows one to see that God's holy city did not forfeit its important role in the Gentiles' conversion.

Luke portrays Jerusalem as the place from which the good news of universal salvation is proclaimed. It is the place whence the mission to the

---

12:19; 15:1; 21:10 (κατέρχομαι; the last three references speak literally of Judea but the context indicates that Jerusalem is in mind). Lk. 2:51, 10:30, Acts 8:15, 26, 24:1 (implied) and 25:6, 7 use καταβαίνω to denote "going down" from Jerusalem. Κατάγω is used with respect to "going up" to Jerusalem in Acts 9:30. 'Αναβαίνω is used similarly in Lk. 2:42, 18:10, 18:31, Acts 3:5, 15:2, 21:4, 12, 15, 24:11 and 25:1, 9.

nations finds its starting point. It is the place which sanctions the conversion of the nations through its leadership. And Luke makes clear that those who actually carried the news of salvation from Jerusalem did so with Jerusalem's blessings and as persons who were loyal to this center of salvation: the Hellenists and Paul were depicted as personified extensions of the city. It is true that Jerusalem was not the literal gathering place where the nations found salvation. Nonetheless, one cannot read the book of Acts and walk away with the impression that Luke could have envisioned the nations' conversion without Jerusalem. To that extent, it was for Luke the place of the nations' salvation.

If this was the case, then the destruction of the city and the temple would have been no small matter for Luke. He could not understand their destruction as the obliteration of satanic and worthless structures. For Luke, the reason for their destruction must come from elsewhere. This is the issue of the next chapter.

The Destruction and Restoration
of Jerusalem and the Temple

Chapter V

Luke's Emphasis on the Destruction of Jerusalem and the Temple

There is no question that Luke wished to emphasize the destruction of Jerusalem and the temple. The first implicit reference to the coming destruction is found in Lk. 13:34-35 (‖ Matt. 23:37-39), where Jesus declares to a personified Jerusalem: "Behold, your house is forsaken" (13:35a). The commentators debate whether οἶκος refers to the temple or the city.[1] It makes little difference, for as M. Bachmann has argued, there is no distinction in Luke's mind between the two entities.[2] The point of verse 35a is that punishment will fall on the city and/or the temple.

---

[1]Some who argue that the οἶκος refers to the temple are Klaus Baltzer, "The Meaning of the Temple in the Lukan Writings," HTR 58 (1965): 272; E. Earle Ellis, *The Gospel of Luke,* The New Century Bible (Greenwood SC: Attic Press, 1974) 191. I. H. Marshall, *The Gospel of Luke: A Commentary on the Greek Text,* The New International Greek Testament Commentary (Grand Rapids MI: Eerdmans, 1978) 576, argues that it refers to the city. F. D. Weinert, "The Meaning of the Temple in the Gospel of Luke" (Ph.D. diss., Fordham University, 1979) 247-58, argues that it refers to the Jerusalem leadership in the sense of "ruling house." This interpretation robs the text of sharing the ominous attitude toward the city and temple which is found in other places (to be discussed immediately below).

[2]Michael Bachmann, *Jerusalem und der Tempel: Die geographische-theologischen Elemente in der lukanischen Sicht des judischen Kultzentrums,* Beitrage zur Wissenschaft vom Alten und Neuen Testament Sechste Folge, Heft 9 (Stuttgart: Kohlhammer, 1980) 13-66.

The second destruction saying is found in Lk. 19:41-44. Jesus has just drawn near to Jerusalem and the Pharisees have encouraged him to rebuke his disciples (Lk. 19:39). Following Jesus' hyberbolic response of verse 40, he utters what is probably the most severe of the destruction sayings.

> For the days shall come upon you, when your enemies will cast up a bank about you and surround you, and hem you in on every side, and dash you to the ground, you and your children within you, and they will not leave one stone upon another in you. (Lk. 19:43-44a)

This material, which is peculiar to Luke, is probably traditional,[3] but it shows clearly the Evangelist's desire to emphasize the destruction of Jerusalem.

Luke 21 also contains clear references to the destruction of both the temple (vv. 5-6) and Jerusalem (vv. 20-24). It appears that Luke wanted to emphasize this destruction. First, whereas Mk. 13:1-2 refers to the destruction of all the "wonderful buildings," Luke specifically makes the temple the object of destruction (21:5-6). Second, whereas Mk. 13:14-20 refers to the "desolating sacrilege" (v. 14), Luke makes specific reference to "Jerusalem surrounded by armies" (Lk. 21:20). Third, in verse 24 Luke adds another reference to the downfall of Jerusalem which is not found in Mark. Hence, chapter 21, while based on Mark, does betray Luke's emphasis on the destruction of Jerusalem and the temple.

The final passage that emphasizes the destruction of Jerusalem and the temple is Lk. 23:28-31. Though no specific reference to Jerusalem's impending destruction is offered, it is clear from the passage that apocalyptic-type woes await both the city and her inhabitants, both of whom will suffer persecution.

The Cause of the Destruction of Jerusalem and the Temple

The Rejection of Jesus and His Church. Luke believed that the fall of Jerusalem and the temple was rooted in the Jews' rejection of Jesus and his church.[4] The connection between the rejection of Jesus and the fall of Je-

---

[3]So Joachim Jeremias, *Die Sprache des Lukasevangeliums: Redaktion und Tradition in Nichtmarkusstoff des dritten Evangeliums* (Göttingen: Vandenhoeck und Ruprecht, 1980) 282.

[4]This is a common explanation. See, e.g., Georg Braumann, "Die lukanische Interpretation der Zerstörung Jerusalems," NovT (1963): 120-27; W. C. Robinson, *The Way of the Lord: A Study of History and Eschatology in the Gospel of Luke* (Ph.D. diss., University of Basel; privately published, 1962) 80; Josef Zmijewski, *Die Eschatologiereden des Lukas-Evangeliums: Eine traditions-und redaktionsgeschichtliche Untersuchung zu Lk 21,5-36 und Lk 17,20-27,* Bonner Biblische Beitrage 40 (Bonn: Peter Hanstein Verlag, 1972) 204-220.

rusalem is readily emphasized by Luke. In each passage in the gospel that speaks of the judgment that is to befall the city and sanctuary, some allusion is made to the guilt of the Jews for rejecting Jesus.

Lk. 13:34-35 associates the forsaking of Jerusalem's house with Jerusalem's consistent pattern of "killing the prophets and stoning those who are sent to you!" (v. 34). Luke apparently views the rejection of Jesus as a repetition of this notorious pattern.[5] The city's rejection of Jesus is affirmed in verse 34b: "How often would I have gathered your children together as a hen gathers her brood under her wings, and you would not!" The effect of such rejection is explained: "Behold, your house is forsaken" (v. 35a).

The second reference to the destruction of Jerusalem is found in 19:41-44, where the violent overthrow of the city is vividly portrayed. Verse 44b offers the reason: "Because you did not know the time of your visitation." For Luke an important nuance of "visitation" was the eschatological, redemptive work of God among his people (see Lk. 7:11-17). The one in whom such visitation comes is Jesus (Lk. 7:16; cf. 1:68). Not knowing the time of visitation can only be understood by Luke as failure on the part of Jerusalem to recognize the salvation that has come in the person of Jesus.[6]

Chapter 21 constitutes the major discourse concerning the fall of Jerusalem and the temple. Interestingly, no explicit mention is made of the rejection of Jesus in the discourse itself. The context, however, does indicate that Luke saw a relationship between the rejection of Jesus and the fall of Jerusalem and the temple. The material preceding the discourse of chapter 21 serves to set this chapter in a context that speaks of the rejection of Jesus by the authorities of Jerusalem. Lk. 20:1-8 makes it clear that the Jewish leaders do not accept the authority of Jesus. The parable that follows (vv. 9-18) indicates that the rejection of this authority is tantamount to the rejection of God's messenger. In the following scenes of controversy the tension heightens. The scribes and the chief priests (v. 19) and the Sadducees (v. 27) ask Jesus questions in order that "they might take hold of what he said, so as to deliver him up to the authority and the jurisdiction of the governor" (v. 20b). These pericopes end with a word of Jesus against the hypocrisy of the scribes (vv. 45-47), followed by an example of true versus false piety (21:1-4). Only after this context of polemical tension between Jesus and the Jerusalem leaders has been established does Luke present the destruction discourse of chapter 21.

---

[5]On the motif of Jesus as the rejected prophet see esp. David L. Tiede, *Prophecy and History in Luke-Acts* (Philadelphia: Fortress Press, 1980) 24-64.

[6]Marshall, *Luke* 719.

Lk. 23:28-31 contains the final prediction in the gospel of the destruction of Jerusalem. In this passage, the woes that await Jerusalem are clearly associated with the guilt of the city. "For if they do this when the wood is green, what will happen when it is dry?" J. Schneider sees in this proverb a contrast between Jesus and Jerusalem. Jesus' innocence is represented by the living wood which, despite the fact that it is not easily burned, is about to experience the fate of one who is guilty. How much more easily will the guilty, represented by the dry, brittle, dead wood, burn when judgment comes?[7] The setting of the saying, the road to Golgotha, makes clear the guilt of the city: it is about to crucify Jesus.

Another text that associates the rejection of Jesus with the destruction of the temple is the crucifixion scene in Luke's gospel (Lk. 23:44-48). A comparison with Mk. 15:33-39 makes Luke's emphasis readily apparent.

COMPARISON OF MK. 15:33-39 WITH LK. 23:44-48

MARK 15:33-39	LUKE 23:44-48
1. Reference to the sixth hour and the darkness over the land until the ninth hour (v. 33).	1. Reference to the sixth hour and the darkness over the land until the ninth hour (vv. 44-45a).
2. The cry of dereliction (v. 34).	2. Omit.
3. Derision of Jesus; giving the vinegar (vv. 35-36).	3. Omit.
4. The death of Jesus (v. 37).	4. The rending of the veil (v. 45b).
5. Rending of the veil (v. 38).	5. The death of Jesus (v. 46).
6. The word of the centurion (v. 39).	6. The word of the centurion (v. 47).
	7. Mourning of the crowd (v. 48).

Marshall has observed the omission of the cry of dereliction and suggests that Luke omitted the material from Mark in order to bring the darkness and the rending of the temple veil into conjunction with one another. I would agree that this was Luke's intention, but Marshall's explanation is incomplete. He further argues that in the Lukan narrative the darkness serves to represent God's displeasure caused by the rejection of Jesus.[8]

Marshall is correct to detect significance in Luke's juxtaposition of darkness and rending of the veil. But in actuality there is no reason to interpret the darkness as a symbol of divine displeasure. Luke has provided the reader with the key to understanding the meaning of the darkness. At

---

[7]Johannes Schneider, ξύλον, TDNT 5:38.

[8]Marshall, *Luke*, 873-75.

the arrest of Jesus by the Jewish leaders Jesus says, "This is your hour, and the power of darkness" (22:53). The darkness at the scene of the crucifixion of Jesus represents for the third evangelist the central role in this death of the satanic forces who operate in conjunction with the Jewish leaders.

If the darkness represents the satanic character of Jesus' enemies, the rending of the veil might very well represent the destruction of the temple. There is good reason for supposing that it did. In the first place, if the rending of the veil does not represent the destruction of the temple, the only other likely explanation would be that it represented the tearing down of the barrier to the holy of holies, hence making salvation accessible to all men.

It is unlikely that Luke would have interpreted the tradition this way. First, one cannot be sure that the curtain referred to was the curtain of the holy of holies. In the LXX καταπέτασμα could mean either the curtain between the sanctuary and the holy of holies[9] or the curtain between the temple and the forecourt.[10] With this fluid usage, the interpreter must acknowledge Luke's ambiguity. Second, if καταπέτασμα were a reference to the holy of holies, then probably the rending of the veil did represent the offering of atonement through the death of Jesus. Yet despite the fact that Luke has many references to the death of Jesus, there is attached to it little explicit expiatory efficacy.[11]

There is evidence that the tearing of the veil served as a portent for the destruction of the temple. This is indicated primarily by the fact that such a tradition was in place in late antiquity.[12] Ps.-Clem. Rec. 1:41 reads: "The veil of the temple was rent, as in lamentation for the destruction impending over the place."[13] There is found in Liv. Pro. Hab. 12 the following statement:

---

[9]See Ex. 26:31-35; 27:21; 30:6; 35:12; 37:3; 41:3, 21-26; Lev. 4:6; 16:2, 12-15; 21:3; 24:3; Num. 4:5; 2 Chron. 3:14; 1 Macc. 1:22.

[10]See Ex. 26:37; 35:15; 37:5-6, 16, 38:18; 39:4, 19; 40:5; Num. 3:10, 26; 4:32; 18:7; 3 Kgs. 6:36; Sir. 50:5.

[11]Augustin George, "La Mort de Jesus pour Luc," RB 80 (1973): 186-217.

[12]A detailed survey of the evidence may be found in Dale C. Allison Jr., *The End of the Ages Has Come: An Early Interpretation of the Passion and Resurrection of Jesus* (Philadelphia: Fortress Press, 1985) 31-32.

[13]Translation follows *The Ante-Nicene Fathers: Translations of the Writings of the Fathers down to A. D. 325,* ed. Alexander Roberts and James Donaldson, 12 vols., reprint ed. (Grand Rapids MI: Eerdmans, 1978) 8:88. In its final form, *Recognitions* offers a fourth

Concerning the end of the temple, he foretold that it would be brought to pass by a western nation. Then, he said, the veil of the inner sanctuary will be torn to pieces and the capitals of the two pillars will be taken away and no one will know where they are. . . . [14]

Given that Luke consistently juxtaposed the notion of the rejection of Jesus with the destruction of the temple, it seems likely that Luke is once again bringing these two motifs together in the narrative of Jesus' death. This possibility is rendered more plausible by the fact that in late antiquity the rending of the veil could represent the destruction of the temple.

Luke's motive for rearranging the Markan source, therefore, becomes obvious. Luke wished to bring into close proximity the motif of darkness (representing the satanic character of the Jewish leaders of Jerusalem), the rending of the veil (representing the destruction of Jerusalem), and the death of Jesus (representing the rejection of Jesus by the Jewish leaders). In so doing, he has affirmed once again the direct relationship between the destruction of the temple and Jerusalem and the rejection of Jesus.

The fall of Jerusalem and the temple is not only linked with the rejection of Jesus, but the rejection of his disciples as well. This is seen in Luke in two places. First, Lk. 21 places into close proximity the persecution of the church and the fall of Jerusalem. In verses 12-19 Luke lists the persecutions to be faced by the church at the hands of both Jews and Gentiles. Zmijewski is probably correct to argue that the book of Acts represents the historical fulfillment of this prophecy.[15] Indeed many of the specific incidents spoken of in 21:12-19 do find a parallel in Acts.

Lk. 21:12a speaks of the persecution of Jesus' followers using the phrase (added to Mark) "they will lay their hands on you." Such a violent laying on of hands occurs a number of times in Acts (Acts 4:3; 5:18; 12:1; 21:27). Lk. 21:12b alludes to persecution at the hands of the Jews ("delivering you up to the synagogues," Lk. 21:12b), which finds fulfillment in Acts 5:17-18, 40-41; 6:12-7:70; 8:1; 9:29; 13:44, 50; 14:2-6; 15:19-22; 21:11 and 23:12-15. The same passage (Lk. 21:12b) makes reference to being delivered up to prison (see Acts 5:18; 12:3-5; 16:23-24; 21:13, 31).

---

century Christian interpretation of the rending of the veil. Earlier materials may have been incorporated into these texts, however. See H. Dressler, "Pseudo-Clementines," *New Catholic Encyclopedia*, 15 vols. (New York: McGraw-Hill, 1967) 11:942-43.

[14]C. C. Torrey, *The Lives of the Prophets: Greek Text and Translation*, JBLMS 1 (Philadelphia: Society of Biblical Literature and Exegesis, 1946) 44. Allison, *End of Ages*, 31, tentatively suggests a date as early as the end of the first century A.D. for this text.

[15]See Zmijewski, *Eschatologiereden*, 177-78.

Lk. 21:12c promises that the Christians "will be brought before kings and governors for my name's sake," during which time Jesus' followers are to offer testimony. On numerous occasions in Acts the Christians offer such testimony before various leaders (Acts 4:5-12; 5:29-32; 24:10-21; 26:1-23). Inspiration which induces powerful and persuasive speech is promised in Lk. 21:14-15 (see Acts 2:14-37; 6:10; 9:22; 17:2-3; 18:4, 28; 19:8). Some Christians will be put to death (Lk. 21:16b; see Acts 7:60; 12:1-2; 20:17-35 [implied]). Through all tribulations, the followers of Jesus are assured divine protection (Lk. 21:18-19; see Acts 5:19; 12:6-11; 16:25-26; 27:34). It is hardly coincidental that immediately following Jesus' prophecy of the church's persecution he predicts the fall of Jerusalem (21:20-24). It would seem that in some way the fall of Jerusalem is causally related to the persecution of the church.

This is confirmed by the Lukan account of Paul's arrest in Jerusalem. Luke offers the following description of the event:

> When the seven days were almost completed, the Jews from Asia, who had seen him in the temple, stirred up all the crowd and laid hands on him, crying out, "Men of Israel, help! This is the man who is teaching men everywhere against the people and the law and this place; moreover he also brought Greeks into the temple, and he has defiled this holy place." For they had previously seen Trophimus the Ephesian with him in the city, and they supposed that Paul had brought him into the temple. Then all the city was aroused, and the people ran together; they seized Paul and dragged him out of the temple, and at once the gates were shut. (Acts 21:27-30)

This text very likely alludes to the destruction of the temple. According to Luke's narrative, "the people ran together; they seized Paul and dragged him out of the temple, and at once the gates were shut" (21:30b). There are two reasons why this text points to the temple's destruction.

In the first place, Luke may intend to offer a parallel to the rending of the temple veil which occurs at the moment of Jesus' death (Lk. 23:45). Charles Talbert has argued that Luke has consciously placed both Paul's and Jesus' final trips to Jerusalem in a parallel relationship.[16]

The following parallels noted by Talbert will illustrate this point. Lk. 19:45-48 and Acts 21:26 describe Jesus and Paul respectively as going to the temple and having an initially positive attitude toward it. Each has an encounter with the Sadducees concerning the issue of resurrection (Lk. 20:27-39; Acts 23:6-9). Each is seized by a mob (Lk. 22:54; Acts 21:30).

---

[16]*Literary Patterns, Theological Themes and the Genre of Luke-Acts* (Missoula MT: Scholars Press, 1974) 17-18.

Each is abused by the priestly court (Lk. 22:63-64; Acts 23:2). Each is unjustly condemned with a similar cry (Lk. 23:18, αἶρε τοῦτον; Acts 21:36 αἶρε αὐτόν). With the abundance of literary allusions it is likely that the shutting of the temple gates corresponds to the rending of the temple veil. It will be recalled that the rending of the veil represented for Luke the destruction of the temple. If Acts 21:30 does correspond to Lk. 23:45, then Luke is writing to indicate that as a direct result of the mob's violent seizure of Paul, the temple faces destruction.

Interpreting the shutting of the temple gates as a representation of the destruction of the temple itself is supported, in the second place, by similar imagery in Josephus:

> . . . moreover, the eastern gate of the inner court—it was brass and very massive, and, when closed towards evening, could scarcely be moved by twenty men; . . . this gate was observed at the sixth hour of the night to have opened of its own accord. . . . The learned understood that the security of the temple was dissolving of its own accord and that the opening of the gate meant a present to the enemy, interpreting the portent in their own minds as indicative of coming desolation.
>
> (War 6:293, 295-96)

Further, rabbinic texts include the following statement attributed to R. Eleazar, dating possibly to the first century C.E.

> Since the destruction of the Temple, the gates of prayer are locked, for it is written, Also when I cry out, he shutteh out my prayer. (b. Baba Metzia 59a)

In each instance the parallels are not exact. In Josephus, it is the opening of the temple gates that portend the desolation of the temple. In the statement of R. Eleazar, the locked gates are the result of the temple's destruction, not a portent of such destruction. Nonetheless, the motif of the destruction of the temple did incorporate imagery of the temple gates.

It seems clear that Luke detected a causal relationship between the fall of Jerusalem and the temple and the Jewish rejection of Jesus and his church. But Luke has gone further; in his writings he has offered an explanation for such Jewish rejection of their Messiah and his followers.

The Rejection of the Universal Mission of Jesus and his Church. It is not enough simply to show that Luke viewed the fall of Jerusalem and the temple as due to the rejection of Jesus and the church. More specifically, Luke believed that it was the Jewish rejection of the universal mission of Jesus and his church that led to the fall of the city and the sanctuary. In rejecting the proposition of a universal gospel, Luke believed the Jews to be rejecting their purpose, and indeed their holy sanctuary's very purpose of existence. Luke believed the salvation of the Gentiles to be an integral part of God's salvific plan. The Gentiles were to be fully admitted as Gentiles to the status of λαὸς θεοῦ (Acts 10:44-48; 11:15-18; 15:7-9, 13-14). Furthermore, Luke has offered the view that the restored Jewish nation was to be an integral instrument in the salvation of the nations (Acts 3:24-26; 15:16-18). In accordance with traditional expectations, the temple and Jerusalem were also to play integral roles in this conversion of the nations. God's eschatological work of salvation had been put into effect—the time of Jesus and the church was the beginning of the "restoration of all things" (Acts 3:21). However, Luke believed that the Jews gradually came to resist this divine intention, thereby stalling the return of Jesus and the restoration of all things (see Acts 3:19-21). The end result was the rejection of Jesus and his church. For this, the Jews are punished.

The programmatic Nazareth pericope makes the reader aware that the Jews as a people will eventually reject the universal thrust of Jesus' gospel.[17] Here Luke leaves the impression that Jesus' announcement of the dawn of the jubilary end-time salvation was happily received by his audience (Lk. 4:22). But when Jesus made it clear that God's blessings of salvation were to extend beyond the Jews (Lk. 4:25-27), his hearers tried to kill him (4:28-29). At this juncture, the reader knows the ultimate fate of Jesus and the ultimate response of the Jews to his mission. Yet Luke will only gradually unfold for the reader how this rejection of Jesus and his mission develops.[18]

The rejection of Jesus' universal gospel begins with the attempts of the Jewish leaders to resist Jesus' ministry to the "outcasts" of Israel. Luke portrays them as wanting to keep the blessings of salvation within the confines of the "righteous."

A number of texts in the gospel portray the "righteous" Jews as resisting Jesus' mission to the outcasts of Israel. Luke has taken over from Mark the material of Lk. 5:17-26 (Mk. 2:1-12), 5:27-32 (Mk. 2:13-17),

---

[17]See J. A. Sanders, "From Isaiah 61 to Luke 4," in *Christianity, Judaism and Other Greco-Roman Cults, Part One. Studies for Morton Smith at Sixty,* ed. Jacob Neusner, Studies in Judaism in Late Antiquity 12 (Leiden: E. J. Brill, 1975) 75-106, and R. C. Tannehill, "The Mission of Jesus according to Luke iv 16:30," in *Jesus in Nazareth* (Berlin: Walter de Gruyter, 1972) 51-75.

[18]The following statement of Robert C. Tannehill is most apropos: " . . . recent theoretical discussions of narrative have noted that events in the narrative may be referred to out of chronological order. There may be previews of coming events and reviews of past events, often in a way that interprets these events from some perspective." "Israel in Luke-Acts: A Tragic Story," JBL 104 (1985): 69.

6:6-11 (Mk. 3:1-6), 12:1 (Mk. 8:14-15,) (to which Luke adds the specific reference to the Pharisees' hypocrisy). Luke shares with Matthew the parable of the lost sheep (Lk. 15:3-7 || Matt. 18:12-14). He has introduced the parable with the comment that the Pharisees and scribes took issue with Jesus on his openness to the tax collectors and sinners.

In a number of passages peculiar to Luke this theme of resistance comes to the fore. Lk. 7:36-50 depicts Simon the Pharisee as reluctant to accept Jesus' authority as a prophet since Jesus accepted the gesture of the sinner-woman. In Lk. 13:10-17 the ruler of the synagogue condemns Jesus for healing on the Sabbath. In Lk. 14:1-6 Jesus knows that his activity of healing will upset Pharisees with whom he is sharing a meal. In the parable of the prodigal son, the obedient, elder brother (who represents the obedient Pharisees) is angered over the father's acceptance of the younger, erring brother. The parable of the rich man and Lazarus (Lk. 16:19-31) portrays the Pharisees' (cf. 16:14) contempt for the poor outcasts of Israel, represented by Lazarus.

In addition to the above texts, Luke plays on the word δίκαιος to show that the Pharisaic concept of ''righteousness'' was perverse in that it led to an attitude of contempt for the outcasts of Israel and the Messiah who ministered to them.[19] Theirs was actually a righteousness before men as opposed to God who considered their activity an abomination (Lk. 16:14-15). The ''lawyer'' strives before Jesus to ''justify himself'' by strictly narrowing his circle of responsibility and love (Lk. 10:25-29). Lk. 18:9-14 explicitly speaks of those ''who trust in themselves that they were righteous and despised others'' (v. 9). The ''others'' denote the sinners, represented in this parable by the tax collector. Finally, Luke speaks of the scribes (Lk. 20:19) as ''pretending to be sincere'' (δίκαιοι, 20:20), though their motives were quite sinister, for they hoped to have Jesus arrested (v. 20b). In Luke, Jesus meets opposition from the ''righteous'' element of Judaism which attempted to inhibit his ministry to the lost and the sinners. They were the first to reject Jesus. What is more, their motivation for rejecting Jesus is grounded in their perverse righteousness which did not allow them to be open to Jesus' offering of salvation to the outcasts and sinners of Israel.

---

[19]Luke identifies the Pharisees with the δίκαιοι in two places. In Lk. 5:30-32 (|| Mk. 2:16-17) Jesus identifies the Pharisees with the righteous when he states: ''I have not come to call the righteous but sinners to repentance.'' One may see a similar identification of the δίκαιοι and the Pharisees in Lk. 15:1-7 where Jesus says to the Pharisees in defense of his mission to the outcast of Israel, ''there will be more joy in heaven over one sinner who repents than over ninety-nine righteous δίκαιοι who need no repentance'' (v. 7).

The resistance of the ''righteous'' Jewish leadership to the offering of salvation to the masses of Israel continues in Acts, as they consistently hamper the work of the apostles (see Acts 4:1-22; 5:17-40). Luke informs his readers that the leaders' motive for resisting the apostolic work was ''jealousy'' (ζῆλος). In passages immediately preceding, Luke indicated that the apostolic ministry was being awarded a wide reception by the ''people.'' Resistance to the universal sweep of the gospel, therefore, finds its origin in the ''righteous'' elements of Judaism which do not favor the incorporation of ''all people'' of Israel into the scope of God's salvific work.

Resistance does not end here, however. As it increasingly becomes clearer that *Gentiles* are also considered the recipients of God's salvation, the Jewish people *as a whole,* who so warmly received the message of salvation in the opening chapters of Acts, now begin to resist the gospel.

As Luke describes the Jewish resistance to the Gentile mission he will employ the words ζῆλος or ζηλόω. Ζῆλος has an affinity with the word δίκαιος in that it can denote ''zeal for law.''[20] Luke is aware of such a nuance, and he can even use it positively (see Acts 21:20). Many Jews, however, have a ''zeal'' for the law that is as perverse as their ''righteousness,'' in that it leads to the exclusion of others from God's promises of salvation, not their inclusion. In Antioch of Pisidia, Paul preaches his ''inaugural sermon'' of Acts. The Jewish reception seems positive in that Luke states that Paul and Barnabas were invited back to the synagogue on the following sabbath (Acts 13:42-43). Yet when Paul and Barnabas returned they found ''the whole city'' (13:44) waiting to hear their message. Here Luke immediately reports: ''But when the Jews saw the multitudes they were filled with jealousy (ζῆλος), and contradicted what was spoken by Paul and reviled him'' (13:45). The Jewish reaction to the Greeks' acceptance of the gospel at Thessalonica is described in the same terms: ''But the Jews were jealous (ζηλώσαντες δὲ οἱ Ἰουδαῖοι, Acts 17:5). The Jews' ''zeal,'' just like their ''righteousness,'' manifests itself in a possessive and selfish attitude with respect to God's gift of salvation. The Jews are receptive to the gospel until it is clear that God intended its blessings to extend to the Gentiles.

Luke brings this motif to a definite climax in his description of Paul's encounter with the Jews at the Jerusalem temple. In Acts 21:27-30, Luke informs his readers that the Jewish mob attacked Paul and tried to kill him

---

[20]See, e.g., 1 Macc. 2:24, 26, 27, 50; cf. Jud. 9:4. See the discussion by Albrecht Stumpff, ζῆλος, κτλ., TDNT 2:882-87.

under the provocation that he was "teaching men everywhere against the people and the law and this place [the temple] . . . [and that he had] brought Greeks into the temple and he [had] defiled this holy place" (v. 28).

This charge against Paul echoes the charge against Stephen found in Acts 6:13-14. In both texts the men are charged with speaking against the law and the temple. What is more, only in Acts 6:13-14 and 21:28 does Luke use τόπος to denote the temple. This seems to indicate that Luke intended his readers to note the connections between the two incidents. I argued in chapter two that Stephen's attack on the temple was not to be construed as a temple polemic per se. Rather, what Luke condemns through Stephen is the temple as it functions to restrict or confine God's presence in the world. The temple as God's stationary οἶκος and place of rest is the object of Stephen's harsh words. The violent killing of Stephen *implies* that it was his criticism of the restricted God which prompted his murder.

Such an implication is made explicit in Acts 21:27-30. Here Luke clearly juxtaposes the charge that Paul speaks against the temple by bringing Greeks into the sanctuary with the attempt to kill Paul. Luke makes it clear in verse 29 that Paul did not violate the temple, but that is not the central point. What is significant is the Jewish reaction to the possibility that a Gentile might have entered the sacred precincts. In their eyes, such would justify the conclusion that Paul "has defiled (κεκοίνωκεν) this holy place" (Acts 21:28b). It is the Jewish view of Gentiles, as common persons who defile the sacred space, which supports their assertion that Paul speaks against the temple. To them, open acceptance of the Gentiles, represented by Paul, is tantamount to a rejection of both Torah and Temple. Their reaction is the rejection of Paul, going so far as to attempt to kill him (21:31).

The reader of Acts knows, however, that the view of the Jews is totally without foundation. It is the will of God that the Gentiles be accepted into the ranks of his people (Acts 15:14-18). He gives them the same Holy Spirit which he has granted to the Jewish Christians (Acts 10:45; 11:17; 15:8). Indeed, it is not accurate of the Jews to assert that the Gentiles' presence would defile (κοινοῦν) the temple. Luke has used the verb κοινοῦν in only two other places (Acts 10:15; 11:9). In both instances it is in reference to the Gentiles where a heavenly voice declares "what God had cleansed you must not call common (κοινοῦν). " God has cleansed the Gentiles; they are not unclean. They do not, therefore, defile the sacred space of Israel. In rejecting the Gentiles as being among the people of God, the Jews are rejecting the very declaration of God himself. Such rejection is manifested in the persecution of Paul.

Luke brings to the fore the Jews' rejection of the Gentiles once again in Acts 22:17-22. Paul has been offering before the Jewish mob the first of a series of defense speeches which he will make in the concluding chapters of Acts. Toward the conclusion of the speech Paul informs his listeners that while in the temple he received a vision from Jesus commanding him to "depart; for I will send you far away to the Gentiles" (Acts 22:21). Luke reports that "up to this word they listened to him; then they lifted up their voices and said, 'Away with such a fellow from the earth! For he ought not to live' " (Acts 22:22). The sole basis of the violent Jewish rejection of Paul is his announcement that he was to involve himself in the mission to the Gentiles.

Luke has gone to great lengths to show that the universal salvation of both Jews and Gentiles was the will of God. The Jews, Jerusalem, and the temple were to play integral roles in the salvation of the latter group. Yet while Luke was aware that many Jews did accept their mission as instruments of salvation, and that Jerusalem and the temple *initially* began to play their important roles in this same salvation, the majority of the Jews rejected God's mission to the Gentiles. Salvation was to be limited to the Jews; and their holy sanctuary was to remain their private domain. The very thought of opening the gates to the Gentiles fills the Jews with such rage that they can only drag Paul from the courts and attempt to kill him. God's response is unequivocal: " . . . and at once the gates were shut" (Acts 21:30). The temple and its city would be destroyed. The question that remains is whether Luke envisioned such a destruction as God's permanent rejection of his people and place.

The Question of the Restoration of Jerusalem and the Temple

A priori considerations would allow one justifiably to argue in favor of both options; either that Luke did envisage a restoration of Jerusalem and/ or the temple or that he did not. Against such a notion of restoration is the fact that Luke would have been cutting solidly against the grain of contemporary Christian tradition. This alone would not preclude Luke's adoption of such a position, but one would perhaps expect from the Evangelist some clear statements affirming such restoration.

In favor of such a notion is the fact that Luke, unlike his Christian contemporaries, did not present Jesus or the church as substitutes for the temple and/or the city. Luke's Christian contemporaries could easily dismiss the literal city and temple for, in their view, there now existed a new temple, "not made with hands" (Mk. 14:58). Old Testament and Jewish expectations concerning Jerusalem and the temple had remained intact in early non-Lukan Christianity; they had been radically redefined, however, being spiritualized in the church or Jesus. Luke's failure to redefine and spiritualize these entities, coupled with no notion of a restoration of these same entities would, in effect, mean that Luke would have left the eschatological expectations concerning Jerusalem and the temple without any kind of ultimate fulfillment. At best, one could say that Jerusalem and the temple had *begun* to fulfill their eschatological roles, but ultimately failed their God-assigned task.

A significant number of Lukan interpreters do maintain that Luke viewed the destruction of Jerusalem and the temple as God's permanent rejection of these places. Conzelmann views the destruction in the context of Luke's attempt to portray Gentile Christianity as finally separated from both the Law and Temple. Hence, the temple's destruction embodies this final and decisive break.[21] W. C. Robinson argues that the destruction represents Christianity's decisive break with Judaism as it moves along its "way."[22] C. H. Giblin's typological and "moral" interpretation of Jerusalem's destruction, wherein the city symbolizes those who reject the gospel, leads him to conclude as well that Luke held to no restoration for the city or sanctuary.[23] W. D. Davies argues that Luke perceived Jerusalem to be the appropriate point of departure for the gospel; but while Christianity began there, it only passed through it. The destruction of Jerusalem and the temple served to indicate that ties to these geographical centers are now broken.[24]

A most thorough study of the destruction of Jerusalem and the temple in Luke is that of J. Zmijewski.[25] It is his contention that the destruction of Jerusalem is indissolubly related to the transferral of salvation from the Jews to the Gentiles. With the irrevocable destruction of Jerusalem, Christianity's links with Judaism are broken forever. Despite the similarities with Rom. 11:25, which also views the present time as "Gentile-time" (see Lk. 21:24c), Luke, unlike Paul, does not view this Gentile period as ending with the conversion of Israel. The Jews have now lost any opportunity to receive the gospel; all the blessings of salvation have now been transferred to the Gentiles.

All the above-mentioned interpreters have at least one thing in common: they perceive Luke as operating from within a salvation-historical

---

[21]Conzelmann, *Theology*, 165.

[22]Robinson, *Way of the Lord*, 80.

[23]*The Destruction of Jerusalem according to Luke's Gospel: A Historical-Typological Moral*, Analecta Biblica 107 (Rome: Biblical Institute Press, 1985).

[24]*The Gospel and the Land: Early Christianity and Jewish Territorial Doctrine* (Berkeley: University of California Press, 1974) 255-60.

[25]Zmijewski, *Eschatologiereden*, 181-224.

context that advocated the transferral of salvation to the Gentiles. To be sure, this salvation has passed through Israel, but Israel (Jerusalem) has rejected the gospel; hence, it too has been rejected by God. Now that Christianity has moved beyond Judaism, the temple and the city are no longer needed. Their destruction simply ends a phase of *Heilsgeschichte*.

It would not be an exaggeration to say that the strength of these salvation-historical interpretations is linked to the conclusion that Jerusalem has been forever left behind by Luke. If, in point of fact, Luke envisioned the literal restoration of Jerusalem, and along with it the redemption of Israel, salvation-historical schemes such as those of the previous interpreters, are severely undermined. One simply cannot speak of leaving Jerusalem and the Jews behind if Luke looked forward to their ultimate restoration.

This is not to say that salvation history is not a helpful concept to describe Luke's perception of God's saving work. Yet Luke viewed the present time not merely as a phase in an ongoing salvation history; rather he viewed it as the time of *eschatological* fulfillment. Hence, the important roles played by Jerusalem and the temple are not transitional as Luke moves the reader from one phase of salvation history to the next. Rather, they are invested with importance precisely because Luke did view the present age as eschatological. Jerusalem and the temple are the places of the eschatologically renewed people of God. Jerusalem is the place of the eschatological apostolic rule of Israel. It is the place of the Messiah's coronation as king. It is the central place from which the universal salvation of the Gentiles goes forth.

Jerusalem and the majority of the Jews have rejected *their* mission. For this reason, the city and temple are destroyed, and the people are the victims of the Roman sword. But this need not imply a *permanent* rejection by God. There are a number of indications in Luke that the third evangelist held out a future hope for the Jews and their city. A number of significant texts point to this conclusion.

Acts 28:23-28. This passage describing Paul's final encounter with the Jews has been interpreted to denote the absolute obduracy of the Jews and to announce the end of any mission to the Jews; the gospel will now go exclusively to the Gentiles.[26] Such an interpretation is easy to offer; yet the

---

[26]Haenchen, *Acts,* 729. Even Jacob Jervell, who has argued so emphatically that one is to locate Luke-Acts within a Jewish matrix, believes that the Jewish mission effectively comes to an end with the conclusion of Acts. See "The Divided People of God: The Restoration of Israel and Salvation for the Gentiles," in *Luke and the People of God: A New Look at Luke-Acts* (Minneapolis: Augsburg, 1972) 68-69. Cf. in this light Jack Sanders,

text is not limited to such an understanding. In the first place, verse 24 clearly states that "some were convinced by what he [Paul] said, while others disbelieved." What is echoed here is a pattern of division which Luke has presented throughout the entirety of Acts.[27] Far from dismissing all Jews forever from salvation, the end of Acts only reiterates what Luke has affirmed throughout his second volume, that wherever the gospel is preached some Jews believed.

Second, the strong scriptural injunction from Isa. 6:9-10 quoted in verses 26-27 need not be understood as a *permanent* deafening and hardening of the Jewish ears to the gospel. To be sure, it affirms that those Jews who refuse to see and hear the will and plan of God (which Luke may know in his time to be the majority of Jews) will not come to see and hear the word of salvation. Like the non-penitent Jews who refuse to accept Jesus as the prophet-like-Moses (Acts 3:22-23), such persons will be destroyed from the people. The text affirms that for healing to come, eyes must be opened and hearts softened. Nothing in the text demands, however, that such repentance can never happen. This conclusion will be confirmed by other texts to be examined below.

Third, Paul's announcement that he would go to the Gentiles (verse 28) need not be understood to mean that only Gentiles would henceforth share in the blessings of the gospel. The declaration appears to be emphatic, but it must be seen in the context of similar announcements in Acts. In Acts 13:46 and 18:6 Paul declares that he will now turn to the Gentiles, but it would be wrong to conclude that following such announcements the Jews were never again permitted the chance to hear the gospel (see Acts 14:1; 17:1-4, 10; 18:1-4; 22:3-21). To be sure, Acts 28:28 betrays Luke's awareness that the Gentile mission is the current focus of the church. But it need not imply that the gospel will never again be offered to the Jews.

Luke 13:35. Following Jesus' "lament over Jerusalem" (13:31-34), where Jesus mourns the failure of the holy city to accept his ministry, he proclaims, "And I tell you, you will not see me until you say, 'Blessed is he who comes in the name of the Lord!' " (v. 35). It is *possible* that Luke

---

"The Jewish People in Luke-Acts," in *SBL Papers, 1986,* ed. Kent H. Richards (Atlanta: Scholars Press, 1986) 110-29, who argues that Luke perceives the Jews to be historically resistant to and rebellious against God. They are villains who get what they deserve, from Luke's perspective.

[27]Throughout Acts, the preaching of the gospel divides Israel into those who accept Jesus as the Messiah and those who do not. In the early chapters of Acts, such division occurs along the lines of the "people" and the "leaders." In later chapters the following texts are pertinent in betraying the pattern of division: Acts 13:42-48; 14:1-7; 17:10-15; 18:1-7; 19:8-10.

understands this prophecy of Jesus as a reference to the Triumphal Entry where the *disciples* say, ''Blessed is the King who comes in the name of the Lord'' (19:38).[28] It is, however, probable that Lk. 13:35 does not find its fulfillment in 19:38, for the former explicitly states that it is *Jerusalem* as a whole which will offer the blessing to Jesus; in 19:38 such blessing is offered only by the disciples.[29] Hence, fulfillment of 13:35 lies in the future.

Careful reading indicates that the cry of blessing does not coincide with the parousia, but rather *precedes* it. Dale Allison has observed that the phenomenon of introducing contingent elements into Jewish statements concerning the fulfillment of eschatological hopes was quite common in Jewish texts.[30] Furthermore, he has compared this text with numerous statements of conditional prophecy found in the Jewish texts, and found there to be close formulaic similarity. In Jewish texts one often finds a contingent element in eschatological statements expressed in the following three-part manner:

Part 1: a negative statement relating to the fulfillment of messianic hope (''The Son of David will not come . . . '').
Part 2: a conditional particle (עד), translated ''until.''
Part 3: a statement of the condition to be met in Israel, the fulfillment of which is necessary to usher in the messianic age.

An example would be: (1) ''The Son of David will not come (2) until (3) there are no conceited men in Israel'' (b. Sanh. 98a).

This is precisely the pattern found in Lk. 13:35b:

Part 1: a statement related to the coming of the messiah expressed negatively: ''You will not see me. . . . ''
Part 2: conditional particle (ἕως) translated ''until.''

---

[28]So Eduard Schweizer, *Das Evangelium nach Lukas* (Göttingen: Vandenhoeck und Ruprecht, 1982) 152.

[29]See Tannehill, ''Israel in Luke-Acts,'' 84-85.

[30]Grundmann views the cry as a *prelude* to salvation. See the excellent discussion by Dale C. Allison, Jr., ''Matt. 23:39 = Luke 13:35b as a Conditional Prophecy,'' JSNT 18 (1983): 75-84. Allison argues that Lk. 13:35b is similar to rabbinic texts that make the coming of the son of David contingent on the fulfillment of certain events (e.g., R. Simeon b Yohai [ca. A.D. 140-160] is reported to have said that if the nation would keep only two Sabbaths, the Lord would immediately usher in salvation). Seen within such a context Lk. 13:35 indicates that acknowledgment of the person and work of Jesus by *Jerusalem* precedes the eschaton.

Part 3: a statement of the condition to be met in Israel. " . . . you say
'Blessed is he who comes in the name of the Lord!' "
Read in the context of Allison's investigation, the text in question indicates that Jerusalem's cry of blessing directed toward Jesus the Messiah
will precede his parousia. Such an acknowledgment of the person of Jesus
on the part of the Jews would lead to their redemption.

Acts 3:19-21. A third text that offers hope for the future salvation of
Israel is Acts 3:19-21. Through Peter Luke emphatically declares that the
repentance of the Jews would serve to usher in the final consummation:
"Repent therefore . . . that he may send the Christ appointed for you, Jesus . . ." (Acts 3:19-20). It has been argued that the concept reflected in
this text actually represents a primitive Jewish Christian eschatology.[31] Its
presence in Acts, however, attests to Luke's agreement with the principle
that the repentance of the Jews would precede, indeed it *must* precede, the
end.

Luke did foresee the genuine possibility of a future salvation for Israel.
Unlike Paul, he does not assert that "*all* Israel will be saved" (Rom. 11:26).
But like Paul he does not believe that the Gentile mission has shut the door
of salvation with respect to the Jews. Furthermore, there is evidence that
such a future salvation of Israel carried with it the restoration of Jerusalem.

Luke 19:11; Acts 1:6. These two texts do not refer explicitly to the
question of the restoration of Jerusalem. Indirectly, however, they could
be interpreted to speak to the issue at hand in a negative way. Lk. 19:11
reads: "As they [the disciples] heard these things, he proceeded to tell a
parable, because he was near to Jerusalem, and because they supposed that
the kingdom of God was to appear immediately." The text is followed by
the parable of the pounds which speaks of the departure of the king (Jesus)
and the rejection of this king by his subjects (the Jews). During his ab-
sence, according to W. D. Davies, the disciples are "to promote the worldwide mission entrusted to them (19:23)."[32] Given that Luke places the parable before the Entry, "it indicates in advance that the event was not to be
understood eschatologically or politically. Jesus did not go to Jerusalem to
set up his kingdom."[33] All of this serves Luke's larger purpose to demote
Jerusalem and the eschatological mystique that surrounded it.

---

[31]See R. F. Zehnle, *Peter's Pentecost Discourse: Tradition and Lukan Reinterpretation in Peter's Speeches of Acts 2 and 3*, SBLMS 15 (Nashville: Abingdon Press, 1971)
61-66. Cf. also, Allison, "Matt. 23:39 = Luke 13:35b."

[32]Davies, *Gospel and the Land*, 256.

[33]Ibid., 257.

Davies is partially right in what he says. The appearance of Jesus in Jerusalem did not mark the advent of the kingdom of God. But one reads too much into this text to assume, as does Davies, that it fits squarely into Luke's larger ideological goal of demoting Jerusalem. The key issue is the *immediate* appearance of the kingdom of God. The parable of the pounds clearly challenges any notion that Jesus' arrival at Jerusalem marks the consummation of the ages.[34] But it simply does not address the issue of the *ultimate* role of this city in the eschatological drama.

Acts 1:6 is related to this issue. Luke states, "So when they had come together, they asked him, 'Lord, will you at this time restore the kingdom to Israel?' " Davies argues that the text speaks to two issues: (1) it challenges the imminence of the parousia and (2) it speaks to Luke's concern to free the gospel from any geographical and nationalistic limitations.[35] It is true that Luke does not want to limit the benefits of salvation to one people or place. Luke is a universalist, and this text, followed as it is by the command of Jesus for the disciples to extend their testimony to the ends of earth, would challenge an ethnocentric gospel. However, the text does not directly challenge a view of an imminent parousia. In the first place, the text must be read in light of other texts. Examination in the previous chapter concluded that Luke did not advocate the view of a far-distant parousia. Second, the question of the disciples is not whether Christ will restore the kingdom imminently, but "at this time" (that is, immediately). Talbert is more on target when he argues that what Luke is combatting here is a radically realized eschatology which advocated that with the ascension, the kingdom of God had fully arrived.[36] The ascension does not mark the time of the restoration of the kingdom to Israel. It does not, however, rule out the hope of an ultimate eschatological restoration of Israel, a restoration which might have some affinities with traditional Jewish hopes. In short, Jesus' response challenges the hope for an immediate restoration of Israel. It does not challenge the hope of such restoration itself.

What has already been observed must be reiterated: Luke never explicitly states that Jerusalem and/or the temple will be restored. Nonetheless, given that he also refuses to ecclesiologize or christologize the temple, and given that he believed the literal Jerusalem and temple played decisive roles in the age of eschatological fulfillment, it would seem logical that

---

[34]See Charles Talbert, "The Redaction Critical Quest for Luke the Theologian," in "Jesus and Man's Hope," *Perspective* 11 (1970): 172-74.

[35]Davies, *Gospel and the Land*. 265-66.

[36]Talbert, "Critical Quest," 176-80.

Luke would expect a literal restoration. Recently, numerous scholars have detected this logic and have affirmed that Luke did foresee a restoration of the city and/or its temple.[37]

Luke 21. Close examination of Lk. 21:24b,c provides a strong hint that Luke did foresee the restoration of Jerusalem. Lk. 21:24b,c reads "and Jerusalem will be trodden down by the Gentiles, until the times of the Gentiles are fulfilled." Zmijewski understands the verse to denote two things. One, the Gentiles are the instruments of God's judgment in his vengeful rejection of the Jews (21:24b); and, two, salvation history has now entered into its Gentile phase. Only Gentiles will be allowed to share in the blessings of salvation (21:24c).[38] Zmijewski's interpretation of 21:24b is partially correct. The Gentiles are instruments of God's judgment against the Jews. But it does not follow from this that Luke envisioned the Jews' permanent rejection by God. Zmijewski's interpretation of 21:24c seems totally incorrect. One is not justified to speak of a definite end of "Jewish-time" and a definite beginning of "Gentile-time" in the offering of salvation. As Acts itself indicates, these times overlap. The gospel was preached first to Jews; but preaching to the Jews did not stop when the preaching to Gentiles began. It would seem that a more appropriate context of interpretation for 21:24b,c can be found than the sharp ethnic division proposed by Zmijewski.

The motif of the desolation of Jerusalem by the Gentiles was widespread in Jewish thought (see, e.g., Zech. 12:3; Ps. 79:1 and 2 Macc. 8:2). Interestingly, a number of texts refer to such Gentile desolation as a "trampling down" of Jerusalem or the sanctuary. "The holy people possessed thy sanctuary a little while: our adversaries have trodden it down" (Isa. 63:18). "She [Zion] is trodden down who ofttimes trod down" (2 Bar. 67:2). "For how long is the vision concerning . . . the giving over of the sanctuary and host to be trampled under foot?" (Dan. 8:13). "The sanctuary was trampled down" (1 Macc. 3:45). "Thy sanctuary is trampled down and profaned, . . ." (1 Macc. 3:51). "Raise up unto them their king . . . that he may purge Jerusalem from the nations that trample (her) down to destruction" (Ps. Sol. 17:23-25). These texts compare nicely with Lk.

---

[37]So, e.g., Tiede, *Prophecy and History,* 92-95; A. J. Mattill, Jr., *Luke and the Last Things: A Perspective for Understanding Lukan Thought* (Dillsboro NC: Western North Carolina Press; Macon GA: Mercer University Press, 1979) 136-42; Eric Franklin, *Christ the Lord: A Study in the Purpose and Theology of Luke-Acts* (Philadelphia: Westminster Press, 1975) 128-130; A. W. Wainwright, "Luke and the Restoration of the Kingdom to Israel," ET 89 (1977): 76-79.

[38]Zmijewski, *Eschatologiereden,* 220-21.

21:24b: "and Jerusalem will be trodden down by the Gentiles." Some common threads of tradition appear probable. Given that Lk. 21:24b is a Lukan addition to his Markan source, it would seem that his phraseology could be understood as an attempt to interpret the fall of Jerusalem in the context of traditional Jewish statements concerning such a fall.

If such be the case, then it cannot be ignored that in the Old Testament and postbiblical Judaism the desolation of Jerusalem and/or the temple was consistently followed by the promise of the restoration of the precincts (see Zech. 12:4, 9; Ps. 79:8-13; 2 Macc. 10:1-5; Isa. 65:17-25; 2 Bar. 67:6-8; Dan. 8:13-14; 1 Macc. 4:36-60; Ps. Sol. 17:23-27). Luke himself offers a hint of such redemption in 21:24c where Jesus speaks of Jerusalem's trampling occurring "until the times of Gentiles are fulfilled." Lk. 21:24c definitely indicates that the period of Gentile domination is one of limited duration. Read in light of 21:24b and its Jewish parallels, this limited duration could be understood to indicate that Jerusalem's restoration would follow the "times of the Gentiles."

Lk. 21:28 offers an explicit word of redemption. "Now when these things begin to take place, look up and raise your heads, because your redemption is drawing near." Luke is the only evangelist to state specifically that redemption stands in some immediate relation to the end of "Gentile-time." To be sure, the immediate recipients of the redemption are said to be Jesus' listeners, and not the city. But the identity of these listeners is most important. While Mark specifically indicates that the recipients of the "little apocalypse" are Peter, James, and John (Mk. 13:3-4), Luke omits the Markan references which limit the audience of Jesus to the disciples.[39] Given that the Lukan discourse takes place in the larger context of Jesus' temple ministry (19:47-21:38), which Luke portrayed as Jesus' encounter with *Israel* (19:47-48; 21:37-38), it would be best to conclude that Jesus' listeners consisted of the Jews.

This conclusion is affirmed by the fact that Jesus' audience, whom Luke identifies only as "some" or "they" (Lk. 21:5, 7, 10), addresses him in the beginning of the discourse as "teacher" (Lk. 21:7). Throughout the gospel of Luke, the third Evangelist often describes Jesus' activity as that of "teaching." Interestingly, with only one exception (Lk. 11:1), the recipients of Jesus' teaching are always described, either implicitly or ex-

---

[39]Lk. 21:5 states: "And as *some* spoke of the temple, how it was adorned with noble stones and offerings he said. . . . " Lk. 21:7 reads: "And *they* asked him. . . . " Note in each instance, the identity is quite general. Some find the antecedent of "they" in 20:45, indicating that the speech is addressed to disciples, with the people as listening in only (see Giblin, *Destruction of Jerusalem*, 75). But see below.

plicitly, generally as the Jewish people.[40] Furthermore, Jesus is always addressed by the title of "teacher" by nondisciples. He is so addressed by Pharisees (7:40; 19:39), lawyers (10:25; 11:45), rulers (18:18), Sadducees (20:28), scribes (20:29), spies of the scribes and chief priests (20:21), Jairus' servant (8:49, cf. 8:41), and Jews within the crowd (9:38; 12:13). Never in Luke do disciples address Jesus as "teacher." It is Jews who are either opposed to Jesus or curious, yet noncommittal, who address him by this title. It is only reasonable to assume the same in Luke 21:7; the audience which asks Jesus concerning the destruction of the temple consists generally of Jews, not just the disciples.

To be sure, some of the words spoken by Jesus are apropos to those who in the future will be his followers (see esp. vv. 12-19). Two explanations account for this. First, if Luke is basing the bulk of the discourse on Mark 13 (which is clearly addressed *only* to disciples, cf. Mk. 13:3), the tradition he inherited from the second Evangelist could account for words which seem to have a narrower focus. Second, Luke would be aware that in his forthcoming volume of Acts the multitudes of Jerusalem Jews would be the group from which myriads of followers of the Way would emerge. It is only appropriate, therefore, that Jesus address words concerning discipleship to these presently noncommitted Jews who, in the future, would become his followers. Hence, when Jesus promises his hearers that their redemption would draw near following the times of the Gentiles, Jesus is proclaiming future redemption to the Jews.

Luke uses the word ἀπολύτρωσις and its cognates quite infrequently. Yet there is a consistency to his usage, for the word is always related directly to the Jews or Jerusalem. Lk. 24:21 states that the despondent disciples on the road to Emmaus lamented the death of Jesus in part because they "had hoped that he was the one to redeem (λυτροῦσθαι) Israel." In the context of the Benedictus Luke declares: "Blessed be the Lord God of Israel, for he has visited and redeemed (λύτρωσις) his people." Finally, Lk. 2:38 states with reference to Anna that "she gave thanks to God, and spoke of him to all who were looking for the redemption (λύτρωσις) of Jerusalem." Luke uses the word redemption selectively, therefore, confining the objects of redemption to Israel *and* Jerusalem.

It is significant that W. D. Davies, in order to take into account the numerous affirmations of Jewish redemption found especially in the birth narrative, must argue that the characters of this opening narrative serve in Luke-Acts to express views to which Luke is strongly opposed.

---

[40]Lk. 4:15, 31; 5:3, 17; 6:6; 13:10, 22, 26; 19:47; 20:1; 21:37; 23:5.

There were Christians whom Luke knew, who did think, we cannot but assume, of the land, concentrated for them in Jerusalem. For them the work of the Messiah was inseparable from God's help to his servant Israel (1:54). . . . It can rightly be implied that Luke stood against much popular Palestinian piety which could easily have been exploited by Zealots. How he countered "the atmospheric pressures" of the popular Christian eschatology we encounter in Luke 1 and 2, we can see in Acts 1.[41]

But would Luke have allowed the spokespersons for this misguided brand of Christianity to be Zechariah, the father of the Baptist, and Mary, the mother of Jesus? There is no indication that those who express the hope of the "consolation of Israel" and the "redemption of Jerusalem" (Simeon and Anna, respectively) represent anything less for Luke than persons who express true piety and faith. Robert Tannehill does not cite Davies' arguments. But he responds well to the position espoused by Davies.

With the possible exception of Zechariah (cf. Lk. 1:20), the four persons named are presented as models of faith within expectant Israel. Furthermore, their words . . . contain many reminders of scripture, so that they seem to share the authority of scripture. Finally, the first proclaimer of the view that Jesus is the messianic redeemer of Israel is the angel Gabriel (1:32-33), who speaks as God's messenger. . . . This evidence indicates that the presentation of God's purpose in Luke 1-2 is being affirmed by the implied author.[42]

Tannehill's interpretation better reflects a natural reading of the Lukan birth narrative. Hence, it is reasonable to conclude that the hopes expressed in this narrative were not seen by Luke to be misguided. Thus, if one is prepared to conclude that the hopes of the pious characters of Luke 1-2 were not vain ones, the announcements of redemption for the Jews *and* Jerusalem are quite consistent with Jesus' own affirmations in Luke 21 concerning the eschatological redemption of Israel following the "times of the Gentiles." Going hand-in-hand with the "consolation of Israel" (Lk. 2:25; cf. 21:28) was the "redemption of Jerusalem" (Lk. 2:38, cf. 21:24). Given Luke's consistent pattern of viewing Jerusalem as the literal city, such redemption is best understood as the trampled city's restoration.

On the basis of what Luke offers, one can provide no further details concerning the content of Jerusalem's redemption. Did Luke envision a new temple? Given the close association between the city and temple through-

---

[41]Davies, *Gospel and the Land,* 263-64.

[42]Tannehill, "Israel in Luke-Acts," 73.

out Luke-Acts, one *might* offer a positive answer, though with great reserve. As to the function and purpose of this "new temple," if such were envisaged, nothing firm can be said. Did Luke envision a final pilgrimage of the Gentiles such as one finds in Jewish expectation? Again, one cannot say.[43] It is quite probable that Luke in some sense believed that Jerusalem would fulfill its eschatological destiny as the city of salvation, a destiny it had begun to fulfill during the ministry of Jesus and the period of the early church; a destiny detained by Jewish disobedience until "the times of the Gentiles are fulfilled" and Jerusalem cries, "Blessed is he who comes in the name of Lord."

---

[43]Wainwright, "Luke and the Restoration," 76-79, and Mattill, *Luke and the Last Things,* 131-42, think that such a pilgrimage was expected by Luke, assuming that Luke's expectations conformed to the pattern in Jewish speculation.

Conclusion:
Reflections and Implications

Eschatology

The present study joins a growing rank of interpretations that maintain that Conzelmann and his followers have missed the track as they argue that Luke has offered a "de-eschatologized" gospel and a view of a far-distant parousia. Luke has not abandoned the conviction of the early Christians that the "Christ-event" marked the dawn of the thoroughly eschatological age of salvation, a salvation that would in the imminent future come to its consummated fulfillment. Rather, Luke understood the ministry of Jesus and the church to be the inauguration of this eschatological new age.

Luke's portrait of the ministry of Jesus as presented in this study is made rich by eschatological colorings and hues. The birth narrative is replete with eschatological language as Mary sings of end-time reversal (Lk. 1:51-53). Both she and Zechariah rejoice over the fulfillment of God's promises of salvation to his people Israel (Lk. 1:54-55, 68-75). The angel Gabriel announces the arrival of the Messiah who will sit on the throne of David forever (Lk. 1:32-33). The same heavenly messenger and the father of the Baptist proclaim the birth of the Elijah-like forerunner who will pave the way for this coming salvation (Lk. 1:16, 76). The old and pious Simeon and Anna, portrayed by Luke as though sitting perched on the watchtower, straining to catch a glimpse of the dawning of the eschatological day of Lord (Lk. 2:25, 38), leave the Lukan stage with thanks to God (Lk. 2:38) and a sense of peace (Lk. 2:29), knowing that the salvation for which they had longed has arrived. Undergirding all of this action, most importantly, was the working of the Spirit of God, whose power Luke perceived as eschatological power.

In the present study the discussion of the ministry of Jesus focused on his "temple ministry" (Lk. 19:45-21:38). Luke summed up such a ministry as one of Jesus' teaching the people of Israel. Luke did not define the precise content of this teaching, but the reader is to take his cue regarding its content from the Nazareth pericope (Lk. 4:16-30). There Jesus taught in the synagogue, and what he taught was nothing short of the fulfillment of the eschatological word of Isaiah the prophet. Jesus' encounter with Israel at the temple, therefore, was portrayed by Luke as Jesus' confronting the nation of Israel with the offering of eschatological salvation.

Luke's description of the ascension of Jesus had a rich eschatological texture, as it was there that Luke described the enthronement of the Messiah. Luke did not tell of Jesus' heavenly enthronement in order to remove him from the stage, but to make clear to the reader that the promise that Jesus would sit on the throne of his father David had now come to fruition. The ministry of the church, therefore, whether the ministry of the apostles to the Jews or emissaries from Jerusalem to the Gentiles, was a ministry that took place under the auspices of Jesus the enthroned Messiah.

Throughout the book of Acts Luke viewed the time of the church as coexistent with the messianic rule of Jesus, or what one might also call the messianic kingdom. Such a disposition on the part of Luke would lead to a presentation of the ministry of the early church as being filled with eschatological significance. The activity of the apostles, as they engaged in their rule of the eschatologically renewed twelve tribes of Israel, was an eschatological rule. The mission of the church beyond the borders of Palestine, both to confront Jews and Gentiles, was an eschatological mission, undergirded by the power of the Spirit, the gift of God for the "last days" (Acts 2:17).

In short, with the arrival of Jesus, the New Age in its fullest eschatological sense, had dawned. The ministry of Jesus and his followers subsequent to his enthronement takes place in the light of this New Day. Furthermore, Luke did not believe that the church was to live long in the dawn of this New Day. Rather, he saw the consummation of this Day as arriving in the imminent future. Many texts, including Lk. 9:27, 10:9, 11, 12:35-48, 18:1-8, 21:32 and Acts 3:19-21, point to Luke's belief that the triumphant coming of the Son of man was not far off.

Hence, this investigation does result in certain implications concerning the eschatological thinking of Luke. Contrary to the arguments of Conzelmann and those who walk under his influence, Luke was no radical innovator of early Christian eschatology.

Israel and the Gentiles in Luke-Acts

There does exist within Lukan studies a broad concensus that salvation history is an appropriate context in which to approach Luke-Acts. In light of the above investigation, however, one must conclude that it does not serve in Luke's mind as a substitute for eschatological expectancy. Rather, salvation history in Luke-Acts is more appropriate as a context for coming to grips with Luke's understanding of Israel and the Gentiles. Luke views the dawn of the New Age, marked by the ministry of Jesus and the church, to be the fulfillment of God's promises of salvation to Israel, and indeed, to the whole world.

The decisive question revolving around Luke's conception of Israel and the nations is whether he interpreted the march of salvation toward the Gentiles as passing through Israel, only to leave Israel behind once the offer of salvation was made, or whether at the end of history Israel would be incorporated into God's saving work. Did Luke, in other words, believe that salvation had passed to the Gentiles at the expense of Israel? I shall not rehearse my arguments, but simply state the implied conclusions which derive from them.

Luke, like Paul, believed that the time in which he lived was predominantely Gentile-time (Lk. 21:24c). The conclusion of Acts (Acts 28:23-30) also betrays Luke's awareness that in his time the most fruitful reception of the gospel would come from the Gentiles. There is also no question but that Luke wanted to affirm quite emphatically that the Gentiles, through confession of Jesus as Messiah, were fully incorporated into the ranks of the people of God. Luke has provided such a smooth transition of emphasis from Israel to the nations, that he can conclude his history confident that the salvific work of God will continue within history, with or without Israel. All of this one would have to affirm.

But it was also argued that Luke did not believe that Israel had had her one and only chance in the history of God's saving work. Luke believed that in the end, Israel would find redemption. To be sure, Luke does not show evidence of personal agony over the present hardness of Israel, as does Paul. But it may be that historical narrative, unlike a letter, is not the place to reveal personal pathos. But he clearly does not write with a vindictive spirit against Israel, as though an irreversible fate of eternal damnation awaits her. Unless one is to affirm that the pious characters of the birth narrative, such as Zechariah, Mary, Simeon, and Anna, are used by Luke as representatives of misguided hopes, one is safe in concluding that Israel will find redemption—she would not merely be made a one-time offer. Luke emphasizes the Jewish roots of the gospel, therefore, not simply in an attempt to legitimize an increasingly Gentile phenomenon. The Jewish roots of God's saving work betray an emphatic declaration on the part of Luke that God's promises to save Israel have begun in the past, can continue in the present (though perhaps with limited results), and will, in the future, find concrete realization.

Luke's hope of the ultimate redemption of Israel, like Paul's, is a more workable solution to the Jews' hardness of heart when one assumes an imminent parousia, as did Luke and Paul. It is not so workable, to be sure, when the "time between the times" has stretched across almost two millennia. But the current fact of history which forces us to concede that Christianity and Judaism are two distinct religions should not color our understanding of the hope of Luke and Paul. Rather, it should be our hope that in "the depth of the riches and wisdom and knowledge of God" (Rom. 11:33) his work of salvation toward his people Israel will find fulfillment.

Luke and His Christian Contemporaries

Luke shows many points of contact with the emerging group of people who, Luke says, were first called Christians in Antioch (Acts 11:26). As stated above, he shares the conviction that the New Age of salvation, in its fully eschatological sense, had dawned and was marching quickly toward its consummation. Like Paul, he holds forth hope for Israel. Like his fellow Christians he sees Jesus and his work as decisive in the offering of salvation, though he apparently did not share with many of his contemporaries a developed understanding of the death of Jesus as an atoning sacrifice.

One of the greatest areas of variance was Luke's perception of Jerusalem and the temple. The tendency among the early followers of Jesus, whether they actually called themselves "Christians" or not, was to spiritualize the temple and its city. Early Christians whose views are now found in the Christian canon were aware of the importance of Jerusalem and the temple in the eschatological age of salvation. They did not dismiss the importance of these entities, they simply spiritualized them and transferred to the church or to Jesus their functions. This fact says something about early Christian hermeneutics. They certainly did not approach their tradition, in this case the Old Testament, with a wooden literalism. The tradition was interpreted to meet the needs of the community, and if that necessitated the dismissal of the literal Jerusalem and temple, then so be it.

Luke's perception of Jerusalem and the temple, which in effect cut squarely against the grain of his contemporaries, indicates what many New Testament theologians have affirmed for a long while: there does not run through the New Testament monolithic and uniform expressions of faith. Luke's perceptions regarding Jerusalem and the temple provide further testimony that the Christian canon is rich in its diversity.

Nonetheless, despite his tendency to understand the significance of Jerusalem and the temple on a more literal level, Luke also, as were his contemporaries, was required to interpret that tradition. Because of the brute facts of history that confronted him, Luke could not maintain that any literal pilgrimage of the diaspora Jews or the nations had occurred. He, with his contemporaries, had to interpret the traditions revolving around Jerusalem and the temple so as to make them meaningful to his situation. So while one might detect more of a literal interpretation regarding Luke's understanding of Jerusalem and the temple, he also was not bound by a woodenly literalistic hermeneutic. For him, as for his contemporaries, the tradition was to live in service to the gospel.

It is also significant that Luke offers his different interpretation of Jerusalem and the temple without any hints of polemical attacks against the spiritualized interpretation that was dominant in early Christianity. The prologue of the gospel, as varied as interpretations of that prologue might be, clearly points to an author who saw himself as being in touch with the larger Christian community. He did not write in a vacuum. It would seem, therefore, that he would have developed his interpretation of Jerusalem and the temple with some awareness that he was not swimming with the mainstream. Assuming his use of Mark, which I do despite the reemergence of Griesbach,[1] and assuming that Luke would have detected Mark's conception of the community as the temple, then it would seem that one is safe to conclude that Luke felt free to offer an alternative understanding without resorting to polemical invective. To be sure, Luke does not betray an attitude that any theological assertions are acceptable—he does write with a concern to provide for his readers what he considers to be a normative understanding of the Jesus tradition.[2] And at times he offers stern warnings against alternative understandings of that tradition which would arise (Acts 20:28-31). At least with regard to Jerusalem and the temple, however, he was able to offer an alternative interpretation with apparent toleration of others.

---

[1]Important bibliography regarding the revival of the Griesbach hypothesis includes W. R. Farmer, *The Synoptic Problem: A Critical Analysis*, (corrected rpt.: Dillsboro NC: Western North Carolina Press; Macon GA: Mercer University Press, 1976); Hans Herbert Stoldt, *History and Criticism of the Marcan Hypothesis*, trans. and ed. D. L. Niewyk (Macon GA: Mercer University Press; Edinburgh: T. & T. Clark, 1980); David Peabody, "The Late Secondary Redaction of Mark's Gospel and the Griesbach Hypothesis: A Response to Helmut Koester," in *Colloquy on New Testament Studies*, ed. Bruce Corley (Macon GA: Mercer University Press, 1983) 87-132.

[2]See esp. Charles H. Talbert, "The Redaction Critical Quest for Luke the Theologian," in "Jesus and Man's Hope," *Perspective* 11 (1970): 171-222; and *What is a Gospel? The Genre of the Canonical Gospels* (Philadelphia: Fortress Press, 1977) 118-24.

While I have problems with much of what Eduard Schweizer says regarding Luke-Acts,[3] I appreciate fully what he says about Luke's refusal to reduce the message of the gospel to petrified assertions which demand thoughtless conformity:

> The gospel is, for [Luke], an event, the living word of God, which may come to people in ever new and unexpected ways, not so much as a message which could be definitely put into one or several sentences to be handed down as the unchangeable truth.[4]

Such a statement argues for a spirit of toleration on the part of Luke. And if this statement properly captures the attitude of the third Evangelist, then it should offer no surprise that he can, with respect to Jerusalem and the temple, swim against the stream of his contemporaries, while at the same time see himself as one with them with respect to the larger cause of the gospel.

The Origin of Luke's Perception of Jerusalem and the Temple

When attempting to explicate the origin of Luke's conception of Jerusalem and the temple, one walks on loose soil and can offer but tentative assertions. Such assertions, however, are in order, if for no other reason than to generate some discussion out of which firmer results might emerge.

Before proceeding with this discussion it would be appropriate to offer some word on Luke's mobility, for the more mobility that can be presupposed, the greater access he would have had to numerous channels of tradition. In an as yet unpublished essay, Dale Allison has offered some good insights to this question.[5] It is Allison's opinion that it is not proper to speak of a particular Lukan community, as though the third Evangelist were a man settled in a particular locale. He argues that there is perhaps internal evidence that Luke was quite a mobile individual. All of his arguments cannot be rehearsed at this juncture, but a summary of the more pertinent points of his thesis will be offered.

Allison notes that the heroes of Luke's gospel and Acts (Jesus, Peter, and Paul) are all itinerants. This could point to a man who viewed geographical mobility as an important dimension of good discipleship. Sec-

---

[3]See my review of Schweizer's *Luke: A Challenge to Present Theology,* in *Faith and Mission* 1 (1983): 94-95.

[4]Eduard Schweizer, *Luke: A Challenge to Present Theology* (Richmond: John Knox Press, 1982) 65.

[5]"Was There a 'Lukan Community' "? Forthcoming.

ond, the author certainly portrays himself as one who was in touch with a broad spectrum of churches. This comes forth in both the prologue and the so-called "we-sections" of Acts, especially if one considers the "we-sections" to be indications of the presence of the author. Third, Luke's use of at least two sources (Mark and Q) and his access to numerous traditions relating to the early history of the church, which takes the reader from Jerusalem, to Antioch, to Asia Minor, to Macedonia and Achaia, and to Rome, point to a man on the move. Fourth, Allison thinks that the inability of modern scholarship to pin down Luke's intent and audience might point in-and-of-itself to a diversity of agendas on the part of the author of this two-volume work. Such a diversity might point to a man who had come into contact with numerous and diverse issues, a situation more likely to exist if the author were mobile as opposed to settled. These observations are worth considering, and if one can work on the assumption that the author of Luke-Acts was a geographically mobile individual, the interpreter is far less restricted in where to look for the "origins" of Luke's conceptions regarding Jersualem and the temple.

The most logical place to begin the search for the origin of Luke's conception is the Christian tradition to which he might have had access. The two-source hypothesis does not immediately lead to fruitful results. Mark did not share Luke's conception, but offered a spiritualized interpretation of the tradition. The hypothetical Q source does not lead much further. The saying of Jesus from Q found in Lk. 13:34-35 (‖ Matt. 23:37-39), speaks with respect to the temple and the city explicitly only of its destruction, with no explicit word of restoration. I did argue that this text in the larger context of Luke-Acts could point to the eventual restoration of Israel prior to the parousia, but it certainly does not help in coming to any conclusions regarding Luke's appreciation of the literal temple of Jerusalem.

It is possible, indeed probable, unless one assumes Luke's creative hand to be behind all the material peculiar to him, that the third Evangelist had access to Christian traditions that are not embodied in either Mark or Q. It is argued by some interpreters of primitive Christian history that the earliest Jerusalem community held to a view of Jerusalem and the temple that was quite similar to traditional Jewish expectations. That is to say that the primitive community viewed these geographical entities as important centers in the eschatological age of salvation.[6] Such a conclusion, however,

---

[6]See Ralph Martin, *New Testament Foundations: A Guide to Christian Students*, 2 vols. (Grand Rapids MI: Eerdmans, 1978) 2:79-80, for a discussion of this thesis and helpful bibliography. Cf. also Hans Conzelmann, *History of Primitive Christianity*, trans. John E. Steely (Nashville: Abingdon Press, 1973) 46.

must be offered with the greatest of caution. If such is assumed to be the case, however, it is quite possible that Luke was privy to the traditions of the most primitive community and found them persuasive. Such a possibility could have existed even if the existence of any possible "Jerusalem source" for Acts is not assumed.[7] Christian tradition is a possible source for Luke's conception of Jerusalem and the temple, but it is only one of several possibilities.

A second possible source was the Old Testament. There is no question but that Luke was well versed in Jewish scripture, and used it often to bolster his positions within Luke and Acts. He was especially fond of arguing from the Old Testament as he defended his assertions that the Gentiles were to be fully incorporated into the people of God. Christology was also a frequent subject for Old Testament exegesis (e.g., Acts 2:25-36; 4:25-30; 13:32-38).

Interestingly, Luke's view of the temple and Jerusalem is not backed by such detailed exegetical argument. Old Testament texts dealing with the temple are actually quite rare, with Acts 7:49-50 being the most prevalent. There, however, the text fed into Luke's larger universalistic thrust in that the text was concerned to state that God and his salvation were not confined to one place or people. Had Luke developed his view of the temple primarily on the basis of his reading of the Old Testament, it is curious that he did not share his texts with his readers. This is certainly not to say the Old Testament was not a source of his thinking. It is only to say that it seems unlikely that Luke, while sitting in some private room, derived his view of the temple primarily from a reading of the Old Testament, only to be silent in his two-volume work regarding the texts that led him to his view.

The investigations of chapter 1 above concluded that the Jewish view of the significance of Jerusalem and the temple in the eschatological age of salvation had thoroughly saturated Jewish thought. In this same chapter it was revealed that the early Christians were aware of this significance, an awareness that would have sprung from the Jewish roots of the earliest followers of Jesus themselves. In short, the speculation concerning the importance of Jerusalem and the temple in the eschatological age of salvation was so pervasive that an early Christian would have met the idea simply

---

[7]The thorny issue of the sources of Acts cannot be discussed in this context. Hence, I have made these statements without assuming any hypotheses regarding such sources. For some discussion of the issue see J. Dupont, *The Sources of Acts: the Present Position* (London: 1964) and Ernst Haenchen, *The Acts of the Apostles: A Commentary*, trans. Bernard Noble and Gerald Shinn, under supervision of Hugh Anderson, rev. trans. R. McLeod Wilson (Philadelphia: Westminster Press, 1971) 81-90.

by virtue of being a part of an emerging religious tradition that sprang out of Judaism. Such could have been the case with Luke as well.

Lk. 21:20-24 offers a unique description of the fall of Jerusalem that concludes with the notification that Jerusalem would experience a temporary trampling by the Gentiles. All of this is in some way tied to the ultimate redemption of Jesus' Jewish audience, as is made clear by 21:28. I. H. Marshall suspects that Luke had access here to Christian tradition, though he lists an impressive array of interpreters who believe that Luke simply rewrote Mark.[8] If—and this is a most tentative "if"—Luke himself, rather than Christian tradition, is responsible for the thrust of these verses, one may deduce that a strong impact was made upon him by Old Testament and postbiblical Jewish tradition. I have argued that the most reasonable context in which to interpret the notion of the temporary trampling of Jerusalem by the nations was the widespread Jewish notion that Jerusalem would experience a temporary denigration prior to its redemption. If Luke developed his version of Jesus' temple discourse primarily on the basis of his familiarity with popular Jewish conceptions, rather than some specific tradition that came to him from Christian channels, it could indicate that the author had some direct contact with Jewish speculation concerning Jerusalem and the temple.

I would be inclined to argue for such contact with Jewish tradition for two reasons. First, Jonathan Smith has argued that there was beginning to emerge within Hellenistic culture a transformation of worldviews which viewed the cosmos not as friend of humanity, but as adversary.[9] Going hand-in-hand with the rising skepticism regarding the cosmos was a degradation of sacred space, which often in ancient culture was believed to embody symbolically this cosmos. People, in their search for salvation, began to turn from temples and the cultus of the temple and look to savior figures and communities revolving around such figures as havens of salvation. What is significant for the purpose of this investigation is that even as Judaism was beginning to show signs of moving in a similar direction, with the sage and synagogue replacing the priest and temple, the dominant pattern within Judaism was to maintain a high regard for traditional sacred space. The predominant pattern within early Christianity, Smith contends, was to conform to the larger Hellenistic cultural trend and to move away

---

[8]I. H. Marshall, *The Gospel of Luke: A Commentary on the Greek Text,* The New International Greek Testament Commentary (Grand Rapids MI: Eerdmans, 1978) 771.

[9]*Map is Not Territory: Studies in the History of Religion,* Studies in Judaism in Late Antiquity 23 (Leiden: E. J. Brill, 1978).

from the valuing of sacred space, and to view the savior figure (Jesus) and his community (the church) as the loci of salvation.

If such be the case, then it is clear that Luke was moving against a powerful stream as he insisted on the ongoing value of Jerusalem and the temple. Not only was he swimming against the stream of early Christianity, but also against a larger cultural tide which was engulfing the whole world. If one were to attempt to find a subcultural stream in which Luke could have developed his understanding of Jerusalem and the temple, Judaism would be the logical place to look. For within Judaism, the temple and its city were not abandoned as important loci for God's saving work.

Second, it needs to be acknowledged that interpreters of Luke-Acts have increasingly recognized the value of understanding Luke against a Jewish backdrop. Jacob Jervell, David Tiede, Eric Franklin, E. Earle Ellis, A. J. Mattill, Donald Juel, Robert Tannehill, and Arthur Wainwright are among recent interpreters who believe that Luke-Acts can be fruitfully interpreted within a Jewish matrix. Even in his recent work, Charles Talbert, who interprets Luke-Acts primarily within the context of hellenistic biography, found Jewish backgrounds helpful in explicating many Lukan texts.[10] When searching for the most appropriate *religionsgeschichtliche* background of a document, the proof is often "in the pudding"—the more a particular background proves helpful in understanding a text, the more confident the interpreter can be that such a background is an appropriate matrix in which to interpret a text. Increasingly, Judaism is offering such a helpful background for Luke-Acts.

One need not make any certain conclusions regarding Luke's identity or ethnic orientation to assert that Judaism fed greatly into his thinking. At the beginning of this concluding discussion, it was stated that Luke may very well have been an itinerant, who therefore could have come into contact with many varying views and interests in his travels. Within his travels he could have had opportunity to come into contact with Jewish points of view, either through friendly dialogue, confrontational debate, or perhaps even through Christian communities who were deeply rooted in Jewish culture and thought. Regardless of any specific scenarios that one might imagine, it would seem that Jewish soil is a rich place to dig in order to uncover Lukan conceptions.

---

[10]Talbert's discussion of Luke-Acts as conforming to a form of hellenistic biography is found in *What is a Gospel?*, 91-109. His work on Luke in which he found reference to Jewish backgrounds helpful in interpreting Luke is *Reading Luke: A Literary and Theological Commentary on the Third Gospel* (New York: Crossroads, 1982).

The Motive for Luke's Conception of Jerusalem and the Temple

In attempting to explicate the motives of an ancient author with whom the modern interpreter can have no direct dialogue, possessing only his literary deposits, one walks on the shakiest of ground. It is one thing to *describe* an author's work, and to derive some conclusions concerning what he or she thought. It is quite another to speculate on motives. Some word is in order, however.

As stated earlier in this conclusion, I do not think that Luke's motive was to offer an alternative understanding of Jerusalem and the temple in a polemical spirit against the dominant view of his Christian contemporaries. He does not speak dogmatically concerning Jerusalem and the temple. One would be correct to argue that Luke would have been unyielding on his notion of the resurrection of Jesus or the universalistic importance of the gospel. He methodically and scripturally argues his point on these issues. But such does not seem to be the case with Jerusalem and the temple. There are no debates staged in the Lukan plot regarding these entities, nor any long speeches coming from the principal characters devoted to them. Luke's conception of Jerusalem and the temple does undergird his presentation of Jesus' ministry and the history of the early church; it is not, however, a matter for heated debate. This might lead one to conclude that Luke's view of Jerusalem and the temple per se was not the decisive issue. It was not, in other words, an end in-and-of-itself. Rather, it seems to function for Luke as a means to an end.

One of Luke's "ends" was to show that God's promises of salvation had come to fruition in the ministry of Jesus and the history of the early church. He was also quite concerned to show how such promises had come to fulfillment on the plane of real history. Scholars have long noted how careful Luke is to integrate his history into the fabric of world history.

Luke also had a tendency to want to describe in literal terms the arrival of this salvation. This is evidenced by his offering of a more literal interpretation of the dove descending "in bodily form" upon Jesus at his baptism (Lk. 3:22). He leaves no question that the darkness that covered the earth during Jesus' crucifixion was a literal phenomenon, as he states that "the sun's light failed" (τοῦ ἡλίου ἐκλιπόντος, Lk. 23:45). Luke offers a very materialistic conception of Jesus' resurrection, as he denies that the resurrected Jesus was a spirit, but rather a body of flesh and bone (Lk. 24:39). Luke offered a very literal description of the messianic enthronement of Jesus, as the disciples witnessed his ascension (Acts 1:9-10). It is also made clear by Luke in this same context that Jesus' parousia would be an objectively observable event (Acts 1:11). The descent of the Holy Spirit upon the church is also described in a literal fashion, as Luke speaks of wind and fire (Acts 2:2-3). In short, as Luke attempted to show that God's salvation was coming to fruition on the plane of real, observable history, it seems that one means of arguing his point was to offer a very literal portrayal of the significant events that marked the dawn of this salvation. Luke wanted there to be no ambiguity that the salvation of God had really come. That the arrival of this salvation had manifested itself in objectively observable events helped Luke to make his case.

By showing how the literal Jerusalem and temple had begun to fulfill their eschatological roles in the real history of Jesus and the church, Luke is being consistent with his tendency to speak of the coming of salvation in literal terms. Jerusalem and the temple were to play significant roles in the age of salvation. Luke knew that, as apparently did many of his Christian contemporaries. If he were to be able to offer his readers assurance of the "truth concerning the things of which you have been informed" (Lk. 1:4), he had to show that the Jewish and Old Testament hope centering upon Jerusalem and the temple was not a vain one. Apparently Luke believed that the best way for him to show this was to speak of a literal Jerusalem and a literal temple as important centers of God's eschatological salvation.

I would offer one final suggestion concerning Luke's motive for interpreting the significance of the literal Jerusalem and temple. Luke was concerned to show that Christianity had its roots in the people of God, the children of Israel. This is commonly acknowledged by interpreters such as Conzelmann and Robert Maddox who argue that Luke wants to legitimize a predominantly Gentile religion.[11] It is also acknowledged by those such as Eric Franklin who believe that Luke has a continued interest in the Jews as the people of God.[12] By showing that in the nascent period the gospel was closely related to the most important physical symbols of Judaism, his description of Christianity as emerging from Jewish roots is enhanced. The reader of Luke-Acts cannot conclude that the group of people who came to be called Christians had no ties with the historic people of God.

---

[11]Conzelmann's discussion of Luke's desire to legitimize Christianity by showing its Jewish roots is found in *The Theology of Saint Luke,* trans. Geoffery Bruswell (New York: Harper and Brothers, 1960) 209-213. For Conzelmann such legitimization includes a political apologetic, 137-44. Cf. in this regard Haenchen, *Acts,* 100-102. Robert Maddox, *The Purpose of Luke-Acts,* ed. John Riches (Edinburgh: T. & T. Clark, 1982) 91-97, rightly rejects any concern on the part of Luke to offer a political apologetic. He does believe that Luke is concerned to legitimize the existence of the church *to Christians* who might have feared that as a result of the break between Judaism and the followers of Jesus, the latter were not the legitimate recipients of the promises of God (183-86).

[12]Eric Franklin, *Christ the Lord: A Study in the Purpose and Theology of Luke-Acts* (Philadelphia: Westminster Press, 1975) 121-40.

I would offer no speculation whether Luke's readers were opting for the position of those Gentiles to whom Paul is speaking in Rom. 11:13-24, Gentiles who apparently thought that they had displaced the historic Israel, and Gentiles who had forgotten that their roots were to be found in Israel. And yet, his two-volume work would address such a mentality by making clear that those who now find their salvation in Jesus Christ are part of a salvation story which would not have existed without Israel. For Luke, the literal temple and Jerusalem cannot be forgotten, displaced, and set aside. The church cannot say that these entities, which stand as permanent symbols of the church's Jewish roots, can be forgotten. Such a forgetting would have been easier if the church could say that it was the new temple and city, but Luke will not permit that.

Furthermore, by offering strong hints that Jerusalem, and perhaps even the temple, would one day experience a literal restoration, Luke indicates that those roots cannot *ever* be forgotten. God has not forgotten them, and neither should his people, though it might be true that in the age of the church it is the Gentiles who, by their positive response to the gospel, make up the majority of God's people. There exists a bond between Jew and Christian which, while it has been severed by Jewish rejection of God's Messiah, will be restored after the "times of the Gentiles" are completed. What was true on the day of Pentecost when Peter spoke to Jews would still have held true for Luke decades later when he wrote: "For the promise is to you and your children and to all that are far off, every one whom the Lord our God calls to him."

Scripture and Other Ancient Texts

New Testament

Apocrypha and Pseudepigrapha

Dead Sea Scrolls

Subject Index